Eyewitness Accounts of the American Revolution

A State of the Expedition from Canada
Burgoyne

The New York Times & Arno Press

A
STATE
OF THE
EXPEDITION
FROM
CANADA,
AS LAID BEFORE THE
HOUSE OF COMMONS,
BY
LIEUTENANT-GENERAL BURGOYNE,
AND VERIFIED BY EVIDENCE;

WITH A
COLLECTION OF AUTHENTIC DOCUMENTS,

AND

AN ADDITION OF MANY CIRCUMSTANCES WHICH WERE PREVENTED
FROM APPEARING BEFORE THE HOUSE BY THE
PROROGATION OF PARLIAMENT.

WRITTEN AND COLLECTED BY HIMSELF,

AND

DEDICATED TO THE OFFICERS OF THE ARMY HE COMMANDED

THE SECOND EDITION.

LONDON:
PRINTED FOR J. ALMON, OPPOSITE BURLINGTON-HOUSE, PICCADILLY.
MDCCLXXX.

T O

MAJOR GENERAL PHILLIPS,

AND THE

OTHER OFFICERS

WHO SERVED IN THE ARMY COMMANDED BY

LIEUTENANT GENERAL BURGOYNE,

UPON AN

EXPEDITION FROM CANADA.

GENTLEMEN,

PROPRIETY and affection alike incline me
to infcribe to you the following undertaking.
We are mutual and peculiar fufferers by the
event of the campaign in 1777. You were
witneffes and judges of my actions; but I owed
you an account of the principles which directed
them.

Another motive for this Addrefs is to avail
myfelf of a proper public opportunity to repeat
to you, what I have omitted no occafion of expreffing in Parliament, in correfpondence, and
in converfation—the fulleft approbation of your
fervices. My errors may have been numberlefs;
your conduct has been uniform—faithful, gal-

lant

lant and indefatigable. Debarred of the power
of doing you juſtice before the King, theſe teſti-
monies are the only means to which my eſteem
and gratitude can reſort.

After vindicating myſelf as a commanding
officer from any inattention to your intereſt or
fame, I next throw myſelf upon your judgment
for my conduct as a friend.

You will find by this publication, and ſome
others, which though not addreſſed to you will
probably engage your curioſity, that I have
been accuſed of ſhrinking from the common
captivity.

I have been ſupported under that aſperſion by
the conſciouſneſs I did not deſerve it, and the
confidence that you (to whom chiefly upon that
charge I was reſponſible) would not adopt it.
After the fortunes we have run together, it is
not ſurely unworthy of belief, that I ſhould
rather have deſired, than avoided to partake the
cloſing ſcene: uniting with a due ſenſe of perſonal attachments, the preſervation of my military fortune, and a retreat from the diſtractions
of my country. The defence of your honour
and my own, at one time, and reſiſtance to an
affront * which my nature could not bear, at another, alone detained me here.

In

* The part of my treatment which I call an affront upon this
and other occaſions, is the refuſal of my ſervice in this country,
even at the head of my own regiment, or as a volunteer, in the
time of exigency, and when other officers *preciſely in my own
ſituation* were employed. My complaint of this partiality has never
been officially anſwered; it has only been evaded by anonymous
writers, who have laid it down as a poſition, that I meant to allude
to the example of Lord Harrington (with which it certainly has
nothing to do) and then have taken a merit in refuting me. The
particular

In regard to my political tranfactions, I have ftated them, and I wifh them to be confidered by my friends, apart from my military conduct, I bear very high refpect to fome eminent and ill-treated characters in our profeffion, who in de-ference to the tranquility of government, have filently refigned the ftations which they could no longer hold with fecurity to their honour, or benefit to the ftate. But the option is not left to thofe, who having a voice in Parliament are obliged to act as citizens as well as foldiers. The number of officers altogether of the army and navy, who with known love to their country and profeffional fpirit equally confpicuous, have voluntarily withdrawn themfelves from employ-ment within thefe two years, exceeds all prece-dent. I do not place my name in the lift with the fame pretenfions; but it is not arrogant to emulate where we cannot compare; and I am defirous of following the high examples before me in no point more than in that of avoiding to difturb the zeal of thofe who are now em-ployed. The officers who have held it their duty to take part in oppofition, have acted open-ly and directly in their place in Parliament; but they may defy malice to fhew an inftance wherein

particular example to which I appeal is that of Lieutenant Colonel Kingfton, of the 86th regiment, appointed to that regiment, em-ployed in it for the defence of Plymouth, and actually now em-barking with it for foreign fervice, under the fame terms of the convention, and the fame terms of parole to the Congrefs verbatim with myfelf. Other objections, and of a nature that could not be afterwards fupported, were tried againft the Duke of Rutland's recommendation of this excellent officer: but the objection of parole, though fully known to be precifely the fame with that which was fo peremptorily urged againft my pretenfions, was never mentioned,

they

they have not encouraged ardour in their profeffion. They contemplate with one and the fame
fentiment the great fupply of honourable men to
occupy their places.

You, Gentlemen, ftand high in that defcription; your trials have made you of fterling value;
and perhaps it will be better difcerned by men in
power, when no longer viewed through the unfavourable medium of my friendfhip. If my
exhortations retain their former weight, let me
be permitted earneftly to apply them upon this
occafion. The examples of generals or admirals
who decline employment, refpect only fimilar
cafes; your honour is fecure: look not at
profeffional difappointments; but point all
your views to the true glory of your King and
country, and truft for the reward.

O focii (neque enim ignari fumus ante Malorum)
O paffi graviora : dabit Deus his quoque finem.

This paffage will bring to the remembrance
of fome among you a hard hour when we before quoted it together, and not without fome
cheer of mind.——May the end of your enduring be near! And with every other wifh and
fentiment that can denote efteem, I have the
honour to be,

Gentlemen,

Your moft faithful and moft obedient

humble fervant,

Hertford-Street,
Jan. 1, 1780.

J. BURGOYNE.

INTRODUCTION.

WHEN it becomes neceffary for men who
have acted critical parts in public ftations to make
an appeal to the world in their own juftification,
there are many prudential confiderations which
might lead them to commit the care of it to
friends, or, which is in many refpects the fame
thing, to defend themfelves under an affumed character. The charge of vanity ufually made on
egotifm is thus eluded : a fuller fcope may be
given to felf-love and particular refentment : even
the lower vexations which attend an author are
to a great degree avoided : the ill-nature of criticifm is feldom awakened by anonymous writ-
ings, and the venal pens of party lofe half their
gall when the object of it is not perfonally and
directly in queftion.

But there are fituations, in which, not only
general affent feems to juftify a man in fpeaking
of himfelf, but in which alfo no little confideration ought to be admitted to the mind. Such
will be the cafe, if I am not deceived, when the
interefts of the public are blended with thofe of
the individual ; and when his very errors may
ferve as inftruction to others. Misfortunes which
awaken fenfibility will be a further, and a perfuafive call, upon the *attention* of the public ; and

I   it

it will amount to a claim upon their *juſtice*, if he can ſhew that he has been injuriouſly treated.

Upon maturely weighing theſe and ſeveral other circumſtances, after I had been denied a profeſſional examination of my conduct, and diſappointed of a parliamentary one, I determined to lay before the public a ſtate of the expedition from Canada, in 1777, in my own name. And my firſt deſign was to do it under the title, and with the latitude of Memoirs ; as a mode by which I could beſt open the principles of my actions, and introduce, with moſt propriety, collateral characters, incidents, and diſcuſſions, as they might occaſionally tend to illuſtrate the main ſubject.

However, in the laſt ſeſſion of Parliament, the enquiry which had not been agreed to the year before, took place. I had preſſed it, and I entered into it under all the diſadvantages which attend a ſtruggle with power, and the prejudice that power can raiſe againſt the perſons it means to deſtroy. The utmoſt that power could do was done ; the Parliament was prorogued pending the proceedings. But though by this contrivance, a final and formal adjudication by that auguſt aſſembly was avoided, their minutes ſtand a ſacred record of truth and juſtice, and the moſt ſatisfactory reliance to which my wiſhes could aſpire, in offering my actions to the judgment of my country at large.

From that time, therefore, I reſolved to publiſh, inſtead of Memoirs, the Proceedings preciſely as they paſſed in Parliament, and to continue my defence by ſuch Obſervations and Comments upon the Evidence, as I ſhould have had a right, and

was

was prepared to make, had the proceedings in the houfe continued.*

Poffibly in this latter part fome colour of my original defign may remain. The fcenes I have been engaged in are uncommon, and it is a natural defire to place them in a full light. The interefts concerned make that defire more urgent; and I dare believe they will be beft guarded by being moft explained.

* The order in which the committe in the Houfe of Commons proceeded was, to hear Sir William Howe's Narrative, refpecting his conduct whilft in command in America, and fuch evidence as he thought proper to bring in fupport of it. They next heard my Narrative and Evidence, refpecting the conduct of the expedition from Canada. Lord George Germain then opened a defence on his part, and fummoned witneffes to fupport it. According to the arrangement made by the committee, Sir William Howe and myfelf were afterwards to be heard in reply; but the proceedings were ended by the prorogation of Parliament before the examination of Lord George's fecond witnefs, Mr. Galloway, was clofed, and there were fixteen or eighteen more upon his lift. The order in which the following papers are placed is—1ft. The Prefatory Speech. 2d. The Narrative. 3d. Minutes of the verbal evidence. 4th. Review of the evidence, with Remarks and Explanations, &c. 5th. An Appendix, containing the written evidence.

ADVERTISEMENT.

In Plan IV. the third and fourth positions of the army in the engagement of 19th of September may appear upon a curfory view to want precifion. The inequalities of the ground could not be diftinctly marked upon fo fmall a fcale; and the continual fhitt of the pofitions of feparate corps, as they were attacked by corps of the enemy, which frequently, from the thicknefs of the wood, they did not fee, made it equally difficult to mark regularly the pofition of the whole at any one time.

The pofition of the armies on the 8th of September in Plate V. requires alfo fome explanation. From the fmallnefs of the fcale, the pofition of the enemy could only be fhewn upon the plain near the river; but it is to be obferved, it extended over the ground of General Burgoyne's former encampment, and in front of the redoubts upon the hill.

The Speech of Lieutenant General Burgoyne, prefatory to his Narrative.

Mr. Montagu,

BEFORE I enter upon the narrative, which the precedent of your late proceedings authorifes me to lay before you, I think it a duty to the committee, to promife that I fhall trouble them with little other matter than fuch as may be neceffary to eludicate the tranfactions of the campaign 1777, in that quarter where I commanded.

I fhall keep in mind, that to explain the caufes of the difafter at Saratoga is the principal point to which all my evidence ought to lead : but at the fame time, I fhall take confidence in the juftice and benevolence of my hearers, that where arguments in exculpation of the commander can aptly be combined with a faithful reprefentation of facts, they will not be deemed foreign to the main object under their confideration.

Upon thefe ideas, though fome introductory explanations are requifite, I fhall fupprefs the inclination I at firft conceived, of ftating my conduct from the time, when, conjointly with my honourable friend who took the lead in this inquiry,* I was called to the unfolicited and unwelcome fervice in America : nor will I enumerate the complicated circumftances of private misfortune and ill health under which I purfued it. Prudence, as well as other propriety, is, I confefs, confulted in this fuppreffion ; for were it feen, that an officer had blended with the refpect due

B   to

* Sir William Howe.

to authority, warm, though difinterefted perfonal attachments; that under a perfuafion of the honour and integrity of the king's fervants, he had united to his zeal for the public caufe an intereft in their private credit and ambition; would it not be conceived, that his guilt muft have been atrocious, beyond all excufe or palliation, to induce the very men to whom his endeavours, and his faculties, fuch as they were, had been thus devoted, not only compleatly to defert him, but to preclude him, as far as in them lay, from every means of defence, and if poffible, to ruin him in the opinion of the king, the army, and the country?

An earneft defire to fave, as much as poffible, the time of the committee, would alfo diffuade me from recurring to any points previous to my inftructions which have been difcuffed upon former occafions; but I find that great ftrefs is ftill laid to my prejudice upon a paper which found its way to the houfe during my abfence: I mean the private letter to the noble lord, fecretary for the American department, dated 1ft January, 1777.*

See Appendix
No. I.

The noble lord has frequently ftated that letter to have flipped inadvertently into the parcel deftined for the houfe, and I give credit in that particular to his affertion; becaufe, whatever other impreffions he might have found it his intereft to make refpecting me, he certainly would not have thought that the imputation on me which that letter tended to fix, a proper one for *him* to put forward: it is a notorious fact, or I would not mention it, that it has been held a reflection upon my character (by the part of the public with whom the noble lord is unpopular) that I addreffed him as a patron and friend.

This is an imputation to which I muft plead guilty; for at the time I wrote that letter, I certainly did hold that noble lord as my friend, and I had acted to deferve he fhould be fo. The next ill tendency of that paper was, as the noble lord well knows, to imprefs the public with an opinion, that I was endeavouring

to

to supplant Sir Guy Carleton in the command of the northern army—an action abhorrent to the honour of an officer and the liberality of a gentleman; and of which, thank God, I can prove the falsehood, by irrefragable evidence upon your table, and in a very small compass. I need only refer to the dispatches to Sir Guy Carleton by his aid de-camp, dated 22d August, 1776,* four months before I came home, to shew that it was at that time determined, that Sir Guy Carleton should remain in Canada; and that determination was made, as I have been informed, not only upon the political reasoning which appears in that dispatch, but also, upon great law opinions, that he could not, under the commission he then held under the great seal, pass the frontiers of his province. Sir, this confutation was urged by me last year; and were collateral proof necessary to my justification upon this subject, I could bring to your bar a tribe of gentlemen, who had imbibed impressions not very favourable to the military proceedings of Sir Guy Carleton in the campaign of 1776: I could shew that I seized numberless, indeed I seized every possible occasion to vindicate the judgment, the assiduity, the activity of that highly respectable officer, careless how ill I paid my court, earnest to meet every attack against his fame.

* See Appendix No. II.

I beg leave also to call the attention of the committee very particularly to one other paper, the date of which is previous to my departure from England: it is entitled, " Thoughts for conducting the War " from the Side of Canada, by Lieutenant General " Burgoyne."* Sir, it will be in the recollection of the committee, whether, when the conduct of the war was under consideration last year in my absence, it was not understood, that the plan of the northern expedition was formed upon that paper as produced upon your table? If so, I must ask the noble lord, why he suffered that error to prevail? The noble lord knew, (and it was peculiarly his duty to declare it) that the two proposals, the first of turning the expedition eventually

* No. III.

tually

tually towards Connecticut; and the second, of em·
barking the army on the river St. Lawrence, in order
to effect a junction with Sir William Howe by sea, in
case the attempt by land appeared " impracticable, or
" too hazardous," were erased while the paper was in
his lordship's hands.

From that paper, as it appeared without erasures,
naturally arose the conclusion, that the plan I had to
execute was completely my own; upon that paper
were founded, as naturally, the doubts which have
been entertained upon the peremptory tenor of my
instructions. I must again ask the noble lord, upon
what principle of justice he suffered those impressions
to exist in this house? Why, in a debate in which he
took a part, did he conceal, that the circumstances in
reality were totally different from those upon which
gentlemen reasoned; that the discretion reserved in the
paper before the house was taken away, and consequently, that my orders were rendered absolute in the
strictest sense by his own alterations?

Let any gentleman who has supposed I had an implied latitude for my conduct, now compare this circumstance with the wording of the letter to Sir Guy
Carleton, dated March 26, 1777, with a copy of which
I was furnished, and extracts from which were afterwards the only orders I had to act upon.*

*
See Ap-
pendix
No. IV.

I shall take no particular notice of what is called the
saving clause, in the latter part of the orders, except
to give the flattest contradiction to the supposition that
I dictated it—a supposition that I know is not yet
abandoned by the men who first suggested it. I have
spoke to it very fully upon a former occasion;† and I
do not wish, when it can be avoided, to enforce or re-
iterate the charges of duplicity and treachery which
must ensue, if that clause could be supposed to have
reference to any conduct previous to my arrival at

† The debate upon Mr. Vyner's motion, May 28, 1778; the
speech was published.

Albany.

Albany. The circumstance of forbidding me the latitude in the two particulars I had proposed in my plan, and many other circumstances, clearly indicated the decided intentions and expectations of the ministers, rendered the sense of the whole order taken together clear and distinct, and shewed that the clause which is pretended to have left me a discretion as to my main object, had no sort of relation to that object. That clause evidently related not to my forcing my way, or not forcing it, to Albany, the place of my destination, but to such collateral and eventual operations as might be adviseable in the course of my march. It related to the making impression upon the rebels, and bringing them to obedience, in such manner as exigencies might require, and in my judgment might seem most proper, previous to receiving orders from Sir William Howe, " of my junction with whom I was never to " lose view."

Notwithstanding there has been so much discussion in debate and print upon the interpretation of absolute orders, the committee, I am confident, will absolve me, though, at the expence of a few moments more, I should continue a subject upon which the merit or blame of the future proceedings in great measure rests.

I do not admit the position, that there can be no case in which an officer acting at a distance is bound at every hazard to pursue orders, that appear absolute *and decisive.* It is easy to conceive circumstances, which might justify a state in hazarding an army, for the sake of facilitating great and decisive objects. Gentlemen, conversant in military history, will recollect many examples of this principle : upon a former occasion, I stated a supposed case ;* and I now entreat

B 3   leave

* The case alluded to was put in a former debate, as follows : suppose the British army that invaded Britany in 1758, had gained a complete victory over the Duke D'Aiguillon : to have marched rapidly towards Paris, abandoning the communication with the fleet, exposing the army possibly to great want of provision, and to the impracticability of retreat, would certainly have been a measure

con-

leave to add a real example of peremptory orders,
which happened in the courſe of my own ſervice.   I
have ever retained the impreſſion, that the circumſtance
I am going to relate, made upon my mind at the time ;
and to thoſe few who may ſtill think, that in any part
of my conduct, I raſhly riſked my peace, my intereſt or
my fame, to forward the wiſhes of others, this pre-
poſſeſſion may in ſome meaſure account for, and ex-
cuſe, my imprudence.

In the campaign of 1762, in Portugal, the Count
La Lippe, a name, which, if it finds a due hiſtorian,
will ſtand among the firſt in military fame, was placed
at the head of about 6000 Britiſh troops, and a Portu-
gueſe army, the greater part of which was little better
than nominal, to defend an extenſive frontier againſt
the whole force of Spain, and a large body of the
veteran troops of France.   The ſalvation of Portugal
depends ſolely on the capacity of that great man, which
united the deepeſt political reaſoning with exquiſite
military addreſs.

I had the honour to be entruſted with the defence
of the moſt important paſs upon the Tagus, and my
orders were peremptory to maintain it againſt any
numbers, and to the laſt man.

A ſelect corps of the enemy, greatly ſuperior to
mine, were encamped within ſight on the other ſide
the river, and our advanced poſts were within half
muſquet ſhot.

In this ſituation, I received intelligence from Count
La Lippe, of a deſign of the enemy to paſs the Tagus

conſummately deſperate and unjuſtifiable, if tried upon military
ſyſtem: yet, will any man ſay, that if that meaſure muſt evidently
have produced ſuch alarm and confuſion in the heart of France,
as to have compelled the recall of her whole force from Germany,
or ſuch part of it, as would have given uncontrouled ſcope to the
armies under the King of Pruſſia and Prince Ferdinand, that the
miniſter of England would not have been judicious, though at the
palpable riſk of the army, as far as capture was concerned, in
ordering the general to proceed by the moſt *vigorous exertions*, and
to force his way to Paris ?

in

in force, about ſix miles above me, and to take poſſeſſion of the open country in my rear, with a large
corps of cavalry, by which means all communication,
ſupply, or ſafe retreat, would be cut off.

Together with this intelligence, the Count's letter
expreſſed, " That every delay to the enemy in getting
" poſſeſſion of the paſs I guarded, was ſo material to
" his other plans and operations, that it juſtified a
" deviation from ſyſtematic rules ; that, therefore,
" after taking timely precautions to ſecure the retreat
" of my cavalry, I muſt abide the conſequence with
" the infantry ; that at the laſt extremity, I muſt
" abandon my cannon, camp, &c. and with ſuch
" proviſion as the men could carry upon their backs,
" throw myſelf into the mountains upon my left, and
" endeavour, by ſmall and diſperſed parties, to gain
" a rendezvous at the northern part of the province."
I muſt obſerve, that when theſe peremptory orders
were given, the commander was at a diſtance that
made all timely communication of circumſtances as
impoſſible, as if the Atlantic had been between us ;
and I cannot cloſe the example without mentioning
the concluding part of Count La Lippe's letter. " He
" participated," he ſaid " in the feelings with which
" an officer would be ſtruck for his reputation, in
" ſuffering himſelf to be cut, and reduced to ſacrifice
" his camp, his baggage, and twenty pieces of can-
" non. But *be at eaſe,*" continued that great and
generous man, " *I will take the meaſure entirely upon*
" *myſelf : perſevere as I have directed, and be confident*
" *of my defence and protection.*" This was a ſaving
clauſe of a nature very different from thoſe it is the
practice in the preſent day to pen ; and if any man
doubts the quotation, I can bring poſitive evidence to
the truth of it verbatim.

Thus much, Sir, I thought it incumbent upon me
to ſtate in argument againſt the poſition that has been
inſiſted upon, that no orders can be worded ſo peremptorily at a diſtance, as not to admit of an im-

plied

plied latitude, in cafe of unforefeen and infurmountable
difficulties: but to prevent all future cavil upon this
fubject, I requeft the committee to recollect, what I
have again and again repeated; that I by no means
put my defence, in paffing the Hudfon's River, folely
upon this reafoning. On the contrary, fuppofing for
the argument's fake, I fhould concede (which I never
have done, nor mean to do) to the noble Lord, and to
every other gentleman, all they can defire to affume
upon implied latitude in given cafes, I fhould equally
prove that no fuch cafe did exift, as would have juftified me upon their own principle, in departing from
the letter of the orders under which I acted.

Having thus cleared my way to the time of my
leaving England, to take upon me the command of
the Northern expedition; I fhall now lay before the
committee a narrative of its progrefs, in as concife and
fimple terms, as the nature of the fubject will allow,
endeavouring to imitate the perfpicuity of the honourable gentleman who took the lead in this bufinefs, and
not without hope of my endeavours producing the
fame effect; and that, in the opinion of the houfe, my
language, as has been expreffed of his, will be deemed
the language of truth.

N A R R A T I V E.

IT is my intention, for the more ready comprehen-
fion of the whole fubject, to divide it into three
periods. The firft, from my appointment to the command, to the end of my purfuit of the enemy from
Ticonderoga; the fecond, from that time to the paffage of the Hudfon's River; and the third to the figning
the convention.

I left

I left London on the 27th of March, and upon my departure from Plymouth, finding the Albion man of war ready to fail for New-York, I wrote to Sir W. Howe by that conveyance, upon the fubject of my expedition, and the nature of my orders. I arrived at Quebec the 6th of May. Sir Guy Carleton immediately put under my command the troops deftined for the expedition, and committed to my management the preparatory arrangements. From thence I wrote a fecond letter to Sir William Howe, wherein I repeated that I was entrufted with the command of the army deftined to march from Canada, and that my orders were to force a junction with his excellency.

I expreffed alfo my wifhes, " that a latitude had " been left me for a diverfion towards Connecticut, " but that fuch an idea being out of queftion, by " my orders being precife to force the junction, it was " only mentioned to introduce the idea ftill refting " upon my mind; viz. to give the change to the " enemy if I could, and by every feint in my power " to eftablifh a fufpicion, that I ftill pointed towards " Connecticut."

" But," I repeated, " that under the prefent pre- " cifion of my orders, I fhould really have no view " but that of joining him, nor think myfelf juftified " by any temptation to delay the moft expeditious " means I could find to effect that purpofe."

I proceeded to Montreal on the 12th, and as my letters, lately laid before the houfe from that place,[*] and from Quebec, will fhew the ftate of things, I fhould not reft a moment upon this period, were it not to add one more public teftimony, to thofe I am not confcious of having omitted upon any occafion, of the affiduous and cordial manner in which the different fervices were forwarded by Sir Guy Carleton. I fhould think it as difhonourable to feek, as I know it would be impoffible to find, excufe for any fault of mine in any failure on the part of Sir Guy Carleton, or of any perfons who acted under him, in any matter refpecting the

* See Appendix No. V.

the expedition. Had that officer been acting for himfelf, or for his brother, he could not have fhewn more
indefatigble zeal than he did, to comply with and expedite my requifitions and defires.

Certain parts of the expected force, neverthefs, fell
fhort. The Canadian troops, ftated in the plan at 2000,
confifted only of three companies, intended to be of
100 men each, but in reality not amounting to more
than 150 upon the whole; nor could they be augmented. The corvées, which are detachments of provincials without arms, to repair roads, convey provifions,
or any other temporary employment for the king's fervice, could not be obtained in fufficient number, nor
kept to their employments, although Sir Guy Carleton
ufed every poffible exertion and encouragement for the
purpofe. Drivers for the provifion carts, and other
carriages, could not be fully fupplied by the contractor, though no expence was fpared; a circumftance
which occafioned much inconvenience afterwards.

To thefe unavoidable difappointments were added
the difficulties occafioned by bad weather, which rendered the roads almoft impracticable at the carrying
places, and confequently the paffage of the bateaux,
artillery, and baggage exceedingly dilatory: we had
befide a great deal of contrary wind. Notwithftanding
all impediments, the army affembled between the 17th
and 20th of June, at Cumberland Point, upon Lake
Champlain.

On the 21ft I held a conference with the Iroquois,
Algonchins, Abenekies, and Outawas, Indians, in all
about four hundred.

This conference appears in your papers*. I thought
at the time that the cordiality of the Indians over
the whole continent might be depended upon, and
their firft operations tended to perfuade me into a belief of their utility. The prieft to whom they feemed
devoted, and the Britifh officers employed to conduct
them, and to whofe controul they engaged to fubmit,
gained advantages, and fpread terror without barbarity.
The

* See Ap-
pendix
No, VI.

The firft party fent out made feveral of the enemy prifoners in the heat of action, and treated them with
European humanity.

During the movement of the different corps to this
general rendezvous, I wrote a third letter to Sir William
Howe. The chief purport of it was to give him " in-
" telligence of my fituation at the time, and of my
" expectation of being before Ticonderoga between the
" 20th and 25th inftant ; that I did not apprehend the
" effective ftrength of the army would amount to above
" 6500 men ; that I meant to apply to Sir Guy Carle-
" ton to fend a garrifon to Ticonderoga when it fhould
" be reduced, but that I was apprehenfive he would
" not think himfelf authorifed by the King's orders to
" comply ; that whenever, therefore, I might be able to
" effect the junction, Sir William would not expect me
" to bring near the original number. I repeated my
" perfeverance in the idea of giving jealoufy on the fide
" of Connecticut, and at the fame time my affurances,
" that I fhould make no manœuvre that could procra-
" ftinate the great object of a junction."

I ftate thefe different letters to Sir William Howe
merely to fhew that my conception of the precifion of
my orders was not upon after-thought, and taken up as
an excufe when I found the expedition had failed ; but
a fixed decided fentiment coeval with my knowledge of
my command.

For a further proof of the fame fact, I beg leave to
ftate an extract from my orders to the army at Crown
Point, June 30th. The words were thefe :

" The army embarks to-morrow to approach the
" enemy. The fervices required of this particular ex-
" pedition are critical and confpicuous. During our
" progrefs occafions may occur, in which, nor diffi-
" culty, nor labour, nor life are to be regarded. This
" army muft not retreat." Were it neceffary, I could
bring abundant collateral proof to the fame effect, and
fhew that the idea of forcing a way to Albany by vi-
gorous

gorous exertions againſt any oppoſition we might meet, was general and fixt through the whole army.

My proceedings from the time of aſſembling the army as before deſcribed, to the date of my public diſpatch from Skeneſborough, comprehending the manœuvres which forced the enemy from Ticonderoga, and the actions at Skeneſborough, Huberton, and Fort Anne, are related at full in that diſpatch.*

See Appendix No. VII. It is the leſs neceſſary to give the Committee further trouble upon this ſubject, becauſe I believe no enemy can be found to arraign my conduct in thoſe days of ſucceſs ; or if there were one, he could not deprive me of the conſolation, that I had his Majeſty's full approbation and applauſe, of which it is known to many, I had a very honourable and diſtinguiſhed proof.

All therefore that is neceſſary before I quit this firſt period of the campaign, is to give a preciſe ſtate of the effective ſtrength of the army, at the time it aſſembled.

On the 1ſt July, the day we encamped before Ticonderoga, the troops conſiſted of

Britiſh rank and file	-	3724
German ditto	-	3016
		————
		6740 regulars, excluſive of artillery-men.
		————
Canadians and Provincials, about	250	
Indians about	-	400
		————
		650

In regard to the artillery, I think this the proper place to rectify the miſrepreſentations that have prevailed reſpecting the quantity employed. It has been ſtated as far beyond the neceſſary proportion for the number of troops, an incumbrance to their movements, and one cauſe of what has been called the ſlow progreſs of the expedition.

In order to juſtify this charge, a view of the whole maſs has been preſented to the public without any explanation

planation of its diftinct allotments; and many have
led to believe, that the whole was attached to the
throughout the campaign, and fell into the en
hands at laft—The intention of this reprefentati
obvious : the allegation is falfe.

The facts, as I fhall prove them to the committee, are
as follow : The whole original train furnifhed by Sir
Guy Carleton confifted of fixteen heavy twenty-four
pounders; ten heavy twelve-pounders; eight medium
twelve-pounders; two light twenty-four pounders; one
light twelve-pounder; twenty-fix light fix-pounders;
feventeen light three-pounders; fix eight-inch howitzers;
fix five and a half inch howitzers; two thirteen-inch
mortars; two ten-inch mortars; fix eight-inch mortars;
twelve five and a half-inch mortars; and twenty-four
four and two fifth-inch mortars. Of thefe, two heavy
twenty-four pounders were fent on board a fhip for the
defence of Lake Champlain, and the other fourteen
were fent back to St. John's. Of the heavy twelve-
pounders, fix were left at Ticonderoga, four ditto in
the Royal George ; four medium twelve-pounders at
Fort George; one light twelve-pounder at Ticonderoga;
two light fix-pounders at Fort George; four light fix-
pounders at St. John's; four light three-pounders at
Ticonderoga; five light three-pounders at St. John's;
two eight-inch howitzers at Fort George; two ditto at
St. John's; two five and a half-inch howitzers at Fort
George; two thirteen-inch mortars in the Royal George;
two ten-inch mortars in ditto; four eight-inch mortars
in ditto; four five and a half-inch mortars at Ticonderoga; four royal mortars in the Royal George; twelve
cohorns at Ticonderoga; and eight cohorns in the Royal
George.

The field-train therefore that proceeded with the
army confifted of four medium twelve-pounders; two
light twenty-four pounders; eighteen light fix-pounders;
fix light three-pounders; two eight-inch howitzers;
four five and a half-inch howitzers; two eight-inch
mortars, and four royals.

The

NARRATIVE.

The carrying the twenty-four pounders (though they were but two) has been spoken of as an error, and it is necessary therefore to inform the committee that they were of a construction lighter by eight hundred weight than medium twelves, and to all intents and purposes field artillery.

This artillery was distributed as follows :

Fraser's corps, estimated at three battalions,
Ten pieces, viz.

Four light six-pounders.

Four light three-pounders, constructed for being occasionally carried on horseback.

Two royal howitzers.

German reserve, under Colonel Breyman, estimated at two battalions.

Two light six-pounders.

Two light three-pounders, and served by the Hesse Hanau artillery men.

The line of British, four battalions,
Germans, five battalions.
Total, nine battallions.

Three brigades of artillery, of four six-pounders each ; viz. one brigade for each wing, and one for the center.

From hence it appears that to fourteen battalions there were allotted twenty-six pieces of light artillery. The customary allotment is two pieces per battalion, consequently the proportion of artillery was less than upon common services.

The forming artillery into brigades, in preference to detaching two guns to each battalion, has been constantly practised in most services during last war under the ablest men, and it is productive of many advantages, as the brigades by that means, either singly or united, fall under the command of a proportionable number of officers. The service is carried on with greater regularity, and the effect of the fire becomes much more formidable than when scattered along the front of the line.

This

This mode of fervice was recommended by Major-general Phillips, and adopted without hefitation by me, my own judgment being confirmed by an officer of his great fkill and experience.

The park artillery confifted of ten peices, viz.

 2 light twenty-four pounders.
 4 medium twelve-pounders.
 2 eight-inch howitzers.
 2 royal howitzers.

I underftood this proportion of field artillery to be the fame as that propofed by Sir Guy Carleton had he commanded; it was the proportion recommended by General Philips, and I formed my opinion conformably to the fentiments of thofe refpectable officers upon the following reafons, viz. that artillery was extremely formidable to raw troops; that in a country of pofts it was effentially neceffary againft the beft troops; that it was yet more applicable to the enemy we were to combat, becaufe the mode of defence they invariably adopted, and at which they were beyond all other nations expert, was that of entrenchment covered with ftrong abbatis, againft which the cannon, of the nature of the heavieft above defcribed, and howitzers, might often be effectual, when to diflodge them by any other means might be attended with continued and important loffes.

In thefe general ideas of the ufe of artillery againft the rebel forces, I have the happinefs to obferve, from the papers before you, the concurrence of Sir William Howe, who ftates fimilar ideas very fully in one of his requifitions to the fecretary of ftate: but further reafons for not diminifhing the proportion of guns of fuperior calibre to fix-pounders in this train, were, firft, their ufe againft block-houfes (a fpecies of fortification peculiar to America); fecondly, a probability that gunboats might be requifite for the fecurity of the water tranfport, on fome part of the Hudfon's River; but principally the intention of fortifying a camp at Albany, in cafe I fhould reach that place, fhould meet with a fufficiency of provifion there (as I was led to expect)

I

and

and fhould find it expedient to pafs the winter there, without communication with New-York.

With refpeƈt to the quantity of ammunition attached to this artillery, it is to be obferved, that the number of rounds accompanying the light pieces, and which were carried in fmall carts, were not more than fufficient for a day's aƈtion.

Light fix-pounders — 124 rounds each.
Light three-pounders — 300 rounds.
Royal howitzers — 90 rounds.

The different referves of ammunition were chiefly conveyed by water in fcows and bateaux : it certainly would not have been advifable, after a communication with Canada was at an end, to depend upon precarious fupplies from the fouthward, and therefore it became neceffary (as far as the fervice would allow) to carry forward fuch ftores, as there was every appearance of an abfolute want of, during the courfe of an aƈtive campaign.

Had the enemy eftablifhed themfelves in force upon the iflands at the mouth of the Mohawk River, or on other ground equally advantageous, to have difputed the paffage of that, or of the Hudfon's River, or had they even waited an affault in their works at Stillwater, it is probable, that recourfe muft have been had to artillery of the heavier nature ; in the latter cafe efpecially they muft have been ufed, in order to derive any advantage from our feizing a poft upon their left flank : I have fince known, that they had iron twelve and nine-pounders mounted upon thofe works, which were in other refpeƈts very formidable.

The Britifh artillery-men, rank and file, were	245
Recruits, under command of Lieutenant Nutt, of the 33d regiment, attached to the fervice of the artillery — —	150
Heffian artillery-men, rank and file —	78
	473
	Add

Add thefe numbers to the former ftate of the army, and it will be found, that the regular ftrength when at the greateft confifted of 7213.

I come now to the fecond period of the campaign, comprehending the tranfactions from the time the purfuit of the enemy from Ticonderoga ceafed, and the corps of Brigadier-general Frafer, and the 9th regiment, rejoined the army, after the refpective actions of Huberton and Fort Anne, to the time when the army paffed the Hudfon's River to attack the enemy near Stillwater.

It had proved impoffible immediately to follow the quick retreat of the enemy farther, from the nature of the country, and the neceffity of waiting a frefh fupply of provifions. But it appeared evident to me, that could a rapid progrefs towards Albany be effected, during their difperfion and panic, it would be decifive on the fuccefs of the expedition.

Queftion has been made by thofe who began at this period to arraign my military conduct, whether it would not have been more expedient for the purpofe of rapidity, to have fallen back to Ticonderoga, in order to take the convenient route by Lake George, than to have perfevered in the laborious and difficult courfe by land to Fort Edward? My motives for preferring the latter were thefe: I confidered not only the general impreffions which a retrograde motion is apt to make upon the minds both of enemies and friends, but alfo, that the natural conduct of the enemy in that cafe would be to remain at Fort George, as their retreat could not then be cut off, in order to oblige me to open trenches, and confequently to delay me, and in the mean time they would have deftroyed the road from Fort George to Fort Edward. On the other hand, by perfifting to penetrate by the fhort cut from Fort Anne, of which I was then mafter, to Fort Edward, though it was attended with great labour, and many alert fituations, the troops were improved in the very effential point of wood fervice; I effectually diflodged the enemy from Fort

C George

George without a blow: and feeing me mafter of one communication, they did not think it worth while to deftroy the other.

The great number of boats alfo, which muft neceffarily have been employed for the tranfport of the troops over Lake George, were by this courfe fpared for the tranfport of the provifion, artillery, and ammunition.

The fuccefs anfwered this reafoning in every point; for by the vigilance of General Phillips, to whom I had committed the important part of forwarding all the neceffaries from Ticonderoga, a great embarkation arrived at Fort George on July 29th. I took poffeffion of the country near Fort Edward on the fame day, and independently of other advantages, I found myfelf much more forward in point of time than I could poffibly have been by the other route.

Another material motive, which could not be known by ftrangers who have reafoned upon this movement, was, that during the time my army was employed in clearing Wook-Creek and cutting roads, and the corps under Major-general Phillips was working to pafs the tranfports over Lake George, I was enabled to detach a large corps to my left, under Major-general Reidefel, and thereby affift my purpofe of giving jealoufy to Connecticut, and keeping in check the whole country called the Hampfhire Grants.

It was at this time Major-general Reidefel conceived the purpofe of mounting his regiment of dragoons. In the country he traverfed during his detached command, he found the people frightened and fubmiffive. He was induftrious and expert in procuring intelligence in parts of the country more remote than Bennington, and entertained no doubt of fuccefs, were an expedition formed under the command of Lieutenant-colonel Baume.

On the arrival of the army at Fort Edward, the great object of attention was the tranfports from Fort George. The diftance was about fixteen miles, the roads wanting great repair, the weather unfavourable, the

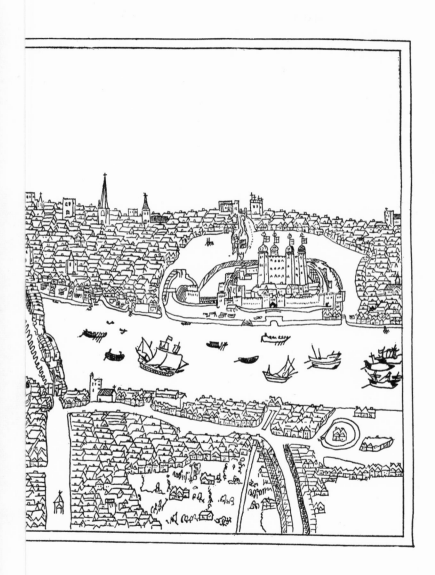

the cattle and carriages fcarce ; part of the latter inconvenience was occafioned by the number of both that were neceffarily detained at Ticonderoga, for the purpofe of dragging the boats and the provifions over the carrying-places, between Lake Champlain and Lake Georg : another part of the inconvenience was caufed by the unavoidable delays, in bringing the different divifions of horfes, as they were collected in Canada, through the defart, for fuch moft of the country is, between St. John's and Ticonderoga.

It was foon found, that in the fituation of the tranfport fervice at that time, the army could barely be victualled from day to day, and that there was no profpect of eftablifhing a magazine in due time for purfuing prefent advantages. The idea of the expedition to Bennington originated upon this difficulty, combined with the intelligence reported by General Reidefel, and with all I had otherwife received.

I knew that Bennington was the great depofit of corn, flour, and ftore cattle; that it was guarded only by militia ; and every day's account tended to confirm the perfuafion of the loyalty of one defcription of the inhabitants and the panic of the other. Thofe who knew the country beft were the moft fanguine in this perfuafion.

Had my intelligence been worfe founded, I fhould not have hefitated to try this expedition with fuch troops, and under fuch inftructions, as I gave to the commanding officer, for fo great a purpofe as that of a fupply fufficient to enable the army to follow at the heels of a broken and difconcerted enemy. The German troops employed were of the beft I had of that nation. The number of Britifh was fmall; but it was the felect light corps of the army, compofed of chofen men from all the regiments, and commanded by Captain Frafer, one of the moft diftinguifhed officers in his line of fervice that ever I met with. The inftructions recommended the utmoft caution refpecting pofts and fecurity of retreat, attention againft expofing the folid part of the

detachment

detachment to affront, or committing it in any inftance, without a moral certainty of fuccefs. I touch with tendernefs and with great reluctance points that relate to the dead. My defence compels me to fay, my cautions were not obferved, nor the reinforcement advanced with the alacrity I had a right to expect. The men who commanded in both inftances were brave and experienced officers. I have ever imputed their failure partly to delufion in refpect to the enemy, and partly to furprife and confequent confufion in the troops.

For further explanation of my motives, and the circumftances attending the conduct of the expedition, I beg leave to refer the committee to the letter laid before the houfe laft year, and more particularly to the private letter laid before the houfe lately.*

See Appendix No. VIII. IX.

The fame letter will fhew the only refource that remained for proceeding towards Albany, after the difappointment of this expedition, viz. to prefs forward a neceffary fupply of provifion, and other indifpenfible articles, from Fort George. I fhall bring proof to your bar to this point, and I truft I fhall fhew, beyond a doubt, that no poffible exertion was omitted. It is not uncommon for gentlemen, unacquainted with the peculiarities of the country to which I am alluding, to calculate the tranfport of magazines, by meafuring the diftance upon a map, and then applying the refources of carriage, as practifed in other countries. I requeft permiffion to fhew their miftake. The firft ftage from Fort George to Fort Edward is by land. The diftance and the roads were defcribed before. At Fort Edward the Hudfon's River becomes navigable for a certain extent, and it is the conftant practice in all tranfports to refume the water carriage. Were it not, new impediments would arife from hills, worfe roads, and fuch an increafed diftance, as would prevent the cattle returning to Fort George the fame day. About fix miles below Fort Edward lie the falls of Fort Miller, where there is another carrying-place, which, though of no
consfiderable

considerable length, makes it neceſſary to unload the boats, to place the contents in carts, and to replace them in freſh boats, at the place the river again admits of navigation. The boats unloaded, return to Fort Edward againſt a rapid ſtream.

Upon this ſhort ſtate of facts, gentlemen will judge of our embarraſſments. In the firſt place, it was neceſſary to bring forward to Fort Edward fourſcore or a hundred boats, as mere carriage-veſſels for the proviſions, each boat made a hard day's work for ſix or more horſes, including the return of the horſes. At the next carrying-place, as above deſcribed, it was neceſſary to place a conſiderable relay of horſes to draw over, firſt, a portion of carriage-boats, and afterwards the proviſion, as it arrived. I have not mentioned the great number of other boats neceſſary to be brought forward, to form bridges, to carry baggage and ammunition, and the number of carriages framed to tranſport the boats themſelves at the enſuing carrying-places, as we ſhould proceed to Albany. This will be ſhewn in detail at the bar, if the committee chuſe to hear it; and I pledge myſelf, it will appear, that the diligence in this ſervice was extreme; that it was performed in the moſt expeditious manner poſſible, regard being had to our reſources, and that no delay was occaſioned by the artillery, becauſe the horſes appropriated to it were ſupernumerary to thoſe for which we had carts, and the artillery, not already with the army, at laſt was all brought up by its own horſes in two days.

On the 13th of September, the ſtore of proviſion, amounting to about thirty days' conſumption, was completed. I have ſtated, in my letter to the ſecretary of ſtate, my reaſons againſt proceeding with leſs quantity. And it is now time to enter upon the conſideration of that object, which is held by ſome to be concluſive upon the executive part of the campaign, the paſſage of the Hudſon's River.

Two errors, reſpecting this paſſage, though of oppoſite and incompatible natures, are ſuppoſed to have

contributed

contributed to the ill fuccefs that enfued ; the one, the error of delay, the other, that of precipitation. In defence againft the firft, I refer to my effort at Bennington to procure fupplies, and to the impediments, I have juft now ftated, after the effort failed. Againft the latter, I refer to the reafons laid down in my private letter to the fecrétary of ftate, dated 20th of Auguft. * The

See Appendix No. IX.

ftate of things at this important crifis, and my reafoning upon it, are expreffed ftill more at large in my difpatch from Albany ; I will now only touch them fhortly. On the one hand, my communications were at an end ; my retreat was infecure ; the enemy was collected in force , they were ftongly pofted ; Colonel St. Leger was retiring from Fort Stanwix. Thefe were difficulties, but none of them infurmountable. On the other hand, I had diflodged the enemy repeatedly, when in force, and more ftrongly pofted ; my army was confcious of having the fuperiority, and eager to advance ; I expected co-operation ; no letters from Sir William Howe removed that expectation ; that to Sir Guy Carleton had never weighed upon my mind, becaufe it was dated early in April, and confequently long before the fecretary of ftate's inftructions, which I muft have fuppofed to relate to co-operation, could be received. The letter of 17th of July,* mentioned that

No. X.

General's return to my affiftance, fhould Wafhington turn his force towards me ; indicated, as I thought, an expectation of my arrival at Albany ; and informed me, that Sir Henry Clinton was left at New-York, and would act as occurrences might direct. I did *net* know Sir Henry Clinton's force. I *did* know, that confiderable reinforcement might be then expected at New-York from England. After all, fhould co-operation from below fail, the whole force of Colonel St. Leger, and Sir William Johnfon, was to be expected from above, in time to facilitate a retreat, though not in time to affift my advance. Under thefe different fuggeftions. and thofe that are more copioufly ftated in the difpatch, to which I have referred, I read again my

orders

orders (I believe for an hundredth time) and I was decided.

And I am ftill convinced, that no proof that could have been brought from appearances, intelligence or reafoning, could have juftified me to my country, have faved me from the condemnation of my profeffion, or produced pardon within my own breaft, had I not advanced, and tried a battle with the enemy.

I will conclude this fubject, with again afferting upon my honour, what I hope to fupport by evidence, though it is impoffible to bring pofitive proof to a negative, that neither General Frafer, nor General Phillips, ever offered, as has been reported, nor can be fuppofed to have conceived any objection againft the paffage of the Hudfon's River.

This refolution being taken, I truft, the manner of approaching the enemy, when explained by witneffes, will not be difgraceful to me as a foldier. The action, which enfued on the 19th of September, verified my opinion of the valour of my army; and I muft, in truth, acknowledge, a very refpectable fhare of that quality in the army of the enemy. To the general defcription given in my difpatch, it will be fit to add, by evidence, the peculiar merits of the troops in that action. The honour of three Britifh regiments, in continual and clofe fire for four hours, all of them fuffering confiderable lofs, and one remaining with lefs than fixty men, and four or five officers, ought not to lofe its due applaufe, becaufe it is faid, their opponents were irregulars and militia.

A victory was at laft obtained, but the clofe of day unavoidably prevented any immediate advantages. On the day following, it was known from prifoners and deferters, that the enemy were in a poft ftrongly fortified; but from the thicknefs of the wood, it was impoffible to catch a view of any part of their pofition. All that could be done, therefore, was to take up ground as near them, as the nature of the country would admit with regard to military arrangement. It appears from the

difpatch

difpatch already alluded to, that the army remained in this pofition till the 9th of October, when the fecond action enfued, employed in fortifying their camp, and watching the enemy, whofe numbers it was now known, had been greatly fuperior to ours in the action.

It may here be afked, why, as foon as it became palpable that no ufe could be made of the victory, I did not retreat?

It will be fhewn, that on the fecond day after the action, I received intelligence from Sir Henry Clinton, of his intention to attack the highlands about that time, and I was hourly in expectation, I thought a juftly founded one, of that meafure operating to diflodge Mr. Gates entirely, or to oblige him to detach a large portion of his force. Either of thefe cafes would probably have opened my way to Albany. In thefe circumftances, could the preference upon thefe alternatives admit of a moment's reflection? To wait fo fair a profpect of effecting at laft the great purpofe of the campaign, or to put a victorious army, under all the difadvantages of a beaten one, by a difficult and difgraceful retreat; relinquifhing the long-expected co-operation, in the very hour of its promife, and leaving Sir Henry Clinton's army, and probably Sir William Howe's, expofed, with fo much of the feafon o the campaign to run, to the whole force of Mr. Gates, after he fhould have feen me on the other fide of Hudfon's River.

Some of the fame confiderations, and other concomitant circumftances, will, in part, ferve to account for my not attacking the enemy during this interval; for in this fituation, as in former ones, my conduct has been arraigned upon oppofite principles.

The committee will obferve, that after receiving intelligence of Sir Henry Clinton's defign, different meffengers were difpatched by different routes, to inform that officer of my fituation, and of the time I thought I could continue in it. To have hazarded a repulfe, under fo reafonable an expectation of a power-

ful

ful diverfion, would, in my opinion, have been very unjuftifiable; but when I add, that from the back-wardnefs, or defection, of the few Indians that remained, the numbers of rifle-men, and other irregulars employed on the enemy's out-pofts, and the ftrength and darknefs of the furrounding woods, it had not yet been practicable to gain any competent knowledge of their pofition, I truft every man will go with me in the fentiment, that all thefe circumftances confidered, an attack would have been confummate rafh-nefs.

Another very powerful reafon, that operated on the fide of delay, was the ftate of my fick and wounded. Numbers of the latter were recovering faft; many excellent officers in particular; and the more I delayed the ftronger I grew. The time alfo entitled me to expect Lieutenant Colonel St. Leger's corps would be arrived at Ticonderoga, and fecret means had been long concerted to enable him to make an effort to join me, with probability of fuccefs.

Upon mature confideration of thefe and other circumftances attending this period, come to my knowledge fince, I am clearly of opinion, that had the re-inforcements from England arrived in time, to have enabled Sir Henry Clinton to have effected the ftroke he afterwards fo gallantly made in the highlands, any time between the two actions, I fhould have made my way.

The difpatch alluded to, proceeds to ftate the reafon that induced me to make the movement on the 7th of October. I fhall only add, to obviate a fuppofed error, in not advancing my whole line, that the part remaining in my camp, operated as effectually to keep the enemy's right wing in check, from fupport-ing their left, as if it had moved, with this additional advantage, that it prevented the danger of their advancing by the plain, near the river, and falling upon my rear.

I have

I have reafon to believe my difappointment on that day proceeded from an uncommon circumftance in the conduct of the enemy. Mr. Gates, as I have been informed, had determined to receive the attack in his lines; Mr. Arnold, who commanded on the left, forfeeing the danger of being turned, advanced without confultation with his general, and gave, inftead of receiving battle. The ftroke might have been fatal on his part had he failed. But confident I am, upon minute examination of the ground fince, that had the other idea been purfued, I fhould in a few hours have gained a pofition, that in fpite of the enemy's numbers, would have put them in my power.

Difagreeable as is the neceffity, I muft here again, in juftice to my own army, recur to the vigour and obftinacy with which they were fought by the enemy. A more determined perfeverance than they fhewed in the attack upon the lines, though they were finally repulfed by the corps under Lord Balcarras, I believe, is not in any officer's experience. It will be the bufinefs of evidence to prove, that in the part, where Colonel Breyman was killed, and the enemy penetrated, the mifchief could not be repaired, nor under it the camp be longer tenable.

The tranfactions of the enfuing night, the day of the eighth, and the whole progrefs of the retreat to Saratoga, will be laid before the committee minutely in the courfe of my evidence, as well as every circumftance, from the time the army arrived there to the figning the convention. I have only to premife, that, I truft, I fhall be able to prove, to the fatisfaction of the committee, that even in this fituation, I had the chance of a favourable event. The enemy had intended to attack by the plain of Saratoga. On the morning of the 11th, a confiderable column had actually paffed the Fifh Kill for that purpofe during the fog, which at that feafon was regular till fometime after fun-rife. The intention was prevented
taking

taking place, by intelligence one of their generals received from a deferter, that I had a line formed behind the brufh-wood, to fupport the poft of artillery, which was their immediate object of attack. The general inftantly retreated his column, and prevented a general action, which my pofition, compared with the propofed one of the enemy, gave me reafon to hope would have been to my advantage.

I have likewife a fatisfactory confidence, that I fhall demonftrate that the intelligence I ftated to the councils of war, refpecting the ftrength of the enemy, did not fall fhort in any part, and in fome parts much exceeded my own belief, particularly on the only poffible routes of my retreat; and that thofe pofts were not taken up during my ftay at Saratoga, as has been reported, but fome of them previous to the action of the 7th, and the reft immediately after it.

I fhall clofe the whole of this by delivering at your table, from the hands of my fecretary, an authenticated return of the force of General Gates, figned by himfelf, and the truth of it will be fupported from ocular teftimony, by every officer of the Britifh army. Many of them are now in England, and after what has been infinuated, not to fay charged in this Houfe, it becomes the duty of the accufers, not only to examine clofely the officers I have called, but to produce any other witneffes, that in their thoughts may be qualified to fpeak to the good or bad order of the rebel troops, when they marched by in their prefence, to their behaviour, when oppofed to our troops in action.

I cannot clofe this long trefpafs upon the patience of the committee, without expreffing one humble hope, that in forming a judgment upon the whole, or any diftinct part of thefe tranfactions, they will be confidered as they muft have appeared at the time; for, I believe, where war is concerned, few men in command would ftand acquitted, if any after-knowledge of facts

and

and circumſtances were brought in argument againſt deciſions of the moment, and apparent exigencies of the occaſion.

I ſubmit all I have ſaid, ſome of it, I fear, not ſufficiently prepared or arranged, with true reſpect to the committee. I ſhall not mention *all* the diſadvantages, under which I have preſſed this buſineſs upon their attention. I have cauſe to regret the abſence of a moſt confidential friend in Major General Phillips; zealous advocates, I truſt, in Major General Reideſel and Brigadier Hamilton. Much of my vindication is in the grave with General Fraſer; much with Colonel Ackland your late member. I truſt my zeal, in promoting this enquiry, as I have done, will be one mark of the ſenſe I bear of the general character of this houſe; that however men may be biaſſed by political attachments upon common occaſions, when the honour of an individual is committed to their hands, they will alone be guided by truth and juſtice. And the next inference I ſhould wiſh to be drawn, from my earneſtneſs for a public appeal, is this; that however others may impute errors to my conduct, I am myſelf conſcious of the rectitude of my intentions.

EVIDENCE.

EVIDENCE.

Jovis 20° *die Maij,* 1779.

Committee to confider of the feveral Papers which were pre-
fented to the Houfe by Mr. De Grey, upon the 19th Day
of March laft, purfuant to their Addrefs to his Majefty.

Mr. F. Montagu in the Chair.

SIR GUY CARLETON was called in and examined by General Burgoyne as follows :

Q. DO you recollect having received a letter from the fe- 1.
cretary of ftate, mentioning the reafons that made
it expedient for you to remain in the province of Quebec ?

A. Yes, very well.

Q. What was the date of it ? 2.

A. I think the 12th of Auguft, 1776—I am fure it was in
Auguft.

Q. Was not the date of that letter long before the return 3.
of General Burgoyne from Canada to Great Britain ?

A. Yes.

Q. During the winter, preceding the campaign of 1777, 4.
was not the artillery prepared at Montreal for field fervice,
upon the fuppofition that you was to command the army beyond the frontiers of the province ?

A. It was.

Q. Was the proportion allotted to General Burgoyne for 5
field fervice more than was intended, had you fo commanded ?

A. I don't precifely recollect that—It does not ftrike me
there was any great difference.

Q. Was the quantity of artillery decided on in concert 6.
with Major-General Phillips, and on his recommendation ?

A. The artillery I had prepared for the campaign, on a
fuppofition that I was to go myfelf, was in concert with General Phillips. That department, as well as others, was put
under the command of General Burgoyne on his arrival ;
and, I fuppofe, he followed the fame method fo far as regarded the artillery.

Q. Did

7.   Q. Did General Burgoyne apply to you for troops from Canada to garrifon Ticonderoga when he advanced ?
A. He did.

.8   Q. What was the purport of your anfwer ?
A. That I did not think myfelf juftified to grant it by my orders—My anfwer will appear more precifely by a copy of my anfwer to General Burgoyne.

9.   Q. Do you recollect that General Burgoyne informed you of the motives on which he proceeded from Skenefborough to Fort Fdward by land in preference to the route by Ticonderoga and Lake George ?
A. I do.

10.   Q. Did you concur in his fentiments ?
A. I remember my anfwer was an anfwer of approbation.

11.   Q. Do you know of any circumftance of General Burgoyne's military conduct, while under your command, that you difapproved ?
A. I had no reafon to difapprove of any part of his conduct while under my command.   [*Withdrew.*
Again called in, and examined by other Members of the Committee.

12.   Q. Whether, when you propofed to take that train of artillery with you that you have mentioned, it was with a view to the reduction ef the forts at Ticonderoga ; or whether you propofed to have taken with you the fame train of artillery in cafe you had marched forward in the country toward Albany ?
A. It was with an intention to reduce the forts and lines at Ticonderoga ; the tr'n of artillery was calculated for that fervice.

13. By General Burgoyne.   Q. Whether you know what proportion of artillery was carried forward by the army under General Burgoyne's command after the reduction of Ticonderoga ?
A. I don't recollect.

14.   Q. Would you not, in cafe you had reduced Ticonderoga and marched forwards towards Albany, have carried with you a train of field artillery ?
A. I probably fhould have taken artillery with me.

15.   Q. Had you forefeen a neceffity of fortifying a camp at Albany, would you not have carried fome guns of the calibre of twelve pounders and light twenty-fours ?
A. It is really a very difficult matter off hand to run into all the minute operations of a campaign ; every meafure of that fort muft have been a matter of confideration and deliberation,

ration, and there are a thousand circumstances that might
have determined me upon the spot—I don't wish to conceal
from this House any thing that I would have done—but I hope
they will consider, that every gentleman may have different
ideas of the state and situation of the army, as expressed by
the question asked, and the least inaccuracy of expression on
my part may convey ideas very different from what I could
wish—In general, so considerable a corps as that was, very
seldom moves without artillery, but the precise number must
depend on a variety of circumstances, which the discretion
and judgment of the officer who commands must determine.

Q. Were not the orders you received from government 16.
positive, for General Burgoyne to march to Albany?

A. The orders have been published I understand—Every
gentleman in this House must be a judge of those orders
whether they were positi.e or not.

Q. Did you not receive a letter, dated the 5th of April,
from Sir William Howe, informing you that he could not 17.
send any force to assist the operations of General Burgoyne's
army?

A. I received a letter from Sir William Howe relative to
his operations, a copy of which was sent to General Burgoyne—I think it was not just in those terms, but a copy
of the letter is on the table.

Q. Whether on that information, you considered that you 18.
had any discretionary power to detain General Burgoyne
after that information?

A. Certainly not.

Q. Whether in case of any difficulty that General might 19.
meet with on his march, there was any latitude given him
(General Burgoyne) to retreat?

A. I said before, that the orders were before the House,
who are competent to judge on that point.

Q. Did you yourself understand those orders to General 20.
Burgoyne to be positive?

. A. That is giving an opinion upon what perhaps may be a
question in the House; whereas I have already said, the
House are as competent to judge as I am.

Q. Is the Committee to understand from that answer, that 21.
you have any objection of giving your opinion on that
question?

A. I have an objection to give an opinion on almost all
points.

                                        Q. Did

22.   Q. Did you give it in orders to General Burgoyne, in case he met with any difficulties during his march in Canada, under your command, not to proceed ?

A. I should have taken care that General Burgoyne met with no difficulties in his march in Canada ; nor do I well see how he could.

23.   Q. Where do the boundaries of the province of Canada end ?

A. Between the Illinois and Point au Fer.

24.   Q. Is the fortress of Ticonderoga in Canada ?

A. No.

25.   Q. Did your commission, as commander in chief of the troops in the northern division, extend beyond the boundaries of Canada to Ticonderoga ?

A. That commission as commander in chief, I understood, did extend so far ; but by the orders already alluded to, or by those which General Burgoyne brought out in the spring 1777, I understood that my command was restrained to the limits of the province, and that General Burgoyne was entirely from under my command, as soon as he passed the limits of the province.

26.   Q. Did you apply to the secretary of state for a reinforcement of 4000 men, as necessary for the campaign of 1777 ?

A. I recollect when General Burgoyne was coming home in the fall of 1776, as I was perfectly satisfied with his conduct in the preceding campaign, I talked over with him, in confidence, what I thought necessary for the following campaign ; among other things I desired him to make a memorandum to demand 4000 men, as a reinforcement for the ensuing campaign, or at least for four battalions. I think I have seen those memorandums were accurately stated and laid before the House.

27.   Q. What part of that 4000 men which you thought necessary for the campaign of 1777, was actually sent out to Canada in that year ?

A. I do not accurately remember how many—I think a very small part—You may have a very precise account from the returns.

28.   Q. Of that small part sent in 1777, did not a certain proportion arrive very late in the year

A. Yes, a part arrived late.

29.   Q. After you had received your orders from the secretary of state, did you apprehend that General Burgoyne, as long as he was within the province of Canada, was positively under your command ?

A. Yes

A. Yes, I did : as long as he was in the province of Canada, I looked on him to be positively under my command; but the load of the expedition being on his shoulders, I thought it proper that he, in all things should direct ; and therefore I gave out immediate orders, that not only the troops he was to command out of the province, but all the departments necessary for the assisting his expedition, should comply immediately, and without delay, with every requisition and order he should give. The reason of my doing so was, that no time might be lost. I only required that they should report to me what orders they had received from General Burgoyne. I believe those orders are also on the table.

Q. Will you explain to the Committee what you mean by 30. the words, *load of the expedition lying on General Burgoyne's shoulders ?*

A. I had no particular meaning ; they are words I should have used on any expedition of importance.

Q. If General Burgoyne had met with very considerable 31. difficulties to impede his progress within the province of Canada, would you have thought yourself justifiable in giving any orders to General Burgoyne, different from those transmitted to General Burgoyne, through you, from the secretary of state ?

A. Had there been any difficulties in Canada, I would not have given him up the command.

Q. Having given up the command to General Burgoyne, 32. and having ordered all the troops to obey him, only reporting their proceedings to you, would you after that, have thought yourself justifiable to change the order to General Burgoyne, upon his meeting with great difficulties on the frontiers of the neighbouring provinces ?

A. I really did not mean to evade the question in the least. It did not appear to me possible that there could be any difficulties. I don't mean to say there could not, from the nature of the country, be difficulties in the march that might occasion delay, but by the nature of the question I understood difficulties from the enemy. In that case I should not have thought myself justifiable in giving up the command.

Q. If you had heard, that on the frontiers, and within 33. the province of Canada, there was the greatest reason to think, that the resistance of General Burgoyne's army was so great as to make it, in your opinion, exceedingly difficult for that general to force his way to Albany, would you think yourself justifiable in giving different orders to General Burgoyne,

D   goyne,

goyne, from thofe given by the fecretary of ftate ; or would
you have thought the fecretary of ftate's orders for General
Burgoyne's army fo peremptory that it would not be proper
for you to interfere ?

A. If I underftood the queftion as it now ftands, it is
what I would have done, had the province been invaded, or
clofe on the point of being invaded, and the enemy entering
the province.

34.   Q. The queftion does not mean an invading army, but a
refiftance from the enemy to the progrefs of General Burgoyne's army, in the cafe ftated in the laft queftion ?

A. In that cafe, that an enemy fhould be found (within
the limits of my command) I fhould have ordered all the
troops deftined for the defence of the province, to have immediately joined thofe deftined for General Burgoyne, and
have reaffumed the command of all, until thofe obftruétions
had been removed, within the limits of my authority.

35.   Q. Suppofe no enemy within the province of Canada,
but pofted in fuch a manner upon the line of communication
with Albany, as to make it exceeding difficult for General
Burgoyne to obey the orders given to him, would you think
yourfelf juftifiable in giving different orders to General Burgoyne, from thofe given by the fecretary of ftate ; or would
you have thought the fecretary of ftate's orders for General
Burgoyne's army fo peremptory that it would not be proper
for you to interfere ?

A. I could not change General Burgoyne's orders one
tittle, that was my opinion ; he received his orders from the
fame power that gave me my authority ; when once he paffed the limits of my command, I neither could give him orders, nor would he be juftified in obeying them.

36.   Q. Do you mean the latter part of that anfwer as an anfwer to a queftion which fuppofes General Burgoyne within
the limits of the province of Canada ?

A. No : while he was within the limits of the province of
Canada, I would have given General Burgoyne orders in all
cafes of difficulty and danger. There being no fuch cafe
when General Burgoyne arrived in Canada, in 1777, nor a
poffibility of an event of that fort, I put the troops and
all things under his command, which concerned his expedition, that he might arrange and combine their motions according to his own plan of operation for the campaign, that
no time might be loft by any unneceffary applications to me,
                                                           which

which the ſtriƈt forms of my command might otherwiſe require. [*Withdrew.*

Again called in.

Q. Should you, if you had been in General Burgoyne's 37. ſituation, and aƈting under the orders which you know he received, have thought yourſelf bound to purſue them implicitly, or at liberty to deviate from them ?

A. I ſhould have certainly thought myſelf bound to have obeyed them to the utmoſt of my power ; but, to ſay as a military man, that in all caſes poſſible, I muſt have gone on, is a very nice thing to ſay indeed ; it muſt have thrown me, and I ſuppoſe every officer, into a moſt unpleaſant and anxious ſituation, to have debated within himſelf, whether he was or was not to go on. Every man muſt decide for himſelf. What I would have done, I really don't know ; the particular ſituation, and a man's own particular feelings, muſt determine the point. If I might be indulged, I would beg leave to ſay, that I did not mean to evade any queſtion ; I meant to anſwer direƈtly ; yet queſtions may be put to me, of ſo delicate a nature, and perhaps no man in the world is in a more delicate ſituation, with reſpeƈt to the preſent caſe in queſtion, and the buſineſs of this Committee, than I am ; when ſuch queſtions are put to me, I ſhall pray the indulgence of the Committee, to be excuſed anſwering them, but I will not evade them. As I now underſtand the meaning of the right honourable member in the former queſtions to be, Whether I ſhould have taken upon me to ſuperſede the King's orders, ſuppoſing I knew of any unſurmountable difficulties in the way, as that I had information of 20,000 men at Ticonderoga, before General Burgoyne left the province of Canada, I ſhould have told General Burgoyne my information ? But it was General Burgoyne who was to carry the orders into execution, and not me, and therefore it was upon his own judgment he was to determine ; I ſhould have given him my opinion, but I think I had no right to give him orders under thoſe circumſtances.

Q. Who was it that made the arrangement and diſtribu- 38. tion of the troops that were to be left for the defence of Canada, independent of thoſe under the command of General Burgoyne ?

A. The orders that are before the Houſe are very full, and I thought very clear. The Committee will ſee in thoſe orders the troops that were deſtined for General Burgoyne's expedition, and the troops that were to remain for the defence of the province.

39.   Q. Who made that diftribution?

A. It came to me from the fecretary of ftate.

40.   Q. Did not the orders from the fecretary of ftate go to the detail of the fmalleft pofts within the province?

A. The letter is before the Committee.

41.   Queftion repeated.

A. I fhould beg for the letter to be read; I don't wifh to avoid any queftion, but I wifh to be accurate.

42.   Q. Was the diftribution of the troops prefcribed to you by the fecretary of ftate, or left to your difcretion?

A. In mentioning the number of troops which were to remain in that province, it was there faid, that thofe troops would be fufficient for garrifoning fuch and fuch places, particularizing them.

43.   Q. Did you ever know an inftance, in your military life, of a minifter making a diftribution of troops for the defence of a province, without taking the opinion or leaving a great deal to the difcretion, of the governor of that province, that governor being an acting military officer of very high rank?

A. I never had the honour to correfpond with a fecretary of ftate, till I was appointed to the command of that province.

44.   Q. Whether you was confulted upon the practicability of penetrating from the frontiers of Canada to Albany by force, with the ftrength allotted to General Burgoyne for that purpofe?

A. No; I was not.

45.   Q. Are you acquainted with the paffage from New York to Canada by the Hudfon's river?

A. I have gone that way.

46.   Q. Have you obferved it with a view to military operations?

A. No; I never made the tour having any military operations in view.

47.   Q. Are you acquainted with the forces which Sir William Howe had under his immediate command at and about New York, on the 17th of July, 1777?

A. I am not.

48.   Q. Suppofing Sir William Howe had 12,000 effective men, befides a fufficient force lodged in New York, Staten Ifland, and Long Ifland, to defend them againft General Wafhington's army, fuppofing General Wafhington's army in the Jerfies, near Quibble Town, and that Sir William Howe

had

had received accounts of General Burgoyne's fuccefs at Ticonderoga, and was acquainted with the orders under which General Burgoyne acted, is it your opinion that the beft movement Sir William Howe could have made for the purpofes of forwarding the execution of the orders, under which General Burgoyne acted, would have been to have failed with his army from New York to Chefapeak Bay ?

A. Had I had the honour to have commanded on that fide, I do not know what I fhould have done myfelf.

Q After you received the letter from Sir William Howe, informing you of his intended expedition to the fouthward, whether you did expect that Sir William Howe's army could co-operate on the Hudfon's River with the northern army that feafon ? 49.

A. I don't know.

Q. Whether you thought, after the receipt of that letter, that it was probable there would be a co-operation from the fouthern army ? 50.

A. I took it for granted, that Sir William Howe knew what he was about, and would do what he thought beft for the public fervice. I really was fo little informed of all the particular circumftances of his fituation and of the provinces under his command, that I could form no judgment of the propriety or impropriety of his conduct, or of the effects of his meafures.

Q. Did your information lead you to believe, that the inhabitants between Saratoga and Albany, were fo well affected to his Majefty and Great Britain, as that there would be much advantage derived from their affiftance to the King's army in the profecution of General Burgoyne's expedition ? 51.

A. I had frequent accounts from that part of the country, that there were numbers ready to take arms and join the King's troops if they fhould penetrate fo far.

Q. Do you mean, by *penetrating fo far*, to Albany, or to the length the army got ? 52.

A. The whole extent of the inhabited country, according to the information brought to me.

Q. Had you no information that a formidable militia might be raifed in that country to oppofe his Majefty's arms ? 53.

A. Yes; I had fuch information.

Q. Did you think that the force which General Burgoyne carried with him from Ticonderoga towards Albany was fufficient to oppofe fuch force ? 54.

A. I

A. I really muſt beg leave to be excuſed anſwering that queſtion.

55.   Q. If you had been conſulted reſpecting General Bur‑ goyne's expedition, knowing the nature of that country, and the force General Burgoyne had, would you or not have adviſed ſuch an enterprize?

A. If I had had the honour to command in that campaign as I had in the former, I don't preciſely know what I ſhould have done myſelf.

56.   Q. Did you give any advice for employing the ſavages?

A. I don't recollect that I ſaid any thing about them.

[*Withdrew.*

Jovis 27° *die Maii*, 1779.

EARL of BALCARRAS called in and examined by General Burgoyne.

1.   Q. IN what ſtation did your Lordſhip ſerve in the cam‑ paigns in America, in 1776, and in 1777?

A. I commanded the Britiſh light infantry.

2.   Q. Was the Britiſh light infantry continually attached to the corps under the command of Brigadier General Fraſer?

A. Yes.

3.   Q. Had you occaſion to obſerve that General Burgoyne and General Fraſer lived together in friendſhip and confi‑ dence?

A. Yes; I had.

4.   Q. Had you reaſon to believe that General Fraſer was conſulted by General Burgoyne in all material operations?

A. I had reaſon to believe that General Fraſer was con‑ ſulted in many material operations.

5.   Q. Does your Lordſhip know or believe that the propor‑ tion of artillery, attached to General Fraſer's corps through the whole campaign, was according to his requiſitions and deſires?

A. I underſtood from General Fraſer, that the proportion of artillery allotted to him was agreeable to his own requi‑ ſitions.

6.   Q. Do you recollect the number of killed and wounded in General Fraſer's corps, at the affair of Huberton?

A. I don't recollect exactly; I think it was about 150.

7.   Q. What was your opinion of the behaviour of the enemy on that day?

A. Cir‑

A. Circumftanced as the enemy was, as an army very hard preffed in their retreat, they certainly behaved with great gallantry.

Q. Was it practicable, the nature of the country, the 8. fatigue of the King's troops, the care of the wounded, and other circumftances confidered, to have purfued the enemy farther after that action ?

A. It was not.

Q. Do you recollect on what day General Frafer's corps 9. rejoined the army at Skenefborough ?

A. On the 9th of July ; I think that it was on that day.

Q. On what day was the action at Huberton ?   10.

A. On the 7th of July.

Q. Do you recollect the difficulties of removing the 11. wounded from Huberton to the hofpital at Ticonderoga ?

A. From the diftance and badnefs of the roads, the difficulties attending the removing of the hofpital muft have been very great.

Q. Was it practicable, unlefs the wounded had been left 12. expofed to the enemy, to have rejoined the army fooner ?

A. It was not.

Q. Does your Lordfhip recollect how the army was em- 13. ployed between that time and the march to Fort Edward ?

A. The Britifh were employed in opening the country and making roads to Fort Anne ; the Germans under General Reidefel were detached about fourteen miles to the left.

Q. Do you recollect the poft the enemy abandoned upon 14. the afcent from the Low Country to the Pitch Pine Plains, in the march from Fort Anne to Fort Edward ?

A. I do recollect fuch a place.

Q. Had the enemy maintained their ground on that poft, 15. do you apprehend that a confiderable portion of artillery would have been neceffary to diflodge them ?

A. Artillery would certainly have been of great ufe to diflodge the enemy.

Q. Did you ever fee an inftance, during your fervice in 16. America, that the rebels continued twenty-four hours on the fame place without entrenching ; and was it not alfo their general practice to add abbaties to their entrenchments ?

A. The rebels were always indefatigable in fecuring themfelves by entrenchments, and in general they added an abbatis to thofe entrenchments.

Q. Do you remember the pofition the enemy abandoned 17. at Schuyler's Ifland ?

D 4

A. I

A. I do remember to have paſſed ſuch a poſt once.

18. Q. Does your Lordſhip think that poſition could have been forced without a numerous artillery or heavy loſs?

A. I do not think it could.

19. Q. From the nature of that country, do you think that poſt could have been turned?

A. Not without greatly riſquing the boats and portable magazines.

20. Q. Is it poſſible at any time in that country, and with a ſmall army, to quit the navigable rivers, without leaving the boats and portable magazines expoſed?

A. I imagine it is not.

21. Q. Did you live in habits of intimacy and communication with General Fraſer?

A. I did.

22. Q. Was General Fraſer of a warmth and openneſs of temper that generally made him communicative of his ſenti-ments, when they differed from the ſentiments of thoſe with whom he acted?

A. General Fraſer's temper was warm, open, and communicative, but reſerved in matters of confidence.

23. Q. Did you ever hear General Fraſer expreſs diſapprobation of the meaſure of paſſing Hudſon's River?

A. I never did.

24. Q. Was not a bridge conſtructed of rafts, and ſome boats thrown over that river, a little before the time of the attack on Bennington?

A. There was.

25. Q. Did not General Fraſer's corps paſs the river by that bridge, and take poſt on the heights of Saratoga?

A. It did.

26. Q. Do you remember that bridge being carried away by the torrents and bad weather, whereby the communication was cut off between that corps and the main body of the army?

A. I do.

27. Q. Was General Fraſer's corps recalled after that action, and obliged to repaſs the river in boats and ſcowls?

A. It was.

28. Q. Do you remember General Fraſer expreſſing his ſorrow for being obliged to return back over the Hudſon's River?

A. I remember General Fraſer mentioning it with regret.

29. Q. Had the rear guard of General Fraſer's corps been attacked during that paſſage over the river, would not a

powerful

powerful fire of artillery from the oppofite fhore have been of great ufe, if not the only means of protecting them ?

A. If the enemy had attacked General Frafer, they would have found him in a very bad pofture ; it was impof-fible to take a better, and, as they could not be fupported by the line, the only means of fafety muft have been to get under cover of the fire of our artillery.

Q. Was there not an expectation and impatience of the troops in general to pafs Hudfon's River, and advance on the enemy ? 30.

A. There was.

Q. Was there not a general confidence and alacrity on the occafion ? 31.

A. There was.

Q. From thefe circumftances, and your other knowledge of the army, do you not believe that to have made no fur-ther attempt on the enemy would have caufed difappointment and dejection in the troops, and reflections on the general ? 22.

A. The troops were in the higheft fpirits, and wifhed to be led on.

Q. Does your Lordfhip recollect the march up to the enemy on the morning of the 19th of September ? 33.

A. I do.

Q. Was the combination of the march fuch, as, that notwithftanding the paffage of the ravines and the thicknefs of the woods, the column of General Frafer's march, and that of the Britifh line, led by General Burgoyne, were in a fituation to fupport each other, and fpeedily to form in line of battle, at the time the enemy began the attack ? 34.

A. After the columns had paffed the ravines, they arrived at their refpective pofts with great precifion in point of time, and every fortunate circumftance attended the forming of the line.

Q. How long did that action laft ? 35.

A. The Britifh were attacked partially about one o'clock. The action was general at three, and ended at feven o'clock.

Q. From the nature of the country, was it poffible to difcern the enemy's pofition or movements, to form any judg-ment what attacks were in force, and what were feints ? 36.

A. I think not.

Q. Did we remain mafters of the field of battle ? 37.

A. We did.

Q. Had

38. Q. Had the field of battle been well difputed by the enemy ?

A. The enemy behaved with great obftinacy and courage.

39. Q. Was it too dark to purfue with effect at the time the action ended ?

A. It was.

40. Q. Did the King's troops take up ground nearer to the enemy, the morning after the action ?

A. It was rather nearer the enemy.

41. Q. How near were the out-pofts of General Frafer's corps to the out-pofts of the enemy from that time to the action of the 7th of October ?

A. I fhould imagine within half a mile.

42. Q. From the nature of the country, and the fituation of the enemy's out-pofts, was it poffible to reconnoitre their pofition ?

A. From the nature of the country, the difficulties attending the reconnoitering muft have been very great.

43. Q. Were not the riflemen, and other irregulars, employed by the enemy at out-pofts and on fcouts, an overmatch for the Indian or provincial troops that were with the army at that time ?

A. They were.

44. Q. Was not General Frafer's corps continually at work during the interval above-mentioned, in fecuring their own pofts, and opening the front to oppofe the enemy ?

A. They were.

45. Q. After General Frafer received his wound, on the 7th of October, on whom did the command of his corps devolve ?

A. On me.

46. Q. Was you in a fituation on that day, to obferve the general difpofition of the army, made by General Burgoyne, previous to the action ?

A. I remember two redoubts having been erected on the left, to cover the boats and provifions to enable General Burgoyne to make a detachment from his army.

47. Q. Was you in a fituation to obferve the difpofition made immediately before the attack by the enemy ?

A. I only recollect the fituation of the two battalions of the advanced corps.

48. Q. After the retreat to the lines, were the lines attacked, and with what degree of vigour ?

A. The lines were attacked, and with as much fury as the fire of fmall arms can admit.

Q. Does

Q. Does your Lordſhip remember that part of the lines 49.
where you commanded, being viſited by General Burgoyne
during the attack ?

A. I don't recollect to have ſeen General Burgoyne.

Q. Was the cannon of great uſe in the repulſe of the 50.
enemy in your poſt ?

A. Of very great uſe.

Q. Do you think that poſt would have been tenable next 51.
morning, the enemy having poſſeſſion of Colonel Briemen's
poſt ?

A. I do not think it would.

Q. Would the poſſeſſion of the poſt by the enemy, toge- 52.
ther with the poſſeſſion of Colonel Briemen's poſts, have
laid open the flank and rear of the camp of the line ?

A. It would.

Q. Was the retreat in the night, and the new diſpoſition 53.
of the whole army made in good order and without loſs ?

A. It was.

Q. Did the army remain under arms, and in momentary 54.
expectation of battle, the whole of the day of the 8th ?

A. It did.

Q. Do you remember the confuſion and difficulties at- 55.
tending the line of baggage in the retreat, in the night of
the 8th ?

A. I do.

Q. Was not the retreat nevertheleſs made in good order 56.
by the troops, and without loſs ?

A. It was.

Q. Does your Lordſhip remember the weather, the ſtate 57.
of the roads, the ſtate of the cattle, and the difficulty of
paſſing the Fiſh Kill, in the retreat to Saratoga, in the day
and night of the 9th?

A. It rained inceſſantly, conſequently the roads were bad ;
the cattle were nearly ſtarved for want of forage, and the
bridge over the Fiſh Kill had been deſtroyed by the enemy;
the troops were obliged to ford the river.

Q. Had there been no enemy to oppoſe us, or no bridge 58.
or roads to repair, would it have been poſſible, from the ſtate
of the fatigue of the troops, to have continued the march
farther immediately after the arrival at Saratoga ?

A. The troops were greatly fatigued, and the artillery
had been left on the other ſide of the Fiſh Kill.

Q. Why were they left on the other ſide of the Fiſh Kill ? 59.
A. The

A. The bridge had been deftroyed by the enemy ; it was exceeding dark, and I do not know whether the ford was paffable for the artillery without being firft examined.

60.   Q. Do you remember the enemy opening a battery on the oppofite fide of Hudfon's River, and the circumftances attending the opening that battery ?

A. The corps I commanded was at that time pofted, and they fired on us at that time, but I do not know from what direction.

61.   Q. Does your Lordfhip remember the fhot from that battery going over the table when you and feveral officers were at dinner ?

A. I did not dine with General Burgoyne that day—I recollect hearing a cannon fhot had difcompofed the company at the general's table.

62.   Q. Confequently muft not that battery have commanded the ford over the Hudfon's River ?

A. I believe I faid, I did not recollect from what direction the fhot came, but they had a battery which commanded that ford.

63.   Q. Do you recollect on what day you was called, with other commanders of corps, to the firft council of war ?

A. On the 13th of October.

64.   Q. Was there a fpot in the whole pofition to be found for holding that council, which was not expofed to cannon or rifle-fhot ?

A. We were not fo fortunate as to find one.

65.   Q. Do you recollect that General Burgoyne, after ftating to the council the difficulties of the fituation, declared, that nothing could induce him to propofe terms to the enemy without the general concurrence of the generals and field officers of the army, and that he was ready to take the lead in any meafure they fhould think for the honour of the Britifh arms, or words to that effect ?

A. I remember words to that effect.

66.   Q. Was the concurrence unanimous for treating on honourable terms ?

A. I hope I fhall ftand juftified with the members of that council, when I have the honour to declare to this Houfe, that our fituation appeared to them fo decided as not to admit of one diffenting voice.

67.   Q. When Colonel Kingfton brought back the firft propofition, wherein it was fpecified by Major General Gates, that the army fhould lay down their arms in their intrenchments

and

and furrender prifoners of war, does your Lordfhip remember, that General Burgoyne, when he read them to the council, declared, he would not fet his hand to thofe conditions, or words to that effect ?

A. I think the words of the propofal from General Gates were, That the Britifh army fhould be ordered, by word of command from their adjutant general, to lay down their arms in the entrenchments. It was rejected with difdain by General Burgoyne, and the council concurred in his indignation.

Q. Were the counter-propofals, penned by General Burgoyne, unanimoufly approved of ? 68.

A. They were.

Q. When thofe propofals had been agreed to by General Gates, but copies not figned by either party, do you remember General Burgoyne informing the council of intelligence he had received from a fpy in the night, and fubmitting to their confideration, whether it was confiftent with public faith, and if fo, expedient to fufpend the execution of the treaty and truft to events ? 69.

A. I do remember it.

Q. Does your Lordfhip recollect what was the refult of that confideration ? 70.

A. The determination of the council, on the queftion being put, was, that the public faith was *bona fide* plighted.

Q. Though that was the opinion of the majority, was there not a difference of opinion in the council ? 71.

A. There was.

Q. Were the opinions of the feveral commanding officers afked refpecting the condition of their refpective corps, and what might be expected from them feverally in defperate cafes ? 72.

A. It was.

Q. Was there not on that queftion alfo difference of opinion ? 73.

A. There was.

Q. After the Convention took place, did your Lordfhip fee the army of General Gates pafs in review before General Burgoyne and General Phillips ? 74.

A. I did.

Q. From the manner and filence of their march, the order obferved in keeping their divifions, and an apparent attention to their officers, did that army appear difciplined ? 75.

A. They marched in good order and were filent, and

3   feemed

feemed to pay attention to their officers. Thefe are effential points of difcipline, but I faw nothing farther of it.

76. Q. From the general behaviour of the rebel troops in the
different actions in which you was prefent in the courfe of
the campaign, did you think them difciplined and refpectable troops?

A. When I anfwered the laft queftion, I fpoke to the manœuvre I faw upon the fpot. At all times when I was oppofed to the rebels, they fought with great courage and obftinacy.

77. Q. Judging by your eye, and the time the rebel army
was marching in review, did you form any judgment of their
number?

A. It requires great experience to make a computation of
numbers by feeing them pafs: as far as I could judge on the
occafion, they feemed to me to amount to thirteen or fourteen thoufand rank and file under arms.

78. Q. Has your Lordfhip reafon to know or believe, that
the troops that paffed in review were exclufive of thofe corps
that had been pofted on the other fide of the Hudfon's River?

A. They were exclufive of thofe corps.

*Examined by other Members of the Committee, and by
General Burgoyne occafionally.*

79. Q. What was the general opinion of the army of General
Burgoyne's behaviour in action and in difficulty?

A. It appeared to me, that General Burgoyne always poffeffed himfelf in every fituation of danger and difficulty, and
I may venture to fay, it appeared fo to the army.

80. Q. Had General Burgoyne the confidence of the army?
A. He had.

81. Q. After the arrival of the troops at Cambridge, were the
officers and foldiers of the army fatisfied with the general's
efforts to contribute to their comfort, and redrefs their grie-
vances?

A. They were.

82. Q. Was the army fatisfied with the general's behaviour
at the court-martial held on Colonel Henley?

A. He carried on that profecution in perfon, and as fuch
they were fatisfied with him.

83. Q. Did your Lordfhip ever hear any officer or foldier of
that army exprefs any diffatisfaction at the general's returning to England?

A. I did not.

84. Q. Does your Lordfhip think that the officers of that army

my wifh to have their refpective merits ftated to their Sovereign, by the general in perfon who had the honour of commanding them ?

A. It was the wifh of that army that General Burgoyne fhould go to Europe, to juftify not only his own conduct, but the conduct of the army he commanded.

Q. Does your Lordfhip apprehend, that the return of 85. General Burgoyne to that army, under perfonal difgrace, and without any diftribution of preferment among the diftinguifhed officers of that army, would be any fort of confolation to the troops under captivity ?

A. General Burgoyne, at all times, fhared the dangers and afflictions of that army in common with every foldier ; as fuch they looked on him as their friend, and certainly would have received him in perfon, or any accounts of him, with every mark of affection.

Q. Your Lordfhip having faid that if the rebels had main- 86. tained their poft, at the afcent from the Low Countries to the Pitch Pine Plains, in the march from Fort Anne to Fort Edward, artillery would have been of great ufe to diflodge them ; will your Lordfhip fay what kind of artillery, of what calibre, would have been neceffary for that purpofe ?

A. Any of the artillery officers now under the order of the Houfe can give a much more fatisfactory anfwer to that queftion than I poffibly can.

Q. Did you fee that poft ?   87.
A. I think I faid I did fee it.

Q. With what kind of work was that poft fortified ?   88.
A. I fpoke of it merely from its fituation.

Q. Were there then any works or none ?   89.
A. I don't recollect there were any works.

Q. If the army, after taking Ticonderoga, had been em- 90. barked, and proceeded directly to South Bay, would there have been any occafion to have attacked the poft at Pitch Pine Plains at all ?

A. The army did proceed by South Bay, excepting a detachment of General Frafer's corps, and fome Germans to fupport him ; and the army affembled at Skenefborough on the 9th or 10th of July.

Q. Was it neceffary to go to the poft at Pitch Pine Plains, 91. in order to go to South Bay ?

A. They had no fort of connection with each other.

Q. Might not the army have proceeded to Fort Edward, 92.

4   and

and omitted the attack of that pafs, fuppofing it had been meant to be defended ?

A. There were two routes to Fort Edward. General Burgoyne might ftill go the fame route without any neceffity of attacking that poft, as there might have been many different ways of diflodging the enemy from that poft without attacking it.

93. Q. In how many inftances do you remember the rebels defending their intrenchments after they had made them ?

A. We never got a view of any of their intrenchments but fuch as they had voluntarily abandoned.

94. Q. Is it then to be underftood that they never defended any entrenchments ?

A. They never did.

95. Q. Did you ever hear General Frafer exprefs his approbation of the paffing the Hudfon's River ?

A. I never did.

96. Q. Did you ever hear General Frafer exprefs his approbation of the Bennington expedition ?

A. That detachment was made, and the bufinefs concluded, before I ever heard of the projeft or execution.

97. Q. Have you occafion to know, when the firft detachment was fent out under Colonel Baume, where they were ordered to rejoin General Burgoyne, after they had performed the fervice they were fent on ?

A. I don't know.

98. Q. Whether, in your Lordfhip's opinion, after the lofs the rebels had fuftained over night, in the aftion of the 19th of September, if they had been attacked brifkly at break of day, the next day, there was a probability that they could have ftood their ground ?

A. I have not hefitated to give an opinion upon fuppofed matters, which muft have been attended with evident and demonftrable confequences ; but I beg the indulgence of the Houfe in declining to give any opinion upon any queftion relative to fpeculation or judgment. Had any general officer of that army under General Burgoyne been prefent in this country, I fhould have confined myfelf merely to the manœuvres of the corps I commanded. As there is no general officer here, I wifh to give this Houfe every information confiftent with my rank in the army.

99. Q. Had you any information that might indicate to you that the rebels were prepared to decamp after the aftion of the 19th of September ?

A. I

A. I was ignorant of any such intelligence being received.

Q. Had you any information of their baggage being pack- 100.
ed up ?

A. I have already answered, that I had no information at
all about it.

Q. In the action of the 7th of October, on which side did 101.
the rebels force our lines and make a lodgment ?

A. The lines to the right were stormed and carried.

Q. Were the lines attacked to the left ?   102.

A. To the left of that post they were, but not to the left
of the army.

Q. Did not the possession of Fort Edward, and the coun- 103.
try thereabouts, cut off the retreat of any garrison that might
have been in Fort George ?

A. It undoubtedly did ?

Q. Had the army proceeded to Fort George by Ticonde- 104.
roga and Lake George, might not the enemy have remained
at Fort George till the trenches were opened, and have still
had their retreat secure ?

A. That is a matter of opinion upon speculation.

Q. Do you not think that the British army, being well 105.
provided with artillery, was a probable reason for their not
defending entrenchments ?

A. The reason they did not defend their entrenchments
was, that they always marched out of them and attacked us.

Q. Does your Lordship think it would have been ad- 106.
visable, in point of prudence, or just to brave troops, who
had suffered severe loss, to attack an enemy the morning after that loss, posted within entrenchments, which it was impossible to reconnoitre ?

A. That attempt was tried on the 7th of October, and
did not succeed.

Q. Were not the enemy reinforced between the 19th of 107.
September and the 7th of October ?

A. I think it is likely they were.

Q. Were they likely to be in better spirits to repel an at- 108.
tack the day after they had been repulsed with great loss, or
when they had been reinforced, and seen an army lie three
weeks inactive in their camp ?

A. I do not judge of the spirit of the enemy but when I
was opposed to them myself.

Q. On the first day of the action, when the enemy was 109.

E   repulsed

repulfed on the 19th of September, had not our army fuffered very confiderably ?

A. They fuffered very confiderable lofs.

110.   Q. Was not the army recruited, and in better order, on the 7th of October, than they were on the 20th of September ?

A. Numbers of the men who had been wounded and difabled in the action of the 19th, joined their corps on the 7th of October.

111.   Q. Was the behaviour of the enemy, oppofed to your Lordfhip, in the actions you have feen, fuch as to make them contemptible in the eye of a foldier ?

A. I have already mentioned, that they fought at all times with courage and obftinacy.

112.   Q. Whether the behaviour of the enemy was fuch as to make advantages obtained by them over his Majefty's troops more humiliating and difgraceful to the Britifh arms than the fame advantages obtained by an equal number of any other troops ?

A. I myfelf felt more humiliation until I confidered that thofe advantages proceeded from the nature of the country, and not from the want of zeal or bravery in the Britifh troops ?

113.   Q. Whether the enemy's troops were fuch bad troops as to make it more difgraceful to have an advantage obtained by them over the King's troops than by the like number of any other enemy over a like number of his Majefty's troops in the fame circumftances of country ?

A. The advantages gained by the rebels over the Britifh troops proceeded from their local fituation, and not from the want of courage in the Britifh troops. We were taught by experience that neither their attacks nor refiftance was to be defpifed.

114.   Q. Did you ever ferve againft any other troops ?

A. I commenced my fervice in America.

115.   Q. Whether the army under General Burgoyne, in general, expected co-operation in their efforts to go to Albany, from the army under the command of Sir William Howe ?

A. General Burgoyne gave it out in general orders, that he had every reafon to believe that powerful armies were acting in co-operation with the army he had the honour to command.

116.   Q. Do you know at what time that order was given out ?

A. The

A. The adjutant general's books will fhew it : I think it was about the 3d of October.

Q. Does your Lordfhip believe that if the army under 117. General Howe had co-operated up the North River with the army under General Burgoyne, that the army under General Burgoyne would have been obliged to have made the convention it did ?

A. That is a matter of judgment. The army looked forward to that co-operation, which they were led to underftand, by the orders General Burgoyne had given out, with pleafure.

Q. What was the general opinion of the officers of the 118. army in which you ferved, on that fubject of co-operation ?

A. I do not think my rank in the army entitles me to give my opinion on that fubject ; I fhall ftill lefs prefume to give that of others. [*Withdrew.*

Then he was called in again, and feveral parts of the examination, particularly that which immediately follows the place where it is faid that his Lordfhip was examined by other members of the Committee, were read, and then the laft queftion which was put to his Lordfhip immediately before he withdrew, was repeated, with this addition, " To the beft of your recollection and information." 119.

A. I have already declined anfwering that queftion.

Q. When did you firft know that there was to be no co- 120. operation from General Howe's army, and that Sir William Howe had carried his army to Chefapeak Bay ?

A. I did not know that we were to expect no co-operation, until after the convention was figned.

Q. When did you firft hear that Sir William Howe was 121. gone to the fouthward ?

A. It was reported fo in the army about the beginning of the campaign, before we croffed the river.

Q. When was that report firft confirmed fo as to make it 122. a matter of belief?

A. I never knew it was confirmed at all.

Q. Whether you yourfelf was not furprifed or difappoint- 123. ed, or both, when you firft underftood that there was not to be any co-operation from Sir William Howe, but that Sir William Howe's army was gone to Chefapeak Bay ? [*Withdrew.*

Again called in.

Q. Whether you yourfelf was furprifed or difappointed, 124. or both, when you firft heard that Sir William Howe's army was gone to Chefapeak Bay ?

E 2 A. I

A. I neither knew the object of the campaign nor its expectations, and therefore cannot speak to any manœuvre of which I could not know the tendency.

125.   Q. Did the army in general express themselves pleased at the news of Sir William Howe's being gone to Chesapeak Bay ?

A. The answer to the last question, as it relates to me in particular, relates to them in general.

126.   Q. Whether your Lordship, as a matter of fact, in the consideration you had in the army, on the news of Sir William Howe's being gone to Chesapeak Bay, heard those you conversed with express themselves pleased, or talk of that expedition to Chesapeak, as a powerful co-operation with General Burgoyne ?

A. I think that question is fully answered in the two preceding ones.

127.   Q. Whether you did not think General Howe's fighting General Washington's grand army at the battle of Brandywine, was a very capital co-operation with the army under General Burgoyne ?

A. I was not at Brandywine.

128.   Q. Whether you was not surprised when you returned home to this country, to learn that the secretary of state for the American department, had information from General Howe, of his intentions of going to the southward, before General Burgoyne departed from this country, and never communicated that information to General Burgoyne before his departure for Canada ?

A. I have the honour to stand before this House as a military man, and not as a politician, and cannot answer any question but those relative to my own profession.

129.   Q. What was your Lordship's opinion of the spirit of your own corps ?

A. The opinion I gave in the council of war, relative to the spirit of the corps I commanded was, that they were willing and zealous to undertake any enterprise that General Burgoyne would please to employ them upon.

130.   Q. When advice was received that Sir Henry Clinton was coming up the North River, did you apprehend the treaty of convention had gone so far that it could not be broken ?

A. My opinion was, with respect to that question, that all military negotiations were fair and justifiable, to make delays and to gain time; I therefore thought and declared my sentiments, that General Burgoyne was at full liberty to
break

break off that treaty in the ftage it then was; and I could not conceive that the public faith was engaged, until the treaty was actually figned and exchanged.

Q. Whether the opinion of General Burgoyne, of Gene- 131. ral Phillips, of Brigadier Hamilton, and feveral other offi- By General cers, did not coincide with your opinion in all the matters Burgoyne. comprifed in the laft queftion?

A. As General Burgoyne feems defirous that I fhould an- fwer that queftion, I declare his fentiments were the fame with thofe I have now delivered. I hope that the other members of that council will foon be in a fituation to ftand forward and to declare the opinion that they gave on that and every other queftion.

Q. When the queftion relative to the point of public faith 132. was decided, by the majority of the council, was not the By General concurrence for figning the convention unanimous? Burgoyne.

A. It was.

Q. What day was it firft known that Sir Henry Clinton 133. had taken the highlands, and was coming up the North Ri- ver?

A. In the night of the 16th of October.   [Withdrew.

CAPTAIN MONEY called in and examined by General Burgoyne.

Q. WAS not you deputy quarter mafter general of the 1. army under General Burgoyne, in 1777?

A. I was.

Q. After Lieutenant Colonel Carleton returned to Cana- 2. da, was you the fuperior officer in that department?

A. I was.

Q. As fuch, did you make it your bufinefs from the be- 3. ginning of the campaign to get a knowledge of the country?

A. Whenever there was any occafion to obtain the know- ledge of any particular part of the country, a party was al- ways fent with me for that purpofe, but the woods were fo thick that it was impoffible to go without a party.

Q. Was you well acquainted with the country between 4. Skenefborough and Fort Edward?

A. I was.

Q. How long was the army employed in making the roads 5. practicable between Skenefborough and Fort Edward?

A. About fix or feven days in making the road between Skenefborough and Fort Anne, and between Fort Anne and

E 3   Fort

Fort Edward. I do not believe the army was delayed an hour on that account; there was a very good road made by the rebels the year before, between Fort Anne and Fort Edward, in which road the rebels had cut down some few trees which took the provincials in our army some few hours to clear.

6. Q. Does not the possession of the country in the neighbourhood of Fort Edward necessarily prevent the retreat of a garrison that might be in Fort George?

A. It prevents the getting off any artillery or stores; but a garrison might get through the woods, in case we were in the possession of the ground in the neighbourhood of Fort Edward.

7. Q. Did not the garrison of Fort George evacuate the fort upon the approach of the King's troops toward Fort Edward?

A. I heard they did; I was not near enough to see.

8. Q. Had the army taken their route by South Bay, Ticonderoga, and Lake George, how many bateaux do you imagine it would have taken to carry the troops solely over Lake George, exclusive of provisions and stores?

A. I think between three and four hundred, which bateaux must have been carried up out of Lake Champlain to Lake George.

9. Q. What time would it have taken, as you imagine, to have drawn those bateaux over the land, between Lake Champlain and Lake George, with the horses then at Ticonderoga?

A. I suppose a fortnight—Four hundred bateaux.

10. Q. Though there were no troops passed over Lake George, how long did it take before the first transport of provisions arrived at Fort George?

A. I can't recollect precisely.

11. Q. Considering the length of time it took to transport the provisions, without the troops, over Lake George, was not the army forwarder in their way to Albany, in point of time, by the route they took, than they could have been by the route of Ticonderoga and Lake George?

A. I have already said, that it would take a fortnight to transport the 400 bateaux from Lake Champlain to Lake George; it therefore would have delayed the army a fortnight longer than they were delayed to have returned from Skenesborough by Ticonderoga, and gone across Lake George.

Q. Was

Q. Was you commiſſary of horſe, as well as deputy 12.
quarter maſter general ?

A. I was.

Q. What is the nature of that department ? 13.

A. It was to take charge of all the horſes furniſhed by
contract for General Burgoyne's army, by any letter of inſtructions from General Burgoyne. I am directed to give
proper orders and directions to the drivers, furniſhed by that
contract, for the purpoſe of tranſporting proviſions and ſtores
brought to Fort George for the uſe of the army.

Q. Did you report from time to time to Major General 14.
Phillips, and take orders from him, as well as from General
Burgoyne ?

A. Yes.

Q. Were not the orders from both the generals invariable, 15.
preciſe, and preſſing, for uſing all poſſible diligence in forwarding the tranſport of proviſions ?

A. They were. There was one order which I will read,
as it will fully anſwer that queſtion : it is dated Auguſt the
18th, Duer-Camp, and is in theſe words ; " It having been
" a practice for officers to order to be taken from the provi-
" ſion train, in the ſervice of the King for this army, the
" carts and horſes, for the carrying baggage and other pur-
" poſes, to avoid for the future the danger and inconve-
" niences to the ſervice, it is in the moſt poſitive manner
" ordered, that no cart or horſe are to be uſed but for the
" public tranſport of the army ; nor is any officer, acci-
" dentally coming to any particular poſt, to interfere with
" the proviſion train, in any other manner than to give it
" every aid and aſſiſtance, which he is on all occaſions to
" do."

Q. Was not the tranſport of merchandize, and even ſut- 16.
lers' ſtores, as well as of officers' baggage, poſitively forbid
till the tranſport of proviſion ſhould be over ?

A. There was ſuch an order, and a ſeizure made of two
barrels of Madeira, and two barrels of rum, which were ordered to the hoſpital.

Q. Do you recollect General Burgoyne's expreſſing, at 17.
ſeveral times, particular anxiety on the ſubject of expediting
the tranſport of proviſions ?

A. I do remember once to have heard General Burgoyne
expreſs his concern at our not being able to bring forward
a greater quantity of proviſion to enable him to proceed with
the army.—I do recollect to have heard him ſay with very

E 4 great

great earneftnefs to General Phillips and Colonel Carleton, that one month's provifion at that particular time (it was about the latter end of Auguft) would be worth 100,000l. to Great Britain ?

18. Q. Do you think that the commiffary of the waggons, and other carriages, was authorifed to buy or hire ox-teams wherever they could be had, and that all draught cattle taken, were appropriated to the tranfport ?

A. He received fuch directions.

19. Q. How many carts and ox-teams could be muftered at any one tiime ?

A. I think only 180 carts could at any one time be muftered ; the number of ox-carts I really forget, but I believe between 20 and 30.

20. Q. About how many days' provifion for the troops, and all other perfons fed from the King's ftores, could that number of carriages convey ?

A. There never was any trial made, but if I may prefume to judge from the proportion brought forward, over and above the daily confumption of the army, fhould fuppofe all thofe carriages would not carry more than four days provifion at moft. I am fpeaking at random, as no trial was made.

21. Q. Did it not fometimes happen, from accidents of weather, and roads, and the tired ftate of the cattle, that not more than one day's provifion could be brought forward in a day ?

A. It did.

22. Q. How many hours did it take, one hour with another, to draw a bateau from Fort George to Fort Edward ?

A. In general about fix.

23. Q. Was not the unloading the carts at Fort Edward, and embarking the contents in bateaux, unloading the bateaux at the upper falls of Fort Miller, and a fecond time unloading them at the lower falls, dilatory as it was, a more expeditious method than it would have been to have carried the provifions the whole way in carts ?

A. I do apprehend it was not poffible, in the feeble ftate I found the horfes furnifhed by contract, to have brought forward the daily confumption of provifions for that army down to Fort Miller. In the month of Auguft, in the latter end of that month, at which time I was appointed a commiffary general of horfe, I made, on the firft of September,

tember, a general mufter, and found 30 horfes unferviceable, from fatigue and hard labour.

Q. Was the tranfport of provifions at any time impeded 24. by the bringing forward the artillery from Fort George?

A. The artillery had a feparate contract for horfes, with which they brought forward their own ftores. I don't recollect that any part of the provifion-train was ever employed in bringing forward artillery or artillery ftores.

Q. Was it poffible, with the means we had, to collect a 25. month's ftore of provifions fooner than it was collected?

A. I believe not, without the utter ruin of the horfes furnifhed by contract for the purpofe of tranfporting ftores.

Q. Was you prefent in the action of the 19th of Septem- 26. ber?

A. I was.

Q. Did the enemy difpute the field that day with obfti- 27. nacy?

A. They did, and the fire was much heavier than ever I faw it any where, unlefs at the affair of Fort Anne.

Q. Do you know how long the regiments of the Britifh 28. line were under that fire?

A. The three Britifh regiments (the 20th, 21ft, and 62d) were engaged from three o'clock in the afternoon till feven in the evening; and whilft I was a prifoner I heard the rebel quarter-mafter general fay, they had nine different regiments in the field, oppofed to the three Britifh I have named.

Q. Do you know the lofs the three Britifh regiments fuf- 29. tained?

A. I can't fay.

Q. Do you remember the ftrength of the 62d regiment 30. when they came out of the action?

A. I can't fpeak to the particular ftrength of the regiment when they came out of action; but I heard that they were not 100 rank and file.

Q. How many officers were left in that regiment at the 31. end of the action?

A. I can't anfwer that queftion.

Q. From the general ftate of the three Britifh regiments, 32. do you think that they would have been in a proper condition to have attacked the enemy the next morning?

A. Certainly not; nor to go on any fervice whatever.

Q. About what time of the day did the enemy finally give 33. way?

A. They

A. They gave way very often; finally about seven in the evening.

34.   Q. Was it practicable, at that time of the evening, and in that kind of country, to have pursued?

A. I should think not.

35.   Q. Was you not often employed, between the day of that action, and the action of the 7th of October, to reconnoitre?

A. I was.

36.   Q. Was you able to obtain a view of the enemy's position?

A. I obtained a view of the position of the right of the rebel entrenchments.

37.   Q. What was the nature of their position to the right, with regard to entrenchments?

A. They were posted on a hill that came very near the river. On the top of the hill was a strong breast-work, at the foot an abbatis.

38.   Q. Did it appear to you that that wing of the enemy was attackable?

A. It is a question that is scarcely in my line of service to answer; but as there are no general officers, nor older officers than myself, who served under General Burgoyne, I hope no military man will think me presuming to give my opinion on that subject. I do think that we could not have attacked the right wing of the rebel entrenchments without risking the loss of the whole army, and with little probability of success.

39.   Q. Could you obtain a view of the left wing of the enemy?

A. I never saw the left wing of the enemy's entrenchments till I was taken prisoner and conducted through their works.

40.   Q. On the 7th of October was you in a situation to see the enemy advancing to the attack of your left?

A. Yes.

41.   Q. Did they advance under a well served fire of grape-shot from our artillery?

A. I was in a situation that gave me an opportunity of seeing the directions of the rebels' columns; and I was very much astonished to hear the shot from the enemy fly so thick, after our cannonade had lasted a quarter of an hour.

42.   Q. When the British grenadiers were forced last from their post, what ensued?

A. I did not see the British grenadiers forced back. I saw them on their march, as I apprehended, taking a different position;

fition ; at that time feveral of them broke their ranks, but on fome aid du camps calling to them for fhame, to continue their rank, they marched away to their ftation in good order. A battalion of Brunfwickers that were on the left of the artillery quitted their ground as foon as the firing began, and, to the beft of my recollection, I did not fee they left a man behind them on the ground. I would add, that after fome difficulty that battalion was brought to make a ftand in the rear of the artillery, but in no order.

Q. Was not that battalion brought to that ftand by the activity and exhortation of Major General Reidefel ? **43.**

A. I did not fee General Reidefel endeavour to ftop the battalion ; but I faw an aid du camp of his and a brigade major, with their drawn fwords, keeping them up. I did fee General Reidefel immediately afterwards, on the right of the artillery, with the battalion perfectly formed, and in good order.

Q. Do you imagine that the giving way of the battalion you firft defcribed was the caufe that the artillery on that fpot was taken, and yourfelf and Major Williams being made prifoners ? **44.**

A. I believe it contributed, in fome meafure, towards the lofs of the action on that day ; but before Sir Francis Clarke died of his wounds, he told me that he received his wound in bringing orders for the artillery and the whole of the detachment to return to camp ; and to the circumftance of Sir Francis Clarke's being wounded, I do attribute the lofs of the artillery, if not the lofs of the whole army.

Q. Had you an opportunity, after you was prifoner, to fee the left of the enemy's entrenchments ? **45.**

A. I had.

Q. Was the ground within cannon fhot of the left open and commanding it ? **46.**

A. All the ground I faw was cleared and entrenched.

Q. Was there not ground within cannon fhot that would have commanded that entrenchment on the left ? **47.**

A. There was.

Q. Had we gained poffeffion of that ground, and been able to erect batteries of our heavieft guns, would not the whole line of the enemy have been enfiladed ? **48.**

A. The ground alluded to was entrenched, and commanded the whole of the rebel camp and lines. If the army had got poffeffion of that ground, I do not believe the rebels would have ftaid one hour in their camp.

Q. Did

49. Q. Did you ever hear, in converfation with the rebel officers, that General Arnold, forefeeing that inconvenience,
had marched out of his lines, and attacked, without orders
from General Gates ?

A. I did hear that General Arnold had marched out on the
7th of October, without orders from General Gates. I did
alfo hear that he advifed the going out to meet General Burgoyne on his march, and engaging him before he approached
their lines ; and the reafon he gave was this : If General
Burgoyne fhould ever come near enough their lines to be able
to make ufe of his artillery, that he would certainly poffefs
himfelf of their camp ; that their troops in that cafe would
never ftand any where ; but if, on the other hand, the rebels
fhould be defeated in the woods, the troops would, after
that, have confidence in their works, for which reafon Arnold advifed rifking an action in the woods before General
Burgoyne came near enough to fee their works.

Examined by other members of the Committee, and by
General Burgoyne occafionally.

50. Q. Did not your fituation, as deputy quarter mafter general, lead you to mix very much with the different officers
of the army ?

A. It did.

51. Q. What do you apprehend to have been the general opinion of the officers of General Burgoyne's conduct, as well
in action as in the many trying occafions which have been
ftated by you at the bar ?

A. They entertained a very high opinion of General Burgoyne's conduct.

52. Q. Had General Burgoyne the full confidence of the army
under his command to the laft moment ?

A. He certainly had.

53. Q. What was the army's opinion of the rebels after their
retreat from Ticonderoga ?

A. The army in general did not think, after they had
evacuated Ticonderoga, that they would make a ftand any
where.

54. Q. What was the reafon given in your army for the expedition to Bennington ?

A. I believe I cannot anfwer that queftion better than by
reading an abftract of the General's orders the day after
that action.   " *Auguft* 17, *Duer Camp.*

" It was endeavoured, among other objects, by the expe-
" dition which marched to the left, to provide fuch a fupply of
" cattle

" cattle as would have enabled the army to proceed without
" waiting the arrival of the magazines.   That attempt
" having failed of fuccefs, through the chances of war, the
" troops muft neceffarily halt fome days for bringing forward
" the tranfports."

Q. Why did the army remain from the 16th of Auguft to 55.
the 13th of September, before they croffed the Hudfon's
River to engage the rebels at Stillwater ?

A. To bring forward a fufficient quantity of provifions and
artillery, to enable the general to give up his communication.

Q. What was the opinion of the army on their croffing 56.
the Hudfon's River ?

A. They did think it was their indifpenfible duty to proceed
forward and fight the rebels, which we heard were then at
Stillwater.

Q. Did you ever forage to the right of General Frafer's 57.
camp before the 7th of Auguft ?

A. We never foraged to the right of the camp at Freeman's Farm, at any one time ; on the 7th of October, while
the troops were in the field, General Frafer ordered all the
batmen and drivers, belonging to his brigade, to come and
forage in the rear of the troops.

Q. Do you know what was General Frafer's opinion on 58.
your foraging to the right ?

A. I do know that General Frafer mentioned to me, on
the 5th of October, that there was forage on the right of
his camp ; but at that time the ground on which that forage
was to be met with was in poffeffion of the rebels' advanced
poft.

Q. Do you think your army would have been loft, if 59.
even the expedition from New York had taken place a few
days fooner ?

A. If the troops had arrived at New York foon enough to
have enabled Sir Henry Clinton to have made his expedition
up the North River a week fooner, I do conceive that our
army would not have been loft.

Q. What was the opinion of the rebels on Sir William 60.
Howe's going to the fouthward ?

A. I was not acquainted enough with the rebel leaders, to
hear their opinion on that queftion.   I do not think that
the peafants of the country were judges of the propriety of
Sir William Howe's conduct.

Q. What

61. Q. What was the opinion of the officers of General Burgoyne's army, after it was loft, relative to the croffing Hudfon's River ?

A. They did think that the alternative of retreating with their army to Canada, or proceeding to Stillwater, under the neceffity of giving up his communication to be an unfortunate fituation ; but I never heard any officers fay that they thought General Burgoyne had done wrong ; many faid, that if they had retreated without rifking an action, at the time Sir Henry Clinton was coming up the North River, the army would never have forgiven him, nor would he ever have forgiven himfelf.

62. Q. Was you at New York after the lofs of General Burgoyne's army ?

A. Yes.

63. Q. What was the opinion or the language of the military at that place, relative to Sir William Howe's expedition to Penfylvania ?

A. Whatever opinion was formed of Sir William Howe's expedition to Penfylvania, or is formed previous to this enquiry, fuch an opinion muft have been ill-founded, as Sir William Howe's reafons were not known, nor his inftructions communicated to the public.

64. Q. From your laft anfwer, is the Committee to underftand that the opinions that were formed refpecting Sir William Howe's expedition to Philadelphia, before this enquiry, were not in favour of that expedition ?

Queftion objected to.   [*Withdrew.*

Again called in.

65. Q. You have faid that the army thought it their indifpenfible duty to pafs over Hudfon's River—Why did they think that that meafure was particularly their indifpenfible duty ?

A. If the Hudfon's River had not been there, the army would have thought it their indifpenfible duty to have gone and rifked an action before they returned to Canada. If I recollect right, I faid, that if the army had returned to Canada, without fighting, that the army would never have forgiven the general, nor the general have forgiven himfelf.

66. Q. Do you know the nature of the country, between the place where we paffed the Hudfon's River and Albany, on the eaft fide of the river ?

A. Yes, I do.

67. Q. Could the army have taken that route, in order to pafs the river oppofite or near to Albany ?

A. The army could not have taken that route, as part of the

the way was a swamp, and on the right of the rebel entrenchments was a mountain very rugged, and not passable nearer than two miles from the river.

Q. Was it not a necessary consequence then, that the boats 68. must have been abandoned, if the army had taken that route?

A. I think I have said the army could not take that route; if the army had marched on the east of the Hudson's River, they could not have marched near enough to have covered their provision bateaux from the rebel force, on the west side of the river?

Q. Did the army under General Burgoyne, on their ap- 69. proach to Albany, expect a co-operation of the army under Sir William Howe, upon the North River?

A. They did; and this is the order of General Burgoyne, given October the 3d at Freeman's Farm:

" There is reason to be assured, that other powerful armies
" are actually in co-operation with these troops; and al-
" though the present supply of provision is ample, it is
" highly desirable, to prepare for any continuance in the field
" that the King's service may require, without the delay of
" bringing forward further stores for those purposes; the ra-
" tion of bread or flour is, for the present, fixed at one
" pound."

Q. Are you acquainted with the North River, from New 70. York to Albany?

A. I am not.

Q. How many days march from Fort Edward to Albany, 71. if no interruption from an enemy?

A. I cannot answer that question, unless I am to suppose that a bridge was ready formed for the troops to pass over, on some part of Hudson's River, between Batten Kill and Fort Edward, or that there were vessels ready to transport the troops over Hudson's River.

Q. Is the distance so great between Fort Edward and Al- 72. bany, that the army could not carry provisions with them to support them during the march?

A. Certainly Albany is not at so great a distance from Fort Edward, but that a corps of troops might certainly carry provisions sufficient for the march to Albany.

Q. Was it not understood, that if you had arrived at Al- 73. bany, that the army would find plenty of provisions there?

A. It was generally believed, and I believe it myself firmly, that if the army had got to Albany, we should have

found

found a number of loyal fubjects, that would have joined and
done every thing in their power to have eftablifhed the army
at that place.

74.   Q. Muft not the army, to march from Fort Edward to
Albany, have neceffarily carried a number of boats to form
a bridge to pafs the river ?

A. There was no paffing the river well without a bridge of
boats, and there were not fcouls enough on that river, to make
a bridge.

75.   Q. Would not the neceffary delay, arifing from carrying
forward thofe boats, and throwing a bridge, fit to pafs an
army, have confumed more time than it was poffible for that
army to fubfift with fuch provifion as they could carry with
them ?

A. I fhould think it would.

76.   Q. You will give the Committee what information you
can, refpecting a road from Fort Edward to Albany on the
left fide of the river.

A. I have anfwered that fully.

77.   Q. Whether by taking a pretty large circuit, the army
would have reached Albany, and avoided the fwamps you
mentioned?

A. Certainly not on the eaft fide of the river, becaufe the
enemy being on the oppofite fhore, would certainly have oppofed General Burgoyne's army croffing the Hudfon's River
at Albany, the river being three times the width it is at
Saratoga.   [*Withdrew.*

Martis 1° *die Junii,* 1779.

Mr. F. Montagu in the Chair.

EARL OF HARRINGTON called in and examined by General Burgoyne.

1.   Q. IN what capacity did your Lordfhip ferve in America
in the campaign 1777 ?

A. I was captain in the 29th regiment of foot, and went
on the expedition with General Burgoyne, with the command
of the grenadier company; I was afterwards appointed fu-
pernumerary aid du camp to the general.

2.   Q. While acting as captain of the grenadier company,
was you at the action of Huberton ?

A. I was.

3.   Q. What was the behaviour of the enemy on that day ?
3   A. They

A. They behaved in the beginning of the action, with a great deal of spirit; but on the British troops rushing on them with their bayonets, they gave way in great confusion.

Q. From the nature of the country, was it practicable to 4. pursue the enemy further than they were pursued on that occasion?

A. Certainly not.—I think we ran some risque even in pursuing them so far.

Q. At what time of the campaign was it that General 5. Burgoyne requested your Lordship to act as his aid du camp?

A. I think about the 12th of July.

Q. Was you present a few days after that time, at a coun-6. cil held with the Indians of the remote nations, then just arrived, under the conduct of Major Campbell and Mr. St. Luc?

A. Yes.

Q. Was you present at a former council of the Indians 7. held at Lake Champlain?

A. Yes.

Q. What was the tenor of General Burgoyne's speeches 8. and injunctions at both those councils respecting the restraint of barbarities?

A. He absolutely forbid their scalping, except their dead prisoners, which they insisted on doing, and he held out rewards to them for bringing in prisoners, and enjoined them to treat them well.

Q. Do you remember being with General Burgoyne, soon 9. after the last council, upon a visit to an out-post near Fort Anne?

A. I perfectly recollect it.

Q. Had General Burgoyne a considerable escort of Indi- 10. ans with him?

A. He had.

Q. Did part of that escort, on a scout from that post, fall 11. in with and take a part of the enemy, who were laid in ambush for the purpose of killing or taking the general, and those who were with him?

A. They did.

Q. What were the sentiments of the captain taken on 12. that occasion respecting his treatment from the Indians?

A. He said he was treated with much humanity, and I perfectly remember that prisoners brought in on many other occasions by the Indians, declared that they had been used with the same degree of humanity.

F

Q. Does

13. Q. Does your Lordfhip remember General Burgoyne's re-
ceiving at Fort Anne, the news of the murder of Mifs
M'Rea ?
  A. I do.

14. Q. Did General Burgoyne repair immediately to the In-
dian camp, and call them to council, affifted by Brigadier
General Frafer ?
  A. He did.

15. Q. What paffed at that council ?
  A. General Burgoyne threatened the culprit with death,
infifted that he fhould be delivered up ; and there were many
gentlemen of the army, and I own I was of the number,
who feared that he would put that threat in execution.
Motives of policy, I believe alone, prevented him from it ;
and if he had not pardoned the man, which he did, I believe
the total defection of the Indians would have enfued, and
the confequences, on their return through Canada, might
have been dreadful ; not to fpeak of the weight they would
have thrown into the oppofite fcale, had they gone over to
the enemy, which I rather imagine would have been the
cafe.

16. Q. Do you remember General Burgoyne's reftraining the
Indian parties from going out without a Britifh officer or
proper conductor, who were to be refponfible for their behaviour ?
  A. I do.

17. Q. Do you remember Mr. St. Luc's reporting difcontents
amongft the Indians, foon after our arrival at Fort Edward ?
  A. I do.

18. Q. How long was that after enforcing the reftraints above
mentioned ?
  A. I can't exactly fay ; I fhould imagine about three
weeks or a month.

19. Q. Does your Lordfhip recollect General Burgoyne's telling Mr. St. Luc, that he had rather lofe every Indian,
than connive at their enormities, or ufing language to that
effect ?
  A. I do.

20. Q. Does your Lordfhip remember what paffed in council
with the Indians at Fort Edward ?
  A. To the beft of my recollection, much the fame exhortation to act with humanity, and much the fame rewards
were offered for faving their prifoners.

Q. Do

Q. Do you recollect the circumstance of the Indians de- 21.
firing to return home at that time ?

A. I do, perfectly well.

Q. Do you remember that many quitted the army without 22.
leave ?

A. I do, immediately after the council, and the next morning.

Q. Was it not the general opinion that the defection 23.
of the Indians, then and afterwards, was caused by the reftraint upon their cruelties and habits of plunder ?

A. It was.

Q. Had you reason to believe that the expedition to Ben- 24.
nington was much desired by General Reidesel, and that it
was his wish to have it conducted by Lieutenant Colonel
Baume ?

A. It was always imagined in the army, that it was his
wish, and that Colonel Baume was appointed to the command of it in compliment to him.

Q. Did you know the corps of British, commanded by 25.
Captain Frafer, which made part of that expedition ?

A. They were volunteers from the British regiments, and
alfo ftood very high in the opinion of the army, from their
gallant behaviour on all occafions.

Q. Do you remember General Burgoyne's vifiting the 26.
detachment after it was affembled, and conferring with Colonel Baume ?

A. I do.

Q. Did Colonel Baume appear fatisfied with the ftrength 27.
of his corps?

A. I converfed with Colonel Baume, and with feveral
officers under his command, and they appeared perfectly fatisfied, at leaft I heard no complaint from them ; the only
anxiety they expreffed was, left the deftination of that corps
fhould become known to the enemy.

Q. Does your Lordfhip remember General Burgoyne's re- 28.
ceiving, in the night, a letter from Lieutenant Colonel
Baume, expreffing he found the enemy in greater force than
he expected ?

A. I do.

Q. Do you remember Sir Francis Clarke, General Bur- 29.
goyne's aid du camp, being fent with orders to Colonel
Breyman to march immediately to fupport him ?

A. I do.

30.   Q. Did you communicate the same order to General
Reidesel at the same time ?
    A. I did.

31.   Q. Was Colonel Breyman's the nearest corps for the purpose of that support ?
    A. It was.

32.   Q. Did Brigadier General Frafer at all times treat your
Lordship with great confidence ?
    A. I was often with General Frafer, and he frequently
talked without referve upon matters which he was not particularly bound to conceal.   There were certain matters of
intelligence which it would have been improper for him to
mention to any body.   In this cafe I cannot boaft fo much
of his confidence, as to fuppofe that he would have opened
his mind to me on matters which he would have concealed
from the reft of his friends.

33.   Q. Have you not frequently been prefent when General
Burgoyne and General Frafer difcuffed the objeét of the
campaign, and converfed freely on the circumftances of the
time ?
    A. I have.

34.   Q. Did your Lordship ever, in prefence or abfence of
General Burgoyne, hear General Frafer exprefs a difapprobation of paffing the Hudfon's River ?
    A. I never did.

35.   Q. Do you know or believe that the idea of forcing our
way to Albany was prevalent throughout the army ?
    A. In every converfation I had with different officers of
the army, I never remember once to have heard it doubted,
but that we were to force our way.

36.   Q. Did the army pafs the Hudfon's River with alacrity ?
    A. It is impoffible for any army to have been in higher
fpirits than they were at that time, or more defirous of coming to an engagement with the enemy.

37.   Q. Do you not conceive, that to have remained pofted
behind the Hudfon's River, at the time the army paffed it
and advanced, would have caft a damp on the fpirits of that
army and a refleétion on their General ?
    A. From the eagernefs of the army to advance, and the
great uneafinefs that was difcernible through it on every delay, I apprehended that it could not have been otherwife;
and I think that General Burgoyne's charaéter would not
have ftood very high either with the army, this country, or
the enemy, had he halted at Fort Edward.

Q. Do

Q. Do you recollect the march up to the enemy on the 38.
19th of September?

A. I do.

Q. Will you pleafe to defcribe it?

A. The army marched in three divifions; the German 39.
line flanking, the artillery and baggage purfued the courfe
of the river through the meadows, and formed the left hand
divifion; the Britifh line marched parallel to it at fome diftance through the woods, and formed the center divifion;
General Frafer's corps, with the grenadiers and light infantry of the Germans, were obliged to make a large detour
through the woods, and formed the right hand divifion or
column. Beyond this, on the right, there were, as I underftand, flanking parties of light infantry and Provincials?

Q. Was the country, over which the army paffed, in- 40.
terfected with a deep ravine?

A. It was one of the deepeft I ever faw.

Q. Which column was firft attacked?

A. The advanced party, confifting of the picquets of 41.
the centre column, being fent forwards, under the command of Major Forbes, to explore the way by which that
column was to pafs, fell in with a confiderable body of the
rebels, pofted in a houfe and behind fences, which they attacked, and after a great deal of fire, the detachment nearly
drove in the body of rebels; but on finding that the woods
quite round them were filled with the enemy, they were
obliged to retire to the main body.

Q. Was the march fo performed that when General Bur- 42.
goyne formed the line of the Britifh infantry, General
Frafer's corps were ready upon their right to fupport them?

A. General Frafer, on hearing the fire of Major Forbes's
party, detached two companies to fupport them, which
came up juft after that engagement was over; and on their
appearance the enemy finding that our troops were in
ftrength, quitted the poft they had before occupied, and,
immediately after this, the whole line was formed with the
utmoft regularity. I would explain, that when I fpeak of
the line, I do not include the left hand column which was
compofed of Germans, and which did not come into the line
or into action till late in the day.

Q. How long did the action laft?

A. From three o'clock, I think, till very near eight. 43.

Q. How long were the 20th, 21ft, and 62d regiments en- 44.
gaged?

A. During

A. During the greateſt part of that time.

45.　Q. Was the action well diſputed by the enemy ?
A. It was, very obſtinately.

46.　Q. Was your Lordſhip near the perſon of General Burgoyne during that action, except when you were employed to carry orders ?
A. Yes.

47.　Q. Were not different attempts made by the General's orders to charge the enemy with bayonets, and did not thoſe attempts fail by the heavineſs of the enemy's fire and thickneſs of the woods ?
A. There were many attempts made for that purpoſe, and they all failed except the laſt, when the Britiſh troops finally drove them out of the field.

48.　Q. When part of the German troops did get into action that day under General Reideſel, how did they behave ?
A. I heard their behaviour ſpoke of in the higheſt terms ; they marched up to the enemy with great coolneſs and ſteadineſs, and gave them, as I was told, three vollies by word of command from their officers.

49.　Q. Can your Lordſhip ſpeak to the loſs ſuſtained by the three Britiſh regiments, the 62d in particular ?
A. The loſs was very conſiderable ; but I don't recollect the numbers.

50.　Q. Were thoſe three Britiſh regiments in a condition to have attacked the enemy the next morning ?
A. Their numbers were ſo reduced, that I apprehend they were not.

51.　Q. From the loſs of killed and wounded, particularly of officers, would it have been deſirable to have brought thoſe three regiments into action for the next ten days ?
A. In leſs than ten days the ſtate of thoſe regiments certainly would not have been much mended ; I therefore apprehend, that if they were not in a condition to be brought into action the next morning, their inability would have ſtill continued for thoſe ten days.

52.　Q. Had the army made a movement to gain the left of the enemy's entrenchments before the redoubts were conſtructed that commanded the plain near the river, would not all the bateaux, ſtores, and hoſpitals have been expoſed to attack ?
A. It certainly would have been ſo.

53.　Q. Do you recollect the ſcarcity of forage on the weſtſide of the river.
A. I do perfectly.

Q. Would

Q. Would not the bridge of boats, conſtructed for the 54. purpoſe of foraging to the eaſt-ſide, have alſo been expoſed before the redoubts, above mentioned, were raiſed?

A. They certainly would, had it not been for thoſe redoubts and a work called the *Tête du pont*, which was raiſed for the protection of the bridge.

Q. Do you recollect how long it took to raiſe thoſe re- 55. doubts, to throw the bridge, and raiſe the *Tête du pont?*

A. If I recollect right, the bridge itſelf was finiſhed in one night; the making and compleating the other works took ſome days.

Q. Does your Lordſhip remember General Burgoyne 56. mentioning to you in confidence, the receipt of a letter from Sir Henry Clinton, and his hourly expectation of his attacking the highlands, and his opinion that his ſucceſs there muſt diſlodge the enemy, without attacking their entrenchments?

A. I perfectly recollect the General's mentioning all this to me.

Q. Was you near General Burgoyne in the action of the 57. 7th of October?

A. I was.

Q. Do you recollect what orders you carried?
A. I do.   58.

Q. What were they?
A. The firſt orders I recollect to have carried, were to 59. poſt fifty men under the command of a captain of the 20th regiment, to the left of the detachment of the army, in order, in ſome meaſure, to join them to the advanced works of General Fraſer's camp, and, in caſe of any accident, to protect the detachment, ſhould they find it neceſſary, to retire thither.

The next orders I carried were to Major General Phillips, at the end of the action, acquainting him, that as that detachment ſeemed much diſordered from the enemy having turned both their flanks, that it was neceſſary to draw it as ſoon as poſſible back to the camp, which ſeemed menaced with an attack; the care of this General Burgoyne committed to General Phillips, while he himſelf returned to the camp, in order to take proper meaſures for its defence. On our return thither the works of the camp were actually attacked as General Burgoyne had forſeen, and I was then employed to collect what troops I ſhould meet, and to order them to thoſe parts where they were moſt wanted. Soon after this, the enemy having got round the right of our camp, we expected an attack upon our rear, and I then was difpatched with orders from General Burgoyne to Brigadier General Hamilton, for all the works in the rear of the camp, which had been previoufly conftructed, to be manned by fuch foldiers as he could fpare from the defence of the front.

60. Q. Does your Lordfhip know what orders Sir Francis Clarke was charged with, at the time he received his wound?

A. I met Sir Francis Clarke as I was fearching for General Phillips, and acquainted him with my orders, telling him at the fame time, that as the thicknefs of the wood might prevent my finding General Phillips directly, I wifhed he would affift me, in order that no time might be loft in delivering thofe orders; that was the laft time I faw Sir Francis Clarke, and I believe that foon afterwards he received the wound of which he died?

61. Q. Was it dark before General Burgoyne had a certainty that Col. Breyman was killed, and his poft carried by the enemy?

A. It was fo dark that the officer, who I believe firft brought the intelligence of it, feeing a number of men round the fires of that camp, took them for Germans, and was not convinced of his error till he was fired upon by them, as they proved to be a part of the enemy who had forced the works.

62. Q. Did General Burgoyne ufe any efforts to rally the Germans who were returning from the action, and to perfuade them to recover Colonel Breyman's poft?

A. He certainly did his utmoft endeavours for that purpofe, which however were ineffectual from the darknefs of the night, and the entire confufion in which they were.

63. Q. Were any other troops at hand that could have been fpared for that purpofe?

A. There certainly were not; every regiment was occupied in defence of its own lines which were not certainly overmanned.

64. Q. In the heat of the action do you recollect feeing General Reidefel about the time that the Germans, on the left of the Britifh artillery, were giving way?

A. I do.

65. Q. Was not General Reidefel exerting himfelf to reftore order in his troops?

A. General Reidefel appeared to me to have behaved, on that

that occasion, in every way as became a brave and intelligent officer.

Q. Was the retreat of the army in the night of the 7th **66.** made in good order, and a new position taken by the time it was day-light?

A. It certainly was.

Q. Was the army under arms the whole day of the 8th, **67.** and in continual expectation of action?

A. They were, and indeed were cannonaded during the greatest part of that day, and the advanced corps in particular, who were posted on a hill, were under almost a continual fire from the riflemen of the enemy.

Q. Do you recollect the circumstance of General Frafer's **68.** funeral on the afternoon of that day?

A. I do, perfectly well; the redoubt in which he was buried was very heavily cannonaded during the ceremony, and even previous to this they fired at those who attended the corpse on its way thither, which I suppose was accidental, and proceeded from the enemy's seeing a number of people together.

Q. Who were the chief persons who attended that fune- **69.** ral?

A. All the generals of the army, their aid du camps, and I believe all those who were not attached to any particular post, which at that time were very few.

Q. Was the retreat of the army on the night of the 8th, **70.** and on the day and part of the night of the 9th, made in good order?

A. It was made in perfect good order.

Q. What was the weather on the day of the 9th?

A. Exceeding wet. **71.**

Q. What was the state of the troops, in point of fatigue, **72.** when they arrived at Saratoga?

A. They certainly must have been much fatigued, from the length of time they had been under arms, and more particularly so from the badness of the roads occasioned by the rains.

Q. When it was day-light the next morning, did you fee **73.** any part of the enemy upon the plain at Saratoga, on the ground where our artillery was afterwards posted?

A. I don't recollect.

Q. Does your Lordship recollect seeing a corps of the **74.** enemy on the other side the Hudson's River opposite to Saratoga?

A. Perfectly

A. Perfectly well; and they feemed in force.

75. Q. Do you remember the circumftance of a battery opening from that corps?

A. I do perfectly well. The general, General Phillips,
and feveral other gentlemen were at dinner. We were all
obliged to remove, from finding ourfelves in the range of
that battery..

76. Q. We being in the range of that battery, muft it not
neceffarily have commanded the ford on the Hudfon's River?

A. It certainly did command that ford.

77. Q. Do you recollect Lieut. Col. Sutherland being fent
with a detachment of regulars and provincials from Saratoga, to cover a party of workmen employed to repair
bridges, and render the road practicable?

A. I perfectly recollect it.

78. Q. Do you recollect for what reafon Colonel Sutherland
and the regulars were recalled?

A. I underftood it was on the apprehenfion of an action.

79. Q. Does your Lordfhip recollect different fcouts bringing
reports of the enemy's being in poffeffion of the country
between Saratoga and Fort Edward, on both fides of the
river?

A. I do.

80. Q. Do you remember General Burgoyne's mentioning,
in confidence to you, different ideas of forcing the ford over
Hudfon's River; of cutting away by the enemy's right, and
attempting a rapid march to Albany; or by a night march
to gain the fords above Fort Edward?

A. I do perfectly remember that he mentioned to me all
thofe ideas.

81. Q. Did you ever hear of an offer made by General
Phillips to make his way to Ticonderoga with a body of
troops?

A. No.

82. Q. In the intimacy in which you lived with Major General Phillips, myfelf, and the officers in General Phillips's
family, do you not think you fhould have heard of fuch an
offer had it been made?

A. I apprehend that I fhould have heard of it.

83. Q. Did your Lordfhip hear of General Phillips offering
to attempt an efcape through the woods, with one or two
guides, for the purpofe of putting himfelf at the head of
the

the troops at Ticonderoga, for the future defence of that place ?

A. I heard it mentioned fince I came to England, in fome common converfation ; but I never heard it hinted at while I was in America.

Q. The day before the councils of the generals and field 84. officers was called, can your Lordfhip fpeak of the ftate of things in general at Saratoga ?

A. The ftate of our army was certainly as bad as poffible. Their numbers were few, their provifions fhort, and their pofition not a good one, owing to the nature of the country, which rofe to the diftance of fome miles, one hill overtopping that which was next to it.

Q. Do you know any officer of that army who, in that 85. fituation, thought we had a right to more than honourable terms ?

A. Our fituation, in the apprehenfion of every one there with whom I converfed, did not entitle us to more.

Q. Did the army in general look on the terms obtained, 86. namely, the power of ferving their country in other places, to be advantageous as well as honourable, and more than they had a right to expect ?

A. I believe they certainly did ; and that few perfons in the army expected fo good terms as thofe which were granted.

Examined by other Members of the Committee, and by General Burgoyne occafionally.

Q. Did the Indians leave the army till after the battle of 87. Bennington ?

A. Great numbers did, and at many different times.

Q. Were not fome Indians on the expedition to Ben- 88. nington ?

A. There were.

Q. Was the expedition originally fent out to Bennington ? 89.

A. My fituation in the army not entitling me to be in the council of war, and not being employed on that expedition, I was of courfe not entrufted with the orders that were given to Col. Baume.

Q. Have you reafon to fuppofe that General Reidefel or 90. Colonel Baume had a particular knowledge of that part of the country, fo as to make it particularly proper to give Colonel Baume the command of that expedition.

A. I believe there was no officer in that army of fufficient
rank

3

rank to have commanded fuch an expedition, who ever had been in that particular part of the country.

91.   Q. The intention of the expedition being, as appears by the papers on the table, to found the difpofition of the people of that country, was that part of the country peopled with Germans, as many other parts of the country are?

A. I can't exactly fpeak to the defcription of the people of that country, as I was never there myfelf; but there were employed on that expedition numbers of provincials, many of whom were of that very country; and I apprehend that the common foldiers of a regular army are not the immediate people who are expected to found the minds of any country to which they are fent.

92.   Q. As your Lordfhip mentioned the alacrity with which the army paffed the Hudfon's River, did the army in general think themfelves at that time inadequate to the purpofe of forcing their way to Albany?

A. The opinions of an army, who cannot be acquainted with the intelligence that has been received, are often erroneous. The army was in high fpirits, and did not, I believe, doubt of reaching Albany.

93.   Q. Did the General then doubt of reaching Albany?

A. I really don't know.

94.   Q. Were the rebels' entrenchments completed on the 19th of September?

A. I never faw the entrenchments at all.

95.   Q. How was our army employed between the 19th of September and the 7th of October?

A. The army itfelf was employed in ftrengthening its pofition.

96.   Q. Did it take the army eighteen days to ftrengthen its pofition before it made any movement?

A. I can't exactly fay. They were working all the time.

97.   Q. What works were executed in that time?

A. There were numbers of redoubts erected; the tête-du-pont; lines before the camp; outworks to the lines, in which guards and picquets were placed; and batteries.

98.   Q. How many redoubts were erected?

A. I think in all there muft have been five or fix.

99.   Q. Was the erecting thofe works full employment for eighteen days?

A. I am not an engineer, or I certainly fhould endeavour to anfwer that queftion.

Q. Were

Q. Were all thofe works neceffary, in your opinion, for 100. an army that meant to march forward and attack the enemy?

A. They were neceffary in our particular fituation, being within half a mile of the enemy to whom we were oppofed, and being inferior in numbers.

Q. Does your Lordfhip know whether the enemy thought 101. it neceffary to fortify themfelves with redoubts?

A. I don't know what the fpecies of their fortification was, but I have been always told that great labour had been employed on their works; and what fmall part I faw of them convinced me of it.

Q. Had you not information from deferters or friends 102. what the enemy was doing?

A. My fituation in that army did not entitle me to receive that intelligence. When any perfon came to me to inform me that he had been employed in gaining fuch intelligence, my duty was to bring him to the general.

Q. Was it not a matter of notoriety in the army, that the 103. enemy received reinforcement between the 19th of September and the 7th of October?

A. The manner of receiving intelligence in an army feldom tranfpires; the army might guefs, but I believe they knew nothing.

Q. Was it not underftood that the rebels had fuffered a 104. much greater lofs than the king's troops on the 19th of September?

A. It was.

Q. Was not the whole, or nearly the whole, of the rebel 105. army engaged?

A. I don't know; I apprehend the whole was not engaged.

Q. Was our army in general, in your apprehenfion, in as 106. good a condition on the 20th of September as the rebel army, who had fuffered much more?

A. The rebel army was fo numerous that their lofs was not equally felt with ours,

Q. What number had you reafon to fuppofe the rebel ar- 107. my confifted of on the 19th of September?

A. I always underftood they were very numerous. I never heard their numbers exactly.

Q. Was not the fcarcity of forage forefeen by every body? 108.

A. Thofe with whom I converfed did not forefee it to the extent in which we experienced it.

Q. Was it prudent, in your Lordfhip's opinion, to bring, 109. or attempt to bring, upwards of fourteen hundred horfes to attend the army, in a country fo deftitute of forage?

A. I never

A. I never heard that the horfes in our army were thought too numerous. On all occafions a fcarcity of them was complained of.

110.   Q. Do you know how many horfes were allowed for the baggage of each regiment?

A. I don't know.

111.   Q. Does your Lordfhip know how many horfes were employed about the train of artillery?

A. I don't recollect; but the returns are on the table.

112.   Q. Was the heavy artillery brought back from Stillwater, on the retreat of the army to Saratoga?

A. We had loft fome fmall part of it, and the reft was brought to Saratoga.

113.   Q. Did the bringing back of that artillery delay that retreat or not?

A. An army with cannon certainly cannot march fo rapidly as one without cannon; but cannon always creates a delay which armies have been content to put up with.

114.   Q. Was it neceffary, in your opinion, in the fituation in which the army retreated, to make their retreat as expeditious as poffible?

A. The army appeared to me that it did make its retreat as expeditious as poffible.

115.   Q. Would the leaving of heavy artillery behind, in your opinion have made a difference of four miles in the march?

A. I can't conceive that it would. The enemy were in force behind us; not having numbers to contend with them, it would have been a very defperate circumftance to have abandoned our cannon, in cafe of an attack.

116.   Q. Were the heavy artillery, in effect, of any ufe in that retreat?

A. I don't recollect as it happened, that they were of any other ufe than that of their not being turned againft us.

117.   Q. Might not thofe cannon have been fpiked, and their trunnions have been knocked off, to have rendered them ufelefs?

A. I underftand that the fpikes in cannon are eafily removed, and that it is not an eafy matter, I believe almoft an impoffibility, with any tools that are carried in an army, to knock off the trunnions of brafs cannon.

118.   Q. Might not the retreat have been accelerated by leaving behind a great part of the baggage?

A. I don't think it would. I do not remember that we were ftopt on account of any particular impediment.

Q. Does

Q. Does your Lordſhip know at what time intelligence 119.
was received in General Burgoyne's army of the failure of
Colonel St. Leger's expedition?

A. I think it muſt have been in the month of Auguſt.

Q. Was not that before the paſſing of Hudſon's river?   120.

A. I don't recollect the exact date of receiving that intelligence.

Q. Was it in the month of Auguſt?   121.

A. I cannot tell. I heard of it ſome time after by accident.

Q. Was there any heavy artillery with the army, properly 122.
ſo called?

A. There was none of the heavy ſort; we had medium
twelve-pounders, and two twenty-four pounders, which we
took from the enemy at Quebec, which were very much
lighter than thoſe twelve-pounders.

Q. From the ſtate of the fatigue of the troops, when they 123.
arrived at Saratoga, do you apprehend they could have con- By General
tinued their march though there had been no artillery?   Burgoyne.

A. The army was certainly very much fatigued. I believe
they could have got but very little further. They certainly
were not in a ſtate for a long march.

Q. If the battle expected at Saratoga had been on the plain, 124.
would not the heavieſt artillery we had have been one of our By General
beſt dependencies?   Burgoyne.

A. It certainly would; it would have given us a manifeſt
ſuperiority in that particular.

Q. If the army had not been provided with the number of 125.
horſes they had, by what means would their proviſions or By General
bateaux have been tranſported in places where the river was Burgoyne.
not navigable?

A. The tranſportation of the bateaux and proviſions could
not certainly have been carried on.

Q. Were there not ſuch places on the Hudſon's River be- 126.
tween Fort Edward and Albany?   By General
A. There were.   Burgoyne.

Q. Is it not at any rate a principal object with every ar- 127.
my, and of a retreating one in particular, to preſerve their By other
artillery if it be poſſible, even at the expence of ſome labour Members.
and delay; and for the uſe they might be of to them afterwards, as well as on the retreat?

A. I apprehend the cannon are ſeldom abandoned, but
through abſolute neceſſity.

Q. Whether in general you can inform the committee, 128.
whether the army had a confidence in the general?

A. They

A. They certainly had a confidence in the general, and I do not believe that they have altered their opinion.

129. Q. Did the army then in general, and the officers in particular, entertain a favourable opinion of the general's conduct, capacity, and attachment to them in the various fcenes in which he was engaged, and more particularly on very trying occafions?

A. I don't recollect that any officer, with whom I have had converfation, has ever exprefled himfelf in different terms, and I believe there never was an army more defervedly pleafed with the conduct of their general.

130. Q. Whether the army exprefled any diffatisfaction at the general's return home; that is, whether they thought he came with any purpofes not friendly to them, or looked on themfelves as deferted by him?

A. I was not with the army when General Burgoyne came away; but I have converfed with many officers who have come from it, and they exprefs no diffatisfaction on that head, much lefs looked on or confidered General Burgoyne's intentions as inimical to them.

131. Q. What was the ftate of the American artillery, and how was it ferved?

A. Except on a few occafions, I do not remember their having made much ufe of their cannon; I thought on thofe occafions that they ferved them flowly, but not ill.

132. Q. Whether, all circumftances confidered at the time of the affair of Saratoga, the retreat of the army was practicable, either with or without artillery?

A. I thought it was impracticable.

133. Q. Whether after the convention at Saratoga you went to Albany?

A. Yes.

134. Q. Whether you had any opportunity of obferving the nature of the country, if it was ftrong or woody, clear or open?

A. Very ftrong and woody, and a great number of hills.

135. Q. What was the diftance?

A. I don't exactly recollect; about thirty-two miles.

136. Q. Was the fituation of Albany a ftrong fituation, or was it commanded by hills round it?

A. The fituation of Albany was in a bottom very much commanded.

137. Q. If the army had penetrated to Albany, from whence might they have drawn their fubfiftence, if the country had been againft them?

A. I don't know enough of the country to anfwer that queftion.

Q. Muft

Q. Muft they not have drawn their fubfiftence from New 138. York?

A. I apprehend fo, if they were not mafters of the Mohawk country.

Q. Had you any opportunity of obferving the extent of 139. clear or cultivated country round Albany?

A. I can't very juftly defcribe it, not having gone out of the town of Albany, from the time I came into it, till I embarked for New York.

Q. Do you think that, circumftanced as the army was 140. after the engagement of the 19th of September, it would have been more advantageous to have returned than to have ftayed and fortified the camp?

A. As matters have turned out, it certainly might; but I believe no one thought fo at that time.   [*Withdrew.*

MAJOR FORBES called in, and examined by General Burgoyne.

Q. WAS you major of the 9th regiment, and prefent 1. with that regiment in the action near Fort Anne?

A. I was.

Q. What was the behaviour of the enemy on that oc- 2. cafion?

A. At half paft ten in the morning, they attacked us in front with a heavy and well directed fire; a large body of them paffed the creek on the left, fired from a thick wood acrofs the creek on the left flank of the regiment; they then began to re-crofs the creek, and attack us in the rear: we then found it neceffary to change our ground, to prevent the regiments being furrounded; we took poft on the top of a high hill to our right. As foon as we had taken poft, the enemy made a very vigorous attack, which continued for upward of two hours; and they certainly would have forced us, had it not been for fome Indians that arrived and gave the Indian whoop, which we anfwered with three cheers; the rebels foon after that gave way.

Q. What command had you on the 19th of September? 3.

A. I commanded the picquets of the Britifh.

Q. Was you attacked on the march, and with what degree 4. of vigour?

A. I was attacked with great vigour from behind railed fences, and a houfe, by a body of riflemen and light infantry.

G

Was

5.   Q. Was you wounded in that affair?

A. Very early in the day.

6.   Q. Do you remember General Burgoyne bringing up the Britifh line to fupport you, and forming at the firft opening of the wood?

A. I do.

7.   Q. Did General Frafer's corps arrive precifely in time to occupy the heights on the right of the Britifh line when the action began?

A. It did, and two companies of light infantry came to my fupport.

8.   Q. Where did General Burgoyne poft the 9th regiment?

A. As foon as they came out of the wood, they filed off to the right, and were drawn off at a fmall diftance from the left of General Frafer's corps, with orders to occupy two houfes, one company in each, and defend them to the laft extremity.

9.   Q. Had you an opportunity in that fituation to obferve the ftrefs of the action?

A. I had while we remained in that pofition.

10.   Q. What was the progrefs of it?

A. The twenty-firft and fixty-fecond regiments were drawn up on our left, and were attacked about three o'clock on the fame ground where the picquets had been attacked. About that time I heard a great deal of firing to my right with the advanced corps; an officer came up to General Burgoyne, and acquainted him that the enemy were endeavouring to turn the left of the fixty-fecond regiment, on which he difpatched an aid-de-camp with orders to the twentieth regiment to form on the left of the fixty-fecond; immediately after, fome companies of light infantry came to occupy the ground the ninth were drawn up on; the ninth were then ordered behind a deep ravine, to form a corps-de-referve. I faw nothing of the action after that.

11.   Q. What was the ftrength of the ninth regiment on that day before they fuftained any lofs?

A. On the 15th of the month the weekly return was given in, and, to the beft of my recollection, they were two hundred and fifty and odd rank and file fit for duty.

12.   Q. What was the ftrength of the other regiments in the Britifh line?

A. I cannot fpeak with any certainty, as I did not fee the returns; but on talking with different commanding officers:

the

the four British regiments were about one thousand one hundred, and the advanced corps about one thousand two hundred.

Q. Where was the twenty-fourth regiment? 13.

A. With the advanced corps.

Q. Where was the forty-seventh regiment? 14.

A. Six companies of the forty seventh regiment that were with that army, were employed as a guard to the bateaux and provisions, and two with the advanced corps.

Q. Where were the other two companies of that regi- 15. ment left?

A. One at Fort George, and another on an island in Lake George.

Q. Of the eleven hundred which composed the line on 16. that day, do you know how many were lost and disabled in the action?

A. I have heard the surgeon of the hospital say, that there were more than five hundred of the whole in the hospital, but I can't speak to how many of the line.

Q. Can you say how many were killed? 17.
A. I can't.

Q. Can you say how many officers were killed and 18. wounded?

A. I can't immediately.

Q. Were the British troops in a condition to have attacked 19. an enemy in intrenchments after the action?

A. After the action of the 19th, I went to the hospital to get my wounds dressed, and did not join the regiment till the 8th of October; I can't therefore give an opinion of my own: but I have heard several officers say, they did not think it would have been prudent or right from the loss they had sustained the day before.

Q. Did the regiments begin to be encreased in their 20. strength from the recovered men to any considerable degree in less than eight or ten days?

A. Not that I know of. I was not at the hospital at the time.

Q. Being in the hospital, had you occasion to know that 21. the regiments were stronger from the receipt of their recovered men on the 7th of October, than they were at any time between the 19th of September and that day?

A. I know that several men were discharged from the hospitals so far recovered as to enable them to do their duty.

Q. At what time did the troops arrive at Saratoga? 22.
A. About eight o'clock at night on the 9th.

G 2

Q. Do

23. Q. Do you know how long the troops had then been under arms, and without repose or regular refreshment?

A. From the 7th in the morning.

24. Q. Had they been in action, or in continual expectation of action, during that whole time?

A. I was in the front of the army, and I heard a great deal of firing in the rear, and we constantly expected and looked for an attack.

25. Q. Did the battery of the enemy on the other side of the river at Saratoga command the fort on that river?

A. It did.

26. Q. Was the ground such on our side as would have enabled our artillery to have silenced that battery?

A. It did not appear to me that it could.

27. Q. Had the passage of the ford been effected, and the army have proceeded towards Fort Edward, on the east side of the river, must they not necessarily have passed Batten Kill?

A. Undoubtedly.

28. Q. Do you remember the ford at Batten-Kill?

A. Yes.

29. Q. Would it have been possible for the army to have passed that ford without artillery to cover them, and the enemy posted on the other side?

A. Certainly not. I had an opportunity of seeing the twentieth regiment pass that ford without an enemy to oppose them, and they took a considerable time, owing to the depth of the water, the rapidity of the current, and the stones being remarkable slippery, so that several of them fell into the river.

30. Q. Was you present at all the councils of war to which the field officers of the army were called at Saratoga?

A. I was.

31. Q. Do you remember whether General Burgoyne stated the difficulties of the time, and that he mentioned his readiness to undertake any measure they should think for the honour of the British arms?

A. I do remember it.

32. Q. Was the council unanimous to treat with the enemy on honourable terms?

A. They were.

33. Q. When the first terms proposed by General Gates were read to them, were they unanimous to reject them?

A. They were.

Q. After

Q. After it was decided by a majority of the council that 34.
the treaty could not be fufpended without breach of faith,
were not the council then unanimous to fign it on that day ?

A. As the majority of the council had given it as their
opinion that the public faith was pledged, the council thought
that there was no time to be loft, and that it ought to be
figned immediately.

*Examined by other Members of the Committee and by General
Burgoyne occafionally.*

Q. Do you know or apprehend that the rebel camp was 35.
completely entrenched on the 19th of September ?

A. I don't know.

Q. Had you any reafon to believe from information that 36.
they completed their entrenchments afterwards ?

A. I underftood they had—I don't fpeak from authority.

Q. Had you reafon to think that the rebels received con- 37.
fiderable reinforcements between the 19th of September and
the 7th of October ?

A. I did not hear that they had.

Q. Suppofing the rebels to have received reinforcements, 38.
could any acceffion of ftrength to our army from the recovery
of any number you can fuppofe of the 500 that were in the
hofpital, be equal to a reinforcement of even 500 men received by the enemy ?

A. I cannot take upon me to fay.

Q. From being in the hofpital yourfelf, how many of the 39.
500 do you judge joined the army ?

A. I can't pretend to fay.

Q. Do you judge in your own opinion, putting all the 40.
circumftances you can together, whether the enemy were
more likely to be forced on the 27th of September or a day
or two after, than on the 7th of October ?

A. It is impoffible for me to judge—I did not know their
ftrength on the 19th of September, or what reinforcements
they received before the 7th of October.

Q. Did you apprehend the army might have made their 41.
retreat good to Canada immediately after the action of the
19th of September ?

A. That depended entirely on circumftances.

Q. Judging from the circumftances you then knew, what 42.
is your opinion ?

A. I was not more acquainted with the circumstances of the 19th of September than with those of the 7th of October.

43.   Q. If the army had had three weeks more provisions when they began their retreat, would not that have been a material circumstance to them towards making good their retreat ?

A. The army could have defended themselves longer in their entrenchments at Saratoga if they had had more provisions.

44.   Q. Had you known, immediately after the action of the
By General Burgoyne. 19th of September, that a letter had been received from Sir Henry Clinton, mentioning his intention to attack the highlands about that time, would you have thought either a retreat or an immediate attack on the enemy adviseable ?

A. Certainly not.

45.   Q. Do you know whether a council of war was called on
By other Members. the 20th of September, or immediately after the engagement of the 19th of September ?

A. I don't know that there was.

46.   Q. Did the army in which you served, in its approach to Albany, expect a co-operation from Sir William Howe on the North River ?

A. We did.

47.   Q. Do you believe if the army under Sir William Howe, instead of going by sea up the Chesapeak to Philadelphia, had operated upon the North River to effect a junction with General Burgoyne's army, considering also the panic that prevailed after the taking of Ticonderoga, that the army under General Burgoyne would have been made prisoners ?

A. I should think not.

48.   Q. Did you expect any great opposition from the rebel army after the taking Ticonderoga ?

A. I did not.

49.   Q. Upon what grounds did you so positively expect a co-operation with Sir William Howe's army ?

A. From General Burgoyne's orders.

50.   Q. Did you ever see General Burgoyne's orders ?

A. Every day during the campaign.

51.   Q. By what orders of General Burgoyne did you expect a co-operation ?

A. Early in October General Burgoyne gave it out in orders that there were powerful armies of the King's then co-operating with ours.

Q. Did

Q. Did not thofe orders give fpirits to General Burgoyne's 52.
army ?

A. Situated as our army was, every profpect of reinforcement muft certainly give us fpirits.

Q. Did you ever hear of any co-operation before thofe 53.
orders of General Burgoyne's in October ?

A. It was generally talked of in the army, but not by
authority.

Q. Whether, if the operations of Sir Henry Clinton on 54.
the North River had taken place in time, it would not have
been looked on as a very advantageous co-operation with
General Burgoyne's army ?

A. It might have been attended with very good confequences.

Q. What fituation in general, and particularly with re- 55.
gard to provifions, was General Burgoyne's army in, at the
time you mentioned thofe encouraging hopes of co-operation
in his orders ?

A. The army was put on fhort allowance at that time.

Q. Whether in military affairs a powerful diverfion, if 56.
well executed, is not known often to anfwer very effectually
the purpofes of co-operation ?

A. Certainly very good effects have accrued from powerful diverfions.

Q. If there had been a council of war on the 20th of 57.
September, or immediately after the engagement of the 19th,
fhould you have known of it ?

A. I think I muft have heard of it.

Q. Whether, confidering the circumftances of Sir Wil- 58.
liam Howe's having carried his army to Chefapeak Bay,
you fuppofed, or ever heard it fuppofed, that Sir Henry
Clinton would have attempted his operations up the North
River fooner than he did, or previous to the arrival of his
reinforcement from Europe ?

A. Not knowing Sir Henry Clinton's ftrength, or his
orders, nor the force the enemy had to oppofe him, it is
impoffible for me to anfwer that queftion.

Q. What effect had it on the fpirits of General Bur- 59.
goyne's army when they found there was to be no co-operation
between that army and the army of Sir William Howe ?

A. We never knew but that there was to be a co-
operation ?

[*Withdrew.*]

CAPTAIN

CAPTAIN BLOOMFIELD, of the Artillery, called in, and
examined by General Burgoyne.

1.   Q. IN what capacity did you serve in the campaign in
America in 1776 and 1777 ?
    A I was major of brigade of the royal artillery.

2.   Q. Was you employed by General Phillips, on your return to England, after the campaign of 1776, to solicit a
further supply of artillery for the service of the ensuing
campaign ?
    A. On my leaving General Phillips at St. John's, in the
month of November, 1776. I was charged with a letter to
Sir Guy Carleton, wherein he recommended it to make a
demand of a further supply of artillery and stores for the
complete equipment of an additional number of gun-boats
for the service of Lake Champlain in the ensuing campaign,
and likewise for the boats themselves to be sent out in frame-
work. Sir Guy Carleton, on perusing the letter, disapproved
of the boats being sent out, but approved of the demand of
the stores and artillery agreeable to General Phillips's request, and they were accordingly sent out in the beginning
of the year 1777.

3.   Q. At what time did you join the army in the campaign
of 1777 ?
    A. I joined the army at Ticonderoga on the 23d of July.

4.   Q. Did you live in the family of General Phillips, and
had you occasion to know his sentiments respecting the artillery department ?
    A. I did chiefly live with the general, and had frequent
occasion to know his sentiments on the subject of the artillery
in the course of my duty as brigade-major.

5.   Q. Did you know, or had you reason to believe, that the
proportion of artillery employed that campaign was according
to the opinion and recommendation of General Phillips ?
    A. I can have no doubt but that an officer of General Phil-
lips's rank and extensive experience must have determined
that point.

6.   Q. What was the distribution of the artillery after the
enemy evacuated Ticonderoga ?
    A. The light brigade of artillery proceeded with the army
by the way of Skenesborough ; the park brigade and stores
were conveyed across Lake George in bateaux.

Q. Was

Q. Was not a confiderable portion of artillery of the 7. heavieft kind either left at St. John's, fent back from Ticonderoga, or difpofed of in veffels?

A. It was: there were left at Ticonderoga fix heavy twelve-pounders, one light twelve-pounder, four light three-pounders, four royal mortars and twelve cohorns. Left on board the Royal George, two heavy twenty-four pounders, two thirteen-inch mortars, two ten-inch mortars, four eight-inch mortars, four royal mortars and eight cohorns. Sent back to St. John's in the Radau, fourteen heavy twenty-four pounders, two eight-inch howitzers. Left at Fort George, four medium twelve-pounders, two light fix-pounders, two eight-inch howitzers, two royal howitzers. With Colonel St. Leger's expedition to Fort Stanwix were fent two light fix-pounders, two light three-pounders, four cohorns. Left at St. John's, four light fix-pounders, five light three-pounders, four cohorn mortars: that was the diftribution of artillery that remained after the army had quitted Fort George. The quantity of artillery brought forward with the army were four medium twelve-pounders, two light twenty-four-pounders, eighteen light fix-pounders, fix light three-pounders, two eighteen-inch howitzers, four royal howitzers, two eight-inch mortars, four royal mortars.

Q. Was not that park artillery, though confifting of fome 8. twenty-four-pounders and fome twelve-pounders, properly field artillery?

A. They certainly were, and have ever been confidered as fuch on all field fervices. Heavy artillery is of a diftinct nature, and confiderably heavier than guns of the fame calibre which we had in the army.

Q. Have you ever known a lefs proportion than the bri- 9. gaded artillery, which was attached to the line and to the advanced corps, allotted to the fame number of troops?

A. The proportion of field artillery certainly fhould vary both in quantity and nature according to the variety of circumftances under which the army is to act; the ufual allotment of light field pieces are two to each battalion; and from a calculation of the number and ftrength of General Burgoyne's army, I do not conceive that our light field artillery exceeded that proportion.

Q. What do you apprehend was the propofed ufe of artil- 10. lery in the country in which we were to act?

A. To diflodge the enemy from fuch pofts as every where prefent themfelves in that part of the country, and from
which

which it may be impoffible to diflodge them without artillery
of a more confiderable calibre than light fix-pounders.

11. Q. Do you remember the pofition which the enemy evacuated at Schuyler's Ifland?

A. I do perfectly.

12. Q. Had that pofition been maintained, would not artillery
of the heavieft nature we had have been particularly ferviceable?

A. Provided the poft could not have been turned, and the
enemy had made ufe of every advantage which the ground
gave them, I have no doubt but the park artillery would
have been abfolutely neceffary.

13. Q. Had the paffage of the Hudfon's River, or of Batten
Kill been difputed, would artillery of that nature have been
ferviceable?

A. Doubtlefs it would.

14. Q. Had the enemy taken a pofition at the Forks of the
Mohawk River, would artillery of that nature have been
ferviceable?

A. From the imperfect manner in which I faw that ground,
it appeared capable of being made extremely defenfible, and,
of courfe, that fort of artillery would have been ferviceable.

15. Q. Had the army reached Albany, and it had been found
expedient to fortify a camp there for the winter, would artillery of that nature have been neceffary?

A. There can be no doubt of it.

16. Q. What do you apprehend to be the chief ufe of howitzers and fmall mortars in the field?

A. I apprehend they are of infinite fervice againft all kinds
of log work, abbatis, and againft entrenchments. The fmall
mortars are particularly ufeful againft redoubts and other
works where the enemy are confined within a fmall fpace.

17 Q. Are not log-works a fpecies of fortification peculiar to
that country?

A. I never faw any elfewhere.

18. Q. Was the carrying forward the artillery from Lake
George to the place where the army croffed the Hudfon's River any impediment to the tranfport of provifions?

A. The tranfport of our artillery and ftores was conftantly made by horfes attached to our department, and therefore
I do not conceive it did in any manner interfere with
the tranfport of provifions—I mean to confine myfelf in this
anfwer to the tranfport from Fort George to the Hudfon's
River; for after croffing the river we had fome oxen and
horfes

horfes attached to the fervice of the artillery, which I believe were before employed in bringing forward provifions
and bateaux.

Q. What time did it take to bring forward the park artil- 19.
lery from Fort George to the bridge of boats over the Hudfon's River?

A. The light brigade and the artillery of the park, with
their proper proportion of ftores and ammunition, had their
horfes, carriages, and drivers conftantly attached to them;
it therefore required no more time to carry thofe ftores than
was neceffary for the carriages themfelves to pafs from Fort
George to the Hudfon's River; but with refpect to the referve which was afterwards tranfported by water in bateaux,
I believe two days with all our carriages would eafily have
conveyed them to the Hudfon's River.

Q. Do you remember the pofition of the King's troops 20.
from the time of the attack on the 19th of September to the
attack on the 7th of October?

A. Yes.

Q. Had the army made a movement to gain the left of 21.
the enemy's entrenchments without previoufly conftructing
redoubts on the heights that commanded the plain, would
not the bateaux, provifions and hofpital have been left open
to an attack from the enemy's right?

A. They would have been left expofed undoubtedly.

Q. Were not the largeft guns we had the propereft pieces 22.
of artillery for thofe redoubts?

A. I think it was a fervice that was exactly adapted to
them.

Q. Do you remember the difpofition made by General 23.
Burgoyne on the 7th of October?

A. I do.

Q. At what time was you wounded in that attack?　　24.

A. I believe in about twenty minutes after it commenced.

Q. What circumftance of the action did you obferve be- 25.
fore you was wounded, particularly refpecting the artillery
and the enemy's advancing under the fire of the artillery, and
what happened to the troops pofted immediately on the left
of the artillery?

A. The ground on which the artillery was pofted was a
clear fpot, in a great meafure furrounded by woods, the
fkirts of which on our left was diftant about two hundred
yards where the attack firft began. The two medium twelve-
pounders were pofted on a fmall eminence, nearly in the cen-

3　　　　　　　　　　　　　　　　　　　ter

ter of this cleared spot between German picquets and
a detachment of the Hesse Hanau regiment. On the enemy's column approaching, the fire of the twelve-pounders
and the four sixes was immediately directed towards the enemy's column, notwithstanding which, they drew up along
the skirts of the wood behind trees, and after driving in the
Germans, kept a pretty warm fire of musketry on the guns
and the troops posted about them ; soon after this I heard a
firing on the right towards a cleared spot, separated from us
by a wood on which the light infantry were posted on very
commanding ground. On their retreating, as also the twenty-fourth regiment who was drawn up in the wood on our
right, the enemy made their appearance on an eminence on
our right, and cut off the retreat of the artillery—At this
moment I received my wound, and therefore can give no
farther account of the circumstances of that day's action.

Examined by other Members of the Committee.

26.   Q. What was the number of horses in general employed
for the artillery after the march from Ticonderoga ?

A. The whole number of horses detached with the British
artillery, previous to the passing the Hudson's River, was
about four hundred.

27.   Q. How many would have been necessary for the field
pieces attached to the battalions only ?

A. Eighteen six pounders at four horses each ; six three-
pounders at three horses each, and two royal howitzers at
three horses each : the remainder were for park artillery,
ammunition, and stores of all kinds to accommodate the army
on its march.

28.   Q. Was the forage for these horses procured in the country on their march, or brought from a distance ?

A. A quantity of oats was brought forward from Canada,
but with respect to other forage they were under the necessity of collecting it in the neighbourhood of the encampment.

29.   Q. How many waggons might the bringing on that quantity of oats employ ?

A. I believe the quantity of oats after passing Fort Edward was so trifling that I don't believe it loaded one wag-
gon.

30.   Q. After the army arrived at Fort Edward, did any delay or not arise to its forward progress from bringing on the
park artillery, waiting for horses and drivers for that purpose,
or to provide forage ?

A. The

A. The park artillery remained at Fort Edward no longer than was neceffary during the time the army remained in that neighbourhood : I do not know of any delay whatever from the want of horfes and drivers. Had the park artillery moved forwards fooner, no end could have been anfwered by it, before the bridge was thrown over the Hudfon's River.

Q. Were there any gun-boats fent out to Quebec for the campaign 1776 ? 31.

A. There were.

Q. Were there a fufficient number fent out, in your opinion ? 32.

A It appeared that the naval force was fuperior to that of the rebels, from the event of that engagement ; and therefore I conclude, that for the ufes of that campaign there were a fufficient number.

Q. Did you apprehend, before the event of the action on the lakes, that the number was fufficient, and went out in time ? 33.

A. We had received very exaggerated accounts of the rebel force on the lakes, and therefore uncommon exertions were ufed to render our force as formidable as poffible ; and probably fome time was loft, and the campaign in fome degree retarded, from that circumftance.

Q. Would the campaign have been retarded fo long if a greater number of gun-boats had been fent out ? 34.

A. Certainly not.

Q. What number of artificers were fent to Canada for the campaign in 1776 ? 35.

A. I don't immediately recollect the exact number : but I think Colonel Chriftie engaged about two hundred. I know of no others being fent out.

Q. Do you know of more being afked for by the artillery or engineers, as neceffary for the campaign ? 36.

A. I did hear of fome fuch intention ; but at this diftance of time I cannot particularly anfwer that queftion.

Q. Whether the number of artificers fent out for that campaign were, in any degree, fufficient for the purpofe of carrying it on ? 37.

A. Certainly not. We were under the neceffity of collecting all the artificers that could be met with in Canada for the armament of St. John's only, moft of the bateaux being built by private contract.

Q. Were not the operations of that campaign confiderably retarded, 38.

retarded, for want of the number of artificers that were
aſked for and not granted ?

A. Had the number of artificers been greater, there can
be no doubt but the work would have gone on much faſter.
With reſpeƈt to the artificers being demanded, I have already
ſaid I do not recolleƈt the number.

39. Q. Were there not horſes neceſſary for conveying the ſtores
and ammunition neceſſary for the field train ; and how many ?

A. The beſt anſwer to that queſtion will, I apprehend, be
a ſtate of the number of horſes aƈtually attached to the ſeveral brigades of artillery, ſince the allotment of ſtores and
ammunition were exaƈtly proportioned to the number of
Anſwer in- pieces which they accompanied.——
terrupted
going into   [The brigade attached to the advanced corps of light ar-
the detail. tillery conſiſted of eighty-five——]

40. Q. How many horſes might have been ſpared, if the
heavy park of artillery had not attended the army ?

A. It would have made a difference of two hundred and
thirty ſeven horſes.

41. Q. Was the army furniſhed with carts to have employed
thoſe two hundred and thirty-ſeven horſes ?

A. I really cannot anſwer that queſtion of my own knowledge.   [Withdrew.

Jovis 3° die Junii, 1779.

LIEUTENANT COLONEL KINGSTON called, in and examined by General Burgoyne.

1. Q. IN what capacity did you aƈt in the campaign of
1777 ?

A. As deputy adjutant general of the province of Quebec; I aƈted as adjutant general of the army under General
Burgoyne, and alſo as ſecretary to General Burgoyne.

2. Q. Did not that double capacity, and the confidence with
which General Burgoyne treated you, lead you to the knowledge of the material circumſtances attending that campaign ?

A. I looked on myſelf to be in the entire confidence of
the general.

3. Q. Did General Burgoyne give any orders for the aug-
mentation of artillery deſtined for this expedition, after his
arrival in Canada ?

A. There was no ſuch order went through me ; nor did I
hear of any ſuch order being given.

Q. Have

Q. Have you reafon to believe that the proportion of ar- 4.
tillery employed was according to the opinion and recommendation of Major General Phillips ?

A. I believe General Burgoyne had the greateft confidence
in General Phillips's knowledge and abilities ; and I believe
the proportion of artillery to have been arranged between
General Phillips and Sir Guy Carleton, becaufe I don't
know of any directions given by General Burgoyne upon
that head.

Q. What were the orders given, at the opening of the 5.
campaign, refpecting the incumbrances of baggage ?
[*The witnefs refers to the orderly book, which he had with him.*]
Read the orders.

They are the original orders, written by myfelf at the
time.

[*Reads.*] " Extracts from orders iffued by Lieutenant General Burgoyne at Montreal, dated 30th May, 1777.

" The regiments deftined for the expedition under Gene-
" ral Burgoyne are to leave in their refpective ftores their
" blanket coats, legging, and all baggage that can be fpared
" during the fummer months ; the officers are depended on
" not to encumber the fervice with more baggage than fhall
" be abfolutely neceffary for a campaign where the move-
" ments may be expected to be fudden and alert ; the por-
" tion of bateaux to each regiment will be regulated on thofe
" principles."

Q. Were thofe orders afterwards enforced ?   6.
A. Orders were iffued again to the fame purport, dated
Skenefborough Houfe, July 12.

[*Reads.*] " It is obferved that the injunction given, before
" the army took the field, relative to the baggage of officers,
" has not been complied with ; and that the regiments in
" general are encumbered with much more baggage than they
" can poffibly be fupplied with means of conveying, when they
" quit the lake and rivers ; warning is therefore again given
" to the officers, to convey by the bateaux, which will foon
" return to Ticonderoga, the baggage that is not indifpen-
" fibly neceffary to them ; or upon the firft fudden move-
" ment, it muft inevitably be left upon the ground. Such
" gentlemen as ferved in America the laft war may remember
" that the officers took up with foldiers' tents and often con-
" fined their baggage to a knapfack for months together."

Q. Have

8. Q. Have you a letter from General Burgoyne to General Reidefel, on the fubject of the incumbrance of baggage?

A. I have an extract of it, taken from the original letter in the letter-book. It is as follows:

Extract of a Letter from Lieut. Gen. Burgoyne to Major General Reidefel, dated Head Quarters at Skenefborough, the 18th July, 1777.

 " Je vous fupplie de faire en forte, que l'efprit de l'or-
" dre par rapport à le renvoye des baggages des offi-
" ciers à Ticonderoga aye lieu.

 " Les baggages des officiers Britaniques font deja ren-
" voyés, et il n'en refte à plufieurs qu'une petite tente,
" et un valife. C'eft réelement pour l'intereft de l'offi-
" cier à la fin, que je fuis fi porté à cet article."

T R A N S L A T I O N.

 " I requeft you to take meafures that the fpirit of
" the order refpecting the fending back officers' baggage
" to Ticonderoga may have due force.

 " The baggage of the Britifh officers is already gone,
" and many of them have only retained a fmall tent and
" one cloak bag. It is really for the intereft of the
" officers, in the end, that I am fo preffing upon this
" fubject."

9. Q. When the contract was made for horfes and carts at Montreal, was it the general opinion of the perfons of beft intelligence confulted, that the number was more or lefs than neceffary for the fervice on which we were going?

A. In general converfation on that fubject I remember to have heard it faid, that though they were infufficient, we might expect to find additional fupplies in the country. I have extracts of letters here that paffed between General Burgoyne and General Phillips on that fubject. They are ex-tracted from the original letter copy-book.

See the Appendix.

10. Q. Have you the returns, or extracts of the returns, of the ftrength of the army at all the different periods of the campaign?

A. I have extracts from the returns.

11. Q. What was the ftrength of the regular troops, at the higheft, at the opening of the campaign, rank and file, fit for duty?

A. The firft returns I received on the firft of July.

The

The Britiſh were   3576 fit for duty.
Germans   2919 do.

     6489

I ſpeak ſolely of the army under Lieutenant General Burgoyne.

Q. What were the numbers of the artillery, and the corps 12. under Lieutenant Nutt, attached to the ſervice of the artillery ?

     Britiſh artillery   257
     Germans   100
     Recruits under Lieut. Nutt   154

Q. Were there any other troops in the army that could be 13. called regulars ?

A. There were Canadians, Provincials, and Indians; but I never conſidered them as regulars, becauſe they were not diſciplined.

Q. Can you ſtate about what was the number of the Ca- 14. nadians ?

A. The Canadians were 148 the higheſt number.

Q. The Provincials ?   15:

A. I would be underſtood to ſpeak to the opening of the campaign the firſt of July. They were low then, and encreaſed afterward. They were then 83.

Q. The Indians ?   16.

A. Between three and four hundred. It was very difficult to colleĉt what their number was exaĉtly.

Q. Was the army ever ſo high in numbers, Provincials 17. and Indians excepted, as at that period ?

A. I believe it never was. On the 3d of September additional companies joined the Britiſh, to the amount of about 300 men; but from killed and wounded, and the garriſon left at Ticonderoga, the army was at no time equal to its firſt number.

Q. What was the force left at Ticonderoga ?   18.

A. The firſt garriſon conſiſted of 462 Britiſh, rank and file; 448 Germans, rank and file, making 910 in the whole.

Q. Do you remember the difficulties which attended mov- 19. ing the wounded to Ticonderoga, after the aĉtion at Huberton ?

A. I remember to have heard they were very great. Different propoſitions were made fo the removing them, ſuch as biers and hand-barrows, which were ſo very incommodious, that I remember to have been told that the wounded

     H   would

would rather be left where they were than move in the then
ftate of their wounds by fuch conveyances.

20.   Q. Do you know what were General Burgoyne's motives
for detaching General Reidefel with a large corps of troops
to the country in the neighbourhood of Caftleton ?

A. I don't remember to have been prefent when General
Reidefel received his orders or inftructions ; but I underftood
it was to create an alarm towards the Connecticut, to give encouragement to the loyal inhabitants, if any fuch there were,
and to protect thofe that were wounded at Huberton or thereabouts.

21.   Q. Was the removal of thofe wounded effected long before General Reidefel was recalled from Caftleton ?

A. I believe not ; for I am not quite certain that the
whole were moved when General Reidefel returned to the
army at Skenefborough, a day or two before the firft divifion
of the army moved towards Fort Anne.

22.   Q. Have you any papers written by General Burgoyne
between the time he was at Montreal and the time he left
Skenefborough, explanatory of the motives on which he
acted ?

See Appen-   A. I have.   They are extracts from the original letter-
dix.   book.

23.   Q. Are you acquainted with any facts that will afcer-
tain whether, on the army's arriving at Fort Edward, it was
forwarder in its progrefs towards Albany, in point of time,
than it would have been had it taken the route by Ticonderoga and Lake George ?

A. In anfwer to that queftion I have to fay, the army, by
taking that route, was a-head of the tranfport of provifions,
which, for the greater part, went from Ticonderoga by the
route of Lake George ?

24.   Q. At our firft arrival at Fort Edward, and previous to
the roads being mended, in what proportion did provifions
arrive at our camp ?

A. Very little more than for the immediate confumption.

25.   Q. Have you the memorandum-books of Sir Francis
Clarke !

A. Yes.

26.   Q. Do you know them to be his hand-writing ?

A. I am fully convinced of it, having feen him enter many
of the articles in thefe books.

27.   Q. Has there been any alteration or addition fince you had
them ?

A. None

A. None.

Q. What was the character of Sir Francis Clarke respect- 28.
ing his accuracy ?

A. I never saw an officer more attentive to the duties of
his station than Sir Francis Clarke, and always found him
exceedingly accurate in the remarks he made.

Q. Are there any memorandums respecting the arrival of 29.
provisions at that time ?

A. There are several.

Q. You will read two or three ?

A. [Reads.] " Fifth August.—Victualling of the army 30.
" out this day, and from difficulties of the roads and tranf-
" ports, no provision came in this night."

" Sixth August.—At ten o'clock this morning, not quite
" enough provisions arrived for the consumption of two
" days."

Q. Was it in general understood, from the combined in- 31.
telligence received by General Reidesel, while he was detached to Castleton, and that received by General Burgoyne
from the Provincials in his camp, that there were many well
affected inhabitants towards Bennington, who would shew
themselves on the approach of troops; and that there was
dejection and submission among the party attached to the
congress in that country ?

A. I did hear several reports to that purpose.

Q. Have you the original rough draft of the expedition to 32.
Bennington, as presented to General Burgoyne from General
Reidesel; with General Burgoyne's alterations and addi-
tions ?

A. I have the original rough draft of the proposals for the
expedition to Bennington ; but not being present at the time,
I can't say whether those proposals were delivered by General Reidesel or not ; but I know of alterations made in
those proposals by General Burgoyne, from a knowledge of
his hand-writing.

Note, The witness delivered in to the Committee the origi- See Appen-
nal rough draft of the Instructions, with a fair copy.   dix.

Q. Whether you have reason to know that all the erasures 33.
and alterations in that plan were made before the expedition
took place ?

A. I believe they were, from the reading of it.

Q. Do you remember taking this plan to General Phillips 34.

the

the day General Burgoyne went to Fort George to infpect the tranfport of provifions?

A. I do remember it very well; it was the rough draft I took.

35. Q. What were General Phillips's fentiments upon it?

A. I remember General Phillips and I had a long converfation on the flownefs of the arrival of the tranfport of provifions; and he faid he looked on this as a very good idea; that he faw no objection, and afked me if I knew of any.

36. Q. Do you remember fhewing the plan to General Frafer?

A. I do very well.

37. Q. What did he exprefs on this fubject?

A. He defired me to leave it with him till the afternoon for his confideration. He came himfelf to my tent the next morning early; he expreffed himfelf to me in a manner that conveyed a difapprobation of the Germans being employed in it. I think I obferved to him that fince the honour gained by the advanced corps at Huberton, I believed General Reidefel was defirous of having the Germans employed. I mentioned to General Frafer my ideas of provifions being obtained by that expedition, and the army thereby enabled to get quicker on to Albany than waiting for the flow tranfport from Fort George. General Frafer faid fomething about Germans, which I don't recollect; which brought this remark from me; I defired General Frafer, from the friendfhip he had for General Burgoyne, if he faw any real objection to this plan, to exprefs himfelf fully and freely to General Burgoyne himfelf; that the fcouts of the army and the guides were attached to his advanced corps, and he might, through them, perhaps know more of the nature of the country than I did; and therefore I preffed him to mention his objections, if he had any, to General Burgoyne. I think he faid, but am not quite certain, "the Germans are not a very active " people; but it may do." I preffed him at parting to go to General Burgoyne, if he thought it would not do. He faid No, and went off.

38. Q. Were not many of the Provincials in the army of the country about Bennington, and towards the Connecticut?

A. I can't pretend to fay they were from that country; but I underftood many of them were well acquainted with that country.

39. Q. Do you remember Captain Sherwood in particular?

A. I do very well.

40. Q. Was he of that country?

A. I

A. I underſtood he was of that neighbourhood.

Q. Did you ever hear Colonel Skeene, or any other Pro-41.
vincial, conſulted on an expedition into that country, expreſs
any apprehenſion of its ſucceſs ?

A. I never did.　Sir Francis Clarke told me he had received favourable accounts from Colonel Skeene ; and I believe after part of the expedition had taken place.

Q. Are there any memorandums of Sir Francis Clarke's, 42.
reſpecting the expedition to Bennington ?

A. Yes.

Q. Is there any that marks the diſtance between Batten 43.
Kill and Bennington ?

A. Yes ; it is his hand-writing.

[*Reads.*] " From the mouth of Batten Kill, Eaſt, for
" two miles ; then ſtrike off South Eaſt for about fifteen
" miles to Cambridge ; and ſo on about twelve miles to
" Bennington."

Q. Have you the original letters, written from Colonel 44.
Baume to General Burgoyne, while he was on the expe-
dition ?　　　　　　　　　　　　　　　　　　　　　　See the
A. They are here.　[*He delivered them in to the Committee.* Appendix.

Q. Is there any memorandum of Sir Francis Clarke's, 45.
marking the time when Colonel Breyman was ordered to
march to ſupport Colonel Baume ?

A. [*Reads.*] " 15th Auguſt.　Expreſs arrived from
" Sancoick, at five in the morning ; corps de reſerve or-
" dered to march.

" 16th Auguſt.　During the night, expreſs arrived from
" Sancoick with an account of the repulſe this evening of a
" detachment of ours on expedition.

" Sunday, 17th of Auguſt.　The general went up to
" the twentieth regiment, advanced on the road to Sancoick,
" and met the corps de reſerve, the men of that expedition
" returning all day."

Q. Do you recollect what time of the day it was Gene- 46.
ral Burgoyne met Colonel Breyman on his return on the
17th ?

A. I think it was ſometime between one and three
o'clock.

Q. Have you the inſtructions given by General Bur- 47.
goyne to Colonel Skeene on that expedition ?　　　See the
A. Here is a copy of them.　　　　　　　　　　　Appendix.
Q. Is there any memorandum of Sir Francis Clarke's, of 48.

any intelligence received from Colonel St. Leger about this time ?

A. There is of the 12th of Auguſt.

[*Reads.*] " This morning received intelligence of an
" action near Fort Stanwix."

49.   Q. After the failure of the expedition to Bennington,
can you ſpeak to the efforts made for forwarding proviſions ?

A. I know that very great efforts were made both before
and after.   I underſtood that General Burgoyne and General
Phillips had been both at different times at Fort George to
forward the proviſions, and I believe ſubſequent to the ill
news from Bennington.   The quarter-maſter-general (I
mean Captain Money) was ſent by General Burgoyne to
Fort Edward, and I believe to Fort George, to collect all
horſes and teams poſſible, and to make every exertion to
bring forward the proviſions.

50.   Q. Have you the calculation, made by the commiſſary-
See the general, of the carriages and horſes neceſſary for different
Appendix. given quantities of proviſions ?

A. It is here.   I believe it is the original.

51.   Q. Did the march of the artillery from Fort George to
the bridge of boats over Hudſon's River, interfere with the
tranſport of proviſions ?

A. I have had many converſations with General Phillips
and the quarter-maſter-general about the tranſport of proviſions, and never remember to have heard from them, or
any other perſon, that the march of the artillery interfered
in any manner with the tranſport of proviſions ?

52.   Q. About what time did the additional companies
arrive ?

A. The 3d of September.

53.   Q. What was the ſtate of the army when we paſſed the
Hudſon's River ?

A. My return goes to the firſt of September.

Britiſh, fit for duty under arms, 2635 rank and file.
Germans   —   1711

The 300 additional did not join the army till the 3d of
September, ſo that this return is excluſive of them.

54.   Q. What was the ſtrength of the artillery and Lieutenant
Nutt's corps at that time ?

A. I believe there was very little variation in either of
them from the former return.

55.   Q. Have you General Burgoyne's application to Sir Guy
                                                    Carleton

Carleton for a garriſon from Canada for Ticonderoga, before
he paſſed the Hudſon's River?

A. I have extracts from letters of General Burgoyne to
Sir Guy Carleton, the 11th of July, 1777, and on the 29th See the
of July, 1777.   Appendix.

Q. Was there any conſiderable alteration in the ſtrength 56.
of the army between the return of the 1ſt of September,
and the action on the 19th?

A. There was a ſkirmiſh or two, but the loſs was not
material in that interval.

Q. In the courſe of the ſervice, did you ever know any 57.
inſtance of a day of action, where there was not ſome deduction from the effective ſtrength upon paper, for baggage
guards, bat-men, care of the ſick, and other indiſpenſible
regimental contingencies?

A. I apprehend there muſt always be deductions of that
ſort?

Q. In the ſervice of our campaign, was there not a con- 58.
ſiderable additional deduction for the care and defence of the
bateaux and moveable magazines?

A. It muſt of courſe make an additional drain from the
army.

Q. Was not all we had of the forty-ſeventh regiment ap- 59
propriated for that particular ſervice?

A. It generally was; I believe always ſo.   60.

Q. Theſe deductions conſidered, about what number do
you compute the Britiſh line to have conſiſted of on the day
of the action of the 19th?

A. I believe the four regiments of the line engaged that
day amounted to little more than one thouſand one hundred
men on the ſpot under arms in the action.

Q. What loſs did the Britiſh ſuſtain in that action?   61.

A. Killed, wounded, and priſoners, rather more than leſs
than five hundred.

Q. Can you ſpeak particularly to the loſs of the line?   62.

A. I believe about ſeventy-ſix killed rank and file, and
between two hundred and forty and two hundred and fifty
wounded, and about twenty-eight or thirty miſſing and
priſoners.

Q. Do you recollect the ſtrength of the 20th regiment 63.
when they made their laſt charge on the enemy?

A. I do very well. I was by General Phillips when the
orders were given for that charge; he was then   the front
of the line: the ranks appeared to be very thin, the regi-
                                                     ment

ment were much fatigued with the length of the action, but moved on to the charge with ſpirit.

64.   Q. Do you remember General Burgoyne going up to the ſixty-ſecond regiment immediately after the firing ceaſed, and the report that was made to him by the commanding officer of the ſtate of that regiment ?

A. I remember it, and the officer reporting the great loſs they had ſuſtained in the action ; I ſaw them, and they appeared to be very conſiderably reduced in number ?

65.   Q. Do you remember the officer mentioning that they had not above fifty or ſixty men in the regiment ?

A. I can't ſpeak poſitively to that ; but in my own judgment they did not exceed that number.

66.   Q. Were not both the field-officers wounded ?

A. Colonel Anſtruther and Major Harnage were both wounded, and a great many other officers were killed and wounded, and the regiment ſuffered greatly.

67.   Q. To what degree did the men of the artillery ſuffer in that action ?

A. I think, but am not quite certain, that the number that were with four guns amounted to forty-eight. I ſaw Captain Jones who was a very gallant man, and commanded thoſe four guns, killed, and ſome other officers wounded, and I believe about thirty-ſix of the men were killed and wounded. I ſhould in juſtice to the artillery ſay, that I think it is not in the power of men to keep a better fire, both of round and grape-ſhot, than was ſucceſſively maintained for ſeveral hours that day.

68.   Q. From your experience in the ſervice, do you conceive it would have occurred to any officer, to engage troops, if he could poſſibly avoid it, in the ſituation in which the Britiſh line was the day after that action ?

A. The experience of an officer of my inferior rank does not lead to much ; but I ſhould have been ſorry to have given orders to thoſe regiments, after the gallant ſufferings of that day, to have attacked an army reported, both from our ſpies and our priſoners, to be very near if not more than four times the number of our whole force : add to this, the country was a very thick wood, and the ſituation of the rebel camp, I believe, could not by any means be reconnoitred within that ſpace of time.

69.   Q. Do you remember General Burgoyne receiving a letter from Sir Henry Clinton the day but one after that action,

informing

informing him, that he intended about that time an attack on Fort Montgomery ?

A. I do remember his receiving a letter from Sir Henry Clinton about that time ; it was the 22d of September ?

Q. Do you imagine that any officer knowing of that let-70. ter would have entertained thoughts of immediately renewing an attack upon the enemy ?

A. As far as an opinion of an officer of my inferior rank goes, I ſhould not have thought of it, nor did I hear any officer of any rank expreſs ſuch an idea at that time.

Q. From what you knew of the country, did you not be-71. lieve that a ſucceſsful attack from Sir Henry Clinton during the time we lay at that camp, would either have diſlodged General Gates entirely, or have obliged him to detach conſiderably from his army ?

A. I remember our ſcouts giving information, that a bridge was laid over the Hudſon's River, very near the enemy's camp ; and it was the opinion of ſome very confidential men that were employed in that army in that capacity, and were much under the direction of General Fraſer, that on the approach of Sir Henry Clinton's army, the army of Mr. Gates could not ſtand us, but would croſs the river, and go towards New England. Whether the idea was right or wrong, I can't tell.

Q. Did you ever hear ſuch perſons, or any others, ex-72. preſs an idea, that the enemy would have taken the ſame meaſure, on our advancing to attack them, without that co-operation ?

A. I don't remember to have heard any ſuch thing.

Q. Do you imagine that any officer knowing of Sir 73. Henry Clinton's letters, would have thought it proper to retreat after the action of the 19th of September ?

A. I never heard any officer expreſs an idea of that ſort. I don't know what officers might be within the knowledge of ſuch a letter ; but I lived intimately with General Phillips, General Fraſer, and with Mr. Twiſs, the engineer ; whether the letter was in their knowledge or not, I don't know : but I never heard them expreſs ſuch an idea.

Q. Did you ever hear any officer of that army, though 74. unacquainted with the letter, before or ſince the time, ex-preſs a diſapprobation of the meaſure of remaining in that camp without either attacking or retreating ?

A. Neither then or at any time while I remained in America, and of courſe not ſince.

Q. From

75.   Q. From your converſation with the chief engineer, and from other circumſtances, have you reaſon to know, that every poſſible means were uſed after the action of the 19th, to obtain a knowledge of the ground on the enemy's left?

A. I had frequent converſations with the chief engineer on that ſubject. I believe his attention was given to that point almoſt every day, and a knowledge of that ground I underſtood to be very difficult to be obtained.

76.   Q. Was not the right of the enemy deemed impracticable?

A. I had no opportunity myſelf of ſeeing the right of the enemy; but I underſtood from others, that the poſition was too ſtrong to be attacked with any proſpect of ſucceſs.

77.   Q. Were there not frequent conſultations held between General Burgoyne, General Phillips and General Fraſer, previous to the movement up to the enemy on the 7th of October?

A. I underſtood there was ſcarce a day paſſed without ſuch conſultation; I believe no day after the action of the 19th.

78.   Q. Did you conceive that the chief purpoſe of that movement was to attain a knowledge of the left of the enemy's poſition, and if expedient to attack them there?

A. I underſtood it was.

79.   Q. Did it appear to you, that the force left in camp, under General Hamilton, was more than ſufficient to keep the enemy in check?

A. I don't think it was.

80.   Q. From the intimacy and confidence in which you lived with General Burgoyne and General Fraſer, do you imagine any diſagreement of opinion could have ſubſiſted between them without your knowledge?

A. I think I muſt have heard of it.

81.   Q. Do you know any inſtance, but more eſpecially reſpecting the periods of paſſing the Hudſon's River, the action of the 19th of September, and that of the 7th of October, wherein General Fraſer expreſſed a diſapprobation of General Burgoyne's meaſures?

A. I do not: but I would beg leave to obſerve, that upon the plan to Bennington, General Fraſer had expreſſed a different opinion, with reſpect to employing the Germans. At the time of paſſing the Hudſon's River, and after it was croſſed, I had a great deal of converſation with General Fraſer: he ſeemed to expreſs ſatisfaction in the manner in which the troops had paſſed.

Q. In

Q. In the action of the 7th of October, after the Ger- 82.
man troops on the left of the artillery had given way, did
you obſerve General Phillips and General Reideſel in perſon ?

A. I was with General Phillips at different times, and I
ſaw General Reideſel more than once ; they were both very
active, and exerted themſelves very much to form the broken
troops, and to make the retreat as regular as the circumſtances would permit.

Q. What was the laſt time you ſaw Sir Francis Clarke in 83.
that action, and do you know what orders he was carrying ?

A. It was after the retreat was become very general.   Sir
Francis Clarke aſked me, if I had given any orders to the
artillery to retreat ?   I told him, that as there was a major-
general of the artillery in the field, who was confeſſed by
the army to be a very excellent officer, I would not take on
myſelf, as adjutant-general, to give orders to any part of the
artillery.   Sir Francis Clarke told me, that a diſpoſition had
been made for a general retreat, and that he was going with
orders from General Burgoyne to bring off the artillery.
About the inſtant we were parting, a very heavy fire came
upon us from the enemy, and I have ſince had reaſon to believe, that Sir Francis Clarke received his wound at that
time.

Q. On the day of the 8th, do you remember the enemy 84.
forming a line in the meadows, and making a demonſtration
of attacking us ?

A. I do remember it very well, and that there was a great
deal of cannonading from the enemy.

Q. Do you alſo remember a cannonading in the afternoon, 85.
about the time of General Fraſer's funeral ?

A. I think I ſhall never forget that circumſtance.   General Fraſer, I underſtood, had deſired to be buried privately,
in one of the redoubts that had been raiſed for the protection
of our magazines and ſtores ; as the corpſe was paſſing by,
General Burgoyne, General Phillips, and I believe General
Reideſel, and ſeveral other officers, out of reſpect to General Fraſer's memory, and to do him honour in the eyes of
the army, notwithſtanding his requeſt, attended his funeral
into the redoubt.   The enemy were in this inſtance, I
thought, very defective in point of humanity ; they pointed
a gun or two at that very redoubt, and kept up a briſk cannonade during the whole of the funeral ſervice, which was
performed with great ſolemnity and very deliberately by
Mr.

Mr. Brudenel, the chaplain. I never saw so affecting a fight.

86. Q. Do you remember on the march to Saratoga seeing a corps of the enemy at work on the plain of Saratoga?

A. I do very well; a working party, and what appeared to be a battalion or more drawn up as a covering party.

87. Q. Was that the corps that afterwards took post on the opposite side of the river!

A. I believe it was the same corps I saw afterwards passing the ford.

88. Q. After the arrival of the army at Saratoga, was Lieutenant Colonel Sutherland detached with a command to cover a party of workmen to repair bridges and roads, in order to continue the retreat on the west side of the river?

A. He was ordered with a party to repair bridges and roads on the west side.

89. Q. Do you remember on what account Colonel Sutherland and the party were recalled?

A. I believe it was on information given by our scouts, that the enemy were preparing to attack us in great force.

90. Q. Have you further reason to know that a general attack on that day was really intended by the enemy?

A. There was particular caution sent round to all the troops to be prepared for that attack, as it was expected it would be attempted under cover of a very thick fog then prevailing. After the convention had taken place, a general officer in the rebel service acquainted me, that such an attack was intended, and from information, I believe from deserters, or from their own scouts, that our army was exceedingly well prepared to receive them, that they would be very much exposed when they came on the plain to our artillery, he not only retreated with his command, but sent word to another general officer to retreat also. The other general officer was his senior; but he had taken that upon him, from the fear of the consequences of such an attack, of which he sent word to General Gates, who approved and confirmed his order.

91. Q. Previous to the council of war to which the field officers were called, do you remember it being determined in the council of the generals, to try a night march, abandoning the carriages and baggage, and orders being given for the delivery of as much provisions as the men could carry?

A. I do remember such a determination very well.

92. Q. What prevented the execution of it?

A. I

A. I underſtood there were ſuch difficulties in getting out the proviſions, that the delivery of the neceſſary proviſions could not be accompliſhed.

Q. Had we intelligence the next day from different ſcouts, 93. that the enemy was in poſſeſſion of the country in force, on both ſides the Hudſon's River, between us and Fort Edward?

A. I underſtood, from ſome of the ſcouts that we had been accuſtomed moſt to depend on, that the enemy were ſo poſted.

Q. Have you reaſon to know that the intelligence General 94. Burgoyne ſtated to the council of war on this ſubject was true?

A. I was aſſured by one of the general officers who con-ducted us towards Boſton, that troops of theirs were in the poſition that our ſcouts had given us information of.

Q. Did you learn at the ſame time at what period thoſe 95. poſts were taken up by the enemy, whether before or after our arrival at Saratoga?

A. I have extracts of minutes made at that time, from the mouth of the general officer I mentioned.

[Reads.]—"When the king's army was returning to Sara-
" toga, a brigade of fifteen hundred men were poſted on the
" eaſt ſide of the Hudſon's River, to diſpute the ford, and
" two thouſand men more were poſted between us and Fort
" Edward, on the ſame ſide of the river."—Fourteen hun-
dred more were alſo poſted oppoſite to Saratoga, a little above the other party I mentioned before, to prevent our paſſing the Hudſon's River. Fifteen hundred of thoſe I have mentioned were poſted on or before the 5th of October. The others, I remember very well now to have heard, were poſted previous to the 7th of October.

Q. Have you an extract of the laſt council of war at 96. which the field officers aſſiſted?

A. The extract is true, excepting the names of the officers, and the votes they gave. I have the original paper, with the names of the officers that compoſed the council; and I See Appen-believe their opinions.   [The extract produced. dix.

Q. Did you ever hear of a propoſal made by General 97. Phillips, to make a way from Saratoga to Ticonderoga with a body of troops?

A. Never with a body of troops; but I remember to have heard General Phillips make an offer, which I thought a very ſpirited one, to riſk his life in attempting, with one or two of our beſt guides, to find a paſſage to Ticonderoga, and

and do his utmoft for the defence of that garrifon, as an artillery officer, fhould the enemy attack that fortrefs after the convention fhould take place.

98.   Q. Have you the return of General Gates's army, figned by himfelf ?

A. I have ; but I have forgot to bring the original. I have the extract.

For the ori-
ginal re-
turn, fee
the Appen-
dix, No.
XVI.

[*Reads.*]   " Copy from General Gates's return, from his camp at Saratoga ; 16th of October, 1777.

" Brigadiers	12
" Colonels	44
" Lieutenant Colonels	45
" Majors	49
" Captains	344
" Firft Lieutenants	332
" Second Lieutenants	326
" Enfigns	345
" Chaplains	5
" Adjutants	42
" Quarter-mafters	44
" Paymafters	30
" Surgeons	37
" Mates	43
" Serjeants	1392
" Drummers	636
" Prefent fit for duty	13,216."

I underftand thefe laft are rank and file, becaufe the others are mentioned before.

" Sick prefent	622
" Sick abfent	731
" On command	3875
" On furlow	180."

I believe that the men on command were explained to me by General Gates to have been detached from his army, in the rear and upon the flanks of the king's troops, previous to the convention.

99.   Q. Do you apprehend that that return includes the corps that were on the other fide of the Hudfon's River, immediately oppofite to Saratoga ?

A. I do recollect the name of one of the general officers who was on the other fide of the Hudfon's River, included in in Mr. Gates's return, and therefore I imagine the men under his command are included alfo. When I fay one, I do not mean to have underftood that the other two general officers, the one who was ftationed with a party oppofite to Saratoga, and the one who was ftationed on the fame fide of the water, between us and Fort Edward, are not alfo included in General Gates's return.

Q. Do the returns to which you referred, of our army, 100. ftate the effective ftrength, at the time of figning the convention ?

A. They do ftate the rough number, collected at that time, of men prefent and under arms.

Q. State the numbers.   101.

A. The Britifh appeared to have been   1905
Germans   ———   1594
I can't be anfwerable for the correctnefs of thofe numbers, as they were taken in a great hurry.

Q. Can there poffibly be a miftake of many hundreds ?   102.

A. I can ftate from a monthly return of the firft of November, fit for duty,

Britifh   ———   2086 } Rank and file.
Germans   ———   1633 }

There might be people recovered from their wounds who were difcharged from the hofpital, and had joined the corps ; or there might have been a miftake in the return, juft before the convention, in the confufion of the army at that time.

Q. Do you know what paffed refpecting the military cheft, 103. while the treaty of Saratoga was depending ?

A. I do remember that it was ftrongly recommended to the commanding officers of corps to take fums of money from the paymafter general, on account of fubfiftence then due to their regiments ; and I believe a great deal of money was fo diftributed, and regularly accounted for to the paymafter general on the fubfequent fettlement of the pay of the army.

Q. What became of the reft of the money in the military 104. cheft ?

A. It was taken by the paymafter general to Albany.

Q. Did any part of it fall into the hands of the enemy ? 105.

A. Not a fhilling that I ever heard of.

Q. Was any proportion of it loft, embezzeled, or fecreted ? 106.

A. If any fuch thing had happened, I think the paymafter general would have applied to me immediately. Never having heard, then or at any time after, of any lofs having

been

been ſuſtained, I do not believe there was any loſs ſuffered in the retreat or after it.

107. Q. Was the ſecret ſervice account, during the campaign, kept by you?

A. It was.

108. Q. Could you produce the ſeveral articles of that account, if called on for it?

A. I have either a copy of it at home of my own, or from the paymaſter general.

109. Q. Did General Burgoyne ever appropriate any part of that expenditure to the extraordinaries of his own expences, or to any other purpoſe for his own uſe?

A. Never that I know of.

110. Q. Muſt not you have known it if it had been ſo?

A. Certainly.

111. Q. Were there not occaſions where General Burgoyne paid, from his own purſe, expences that, in the opinion of others, he might have been juſtified in placing to the public account?

A. I remember to have been told by other gentlemen, that expences of that ſort General Burgoyne had been at, ought to have been charged in that manner.

112. Q. What was the nature of thoſe expences?

A. They were preſents to people who had diſtinguiſhed themſelves, and in acts of charity to women who had loſt their huſbands, and other occaſions which it was very proper for a general officer to give, and very proper to put into a public account.

113. Q. Had not General Burgoyne, from his ſituation, all the expences attending a Commander in Chief?

A. He certainly had, from being obliged to keep a public table for the entertainment and refreſhment of officers and others coming to head quarters, on duty or buſineſs; and I know thoſe expences to have been very great, from the exceeding high price of all the articles of life in that part of the world.

114. Q. Did General Burgoyne ever receive more than the appointment of a lieutenant general?

A. Never.

115. Q. Was there not a board of general officers appointed at Cambridge, to inſpect all the accounts of the campaign; and did not General Burgoyne regulate the payment of the battalions by the report of that board?

A. There was ſuch a board, and the payments were regulated according to the report of that board.

3

Q. Upon

Q. Upon the whole of what you know of General Bur- 116.
goyne's receipts and expences, do you believe he was, in his
own purſe, a gainer or a ſufferer in the campaign 1777?

A. I really believe his appointments were not equal to his
expences in that campaign.

*Examined by other Members of the Committee and by General
Burgoyne occaſionlly.*

Q. What were the numbers of the effective Britiſh, at the 117.
opening of the campaign 1777, including officers and non-
commiſſioned officers?

A. I have not thoſe returns; but they were ſent to the
Commander in Chief, and my extracts are for the rank and
file.

Q. Can you anſwer that queſtion with reſpect to the Ger- 118.
mans?

A. My extracts are the ſame both for the Britiſh and the
Germans.

Q. What was the greateſt number of Provincials in the 119.
army at any time in the campaign?

A. I believe the only queſtion that has been aſked reſpecting them was at the beginning of the campaign; they were
then eighty-three. On the firſt of September they amounted
to about ſix hundred and eighty, which was the greateſt
number they ever amounted to.

Q. What do you mean by Provincials?   120.
A. I underſtand them to be inhabitants of that country,
aſſembled under officers who were to have had different com-
miſſions, provided they had ever amounted to certain numbers.

Q. Do you include Canadians under the name of Pro- 121.
vincials?

A. I believe, in the former part of my evidence, the Canadians were ſtated to be one hundred and forty-eight, and
diſtinguiſhed from the Provincials.

Q. Was General Burgoyne's ſecond order of the twelfth 122.
of July, relating to the baggage, ſtrictly complied with?

A. I conceive it was the duty of the commanding officers
of regiments to enforce an obſervance and obedience to the
general orders.

Q. Was it actually enforced in ſuch a manner to the de- 123.
gree you thought it ſhould have been.

A. I am not quite poſitive whether there was not another order iſſued afterwards.

                      I   [*Queſtion*

124.   [*Queſtion repeated.*]

A. I never had any report made to me by a commanding officer of any corps, of that order not being complied with.

125.   Q. What was your own ocular obſervation of the quantity of baggage carried with the army ; and did it appear to you that that order could have been fairly complied with ?

A. I own I don't recollect, not hearing any complaint nor attending to it. The quartermaſter general of the army muſt naturally know more of the baggage than the adjutant general.

126.   Q. Do you know what allowance of waggons was made to a regiment ?

A. I don't recollect any waggons that we had to allow.

127.   Q. Was none of the baggage brought down in wheeled carriages ?

A. Several officers, I believe, bought waggons and carts of the country people for their own uſe ; but I do not remember any of the King's carts or waggons being appropriated to the carriage of officers' baggage. It might be, but I don't recollect it.

128.   Q. Can you ſay, in a general way, how many horſes might be employed in carrying the baggage of the army, including officers' horſes ?

A. I never had any information upon that ſubject ; it did not belong to my department, and I had much buſineſs on my hands.

129.   Q. How was the regimental baggage carried ?

A. I believe chiefly in bateaux.

130.   Q. How was it carried when there was no water-carriage ?

A. I can't ſpeak to that point, having had no information on that ſubject ; and when I ſpeak of bateaux, I ſpeak generally, having *had* no information on the ſubject.

131.   Q. Can you ſay, in a general way, how many women attended the army ?

A. I had really ſo much to do that I had not much leiſure to pay much attention to the ladies ; and I know very little of their beauty or their numbers.

132.   Q. Would not the feeding of two thouſand women be a conſiderable object with reſpect to the proviſions of the army ?

A. I ſhould have been very ſorry to have had two thouſand women to have experienced that.

Q. How

Q. How many women were there, if not two thouſand ? 133.

A. I would wiſh to give the houſe every information in my power, when I can ſpeak with any degree of accuracy or tolerable gueſs. I have ſeen the commiſſary of proviſions return, and I think the number of women returned, as victualled from the ſtores, was very, very few.

Q. Do you think that a corps of dragoons mounted would 134. have been of great uſe to the army ?

A. I own, I very much wiſhed thoſe few dragoons we had could have been mounted, becauſe, though in that part of America that I ſaw they might not have been neceſſary or uſeful to have made a charge, I think thoſe light dragoons might be always applied to very uſeful ſervices.

Q. How many had you of thoſe dragoons ? 135.

A. They are included in the ſtrength of the Germans, and I really do not remember their particular number.

Q. If none or leſs of the park of artillery had been brought 136. forward, would there not have been horſes to have mounted thoſe dragoons ?

A. I believe there might have been horſes enough taken from the artillery, or from the proviſion train, to have mounted thoſe dragoons, if it had been thought more expedient to have employed the horſes in that manner ; but they were hired or contracted for, for the ſpecial purpoſes of carrying proviſions, and bringing on the artillery, and never meant by the perſons who furniſhed the contract for the dragoon ſervice.

Q If a ſmaller quantity of baggage had been carried, 137. might not the officers have ſpared ſome of their baggage horſes for mounting the dragoons ?

A. I never met with an officer who had horſes to ſpare. I know Sir Francis Clarke and myſelf wiſhed to buy horſes to carry our own ſervants ; cared very little what expence we were at ; and yet I could not obtain any.

Q. Do you know of any corps or party finding their way 138. back to Canada ?

A. I never heard of any corps finding its way there ; and I underſtood from the guides who were with us, previous to the convention's taking place, that if that was attempted, we muſt break into ſmall parties, and go by what is called Indian paths.

Q. Suppoſing there was a ſmall party that found its way to 139. Canada by Indian paths, do you think it would have been poſſible for an army to have done the ſame ?

A. My

A. My idea of that muſt be founded upon the report of thoſe guides who had ſerved us very faithfully as ſcouts upon former occaſions, and who informed me that we muſt break into very ſmall parties, to have any chance of making our way through the woods to Canada; and I remember that when General Phillips offered to attempt to find his way to Ticonderoga, it was talked of and looked on to be as deſperate as gallant.

140.   Q. If any party did make its way to Canada, do you not ſuppoſe it muſt be that party of Provincials that ran away while they were employed to repair roads, and that were never heard of afterwards?

A. I remember ſome were reported to have run away who were making roads, and it is likely to have been that party.

141.   Q. When you mentioned the higheſt number of provincials, did you mean that they were all armed?

A. I know that they were not all armed. We had not arms for them.

142.   Q. Of thoſe that were armed, ſome reſpectable perſons excepted, were they much to be depended upon?

A. A very great part of them were ſuch as I ſhould have placed very little dependence upon.

143.   Q. Before the army left Canada, was there not a ſtrict order, that not more than three women a company ſhould be ſuffered to embark?

A. I do know there was ſuch an order iſſued, and I never heard any complaint of its having been broke through. I don't recollect the date of that order, or I would have turned to my book, and ſtated to the houſe, upon the firſt queſtion relative to the number of women that were employed on our expedition.

144.   Q. Is it not the cuſtom in all armies victualled from the king's ſtores, to prohibit the delivery of proviſions to any women over and above the number allowed by order?

A. It was cuſtomary in all places where I ſerved in the laſt war, and very ſtrong and peremptory orders were given on that ſubject to the commiſſaries in our army.

145.   Q. Do you not then believe, that all women who followed your army were fed from the ration of the men they followed, or found their proviſion in the country?

A. I remember, upon aſking the commiſſaries how there came to be ſo few women in the provincial returns, I was told

3   told

told, it was the cuftom for them to be fupplied out of the
men's rations.

Q. Were the women conveyed on baggage carts or horfes, 146.
or did they walk a-foot ?

A. I never heard of the women's being conveyed on baggage carts or the king's horfes.

Q. If the women neither employed the king's horfes, nor 147.
confumed his provifions, do you think they were more of
impediment, or of comfort to the King's troops ?

A. I never underftood from my converfation with the
commanding officers, or others, that the women were any
impediment.

Q. If after the taking of Ticonderoga there was any 148.
doubt in the army in which you ferved, of their being
able to reach Albany ?

A. I don't remember to have heard any doubts expreffed
upon that fubject, meaning foon after the taking Ticonderoga.

Q. Was it generally underftood in the army, that it was 149.
well fupplied with all the neceffaries, appointments for war,
and articles proper for forwarding the expedition to Albany ?

A. I always underftood that the army had been very well
fupplied with every thing.

Q. Do you believe, if the fecretary of ftate had ordered 150.
the army under General Howe to co-operate with the army
under General Burgoyne for the North River, with a view
to have formed the junction of the two armies, that the difafter which befel General Burgoyne's army could have happened ?

A. If a junction could have been formed, I fhould apprehend that Mr. Gates's army might have been diflodged, and
that the misfortune at Saratoga would not have happened.
This is only matter of opinion.

Q. Do you apprehend, that if the army under Sir Wil- 151.
liam Howe had operated on the North River, with a view to
effect a junction, that fuch a junction would have taken
place ?

A. I had an opinion while in America, that if the expedition which came up the Hudfon's River under General
Vaughan, could have been there about the time of our action of the 19th of September, that Mr. Gates would have
found it difficult to have kept his army together, if he had
not croffed over the Hudfon's River towards New England.
But this is mere matter of private opinion.

I 3   Q. If

152.   Q. If you are of opinion, that the troops under General
Vaughan would have had ſo powerful an effect, even ſo late
as September, what effect do you think Sir William Howe's
army, aſſiſted by all the fleet and craft, would have had as
early as the beginning of July, immediately after the impreſſion which took place among the enemy after the defeat
at Ticonderoga ?

A. I did not know what force there was under the command of General Vaughan, nor do I even now know ; but I
ſhould think moſt certainly, that a great army upon the
Hudſon's River near Albany, would have contributed very
much to our making our way to Albany.

153.   Q. Have you ever conſidered what were the cauſes of the
failure of the expedition under General Burgoyne, and to
what do you impute it ?

A. I looked upon our force not to be equal to the forcing
our way to Albany without ſome co-operation.

154.   Q. Where then did you expect that co-operation ?

A. I had no where to expect it from, but up the Hudſon's
River from New York ; and the ſucceſs of Colonel St. Leger's expedition would have been of uſe certainly.

155.   Q. If General Waſhington's army had not been diverted,
would it not have impeded, or ſtopped the progreſs of any
army up the Hudſon's River ?

A. I don't know the ſtrength of General Waſhington's
army, nor the nature of the country between Albany and
New York ; and therefore I cannot form any judgment of
what would have happened.

156.   Q. Are you not of opinion that there are very ſtrong
paſſes or poſts on that river ?

A. I found them very ſtrong between Ticonderoga and
Albany, and from reports of military men of high reputation in the ſervice, I have underſtood there were many very
ſtrong poſts between New York and Albany.

157.   Q. From whence is the account of the ſtrength of Mr.
Gates's army taken ?

A. From a return voluntarily given by General Gates to
me for my own ſatisfaction when at Albany, and that return
was ſigned by General Gates.

158.   Q. Have you that return ?

A. I gave it to General Burgoyne ; I ſaw it to-day ; he
has it.

Q. Was it by conſent of General Gates that the ſoldiers
after the convention retained their cartouch-boxes ?

A. They

A. They retained their belts, and I really don't recollect whether their cartouch boxes were in general retained or not : but talking with Mr. Gates when the king's troops marched by with the accoutrements on, Mr. Gates aſked me (we had been old acquaintance formerly) whether it was not cuſtomary on field-days for arms and accoutrements to go together ? I told him, there was nothing ſaid in the convention that I had agreed to with him relating to accoutrements, and that he could have no right to any thing but what was ſtipulated in that treaty. He replied, " You are perfectly right;" and turned to ſome of the officers in their ſervice by, and ſaid, " If we meant to have had them, we ought to have in-" ſerted them in the convention." [*Withdrew*.

REVIEW of the EVIDENCE;

Its feveral Parts compared with the prefatory Speech and Narrative; and additional Remarks and Explanations.

THE noble Lord who is at iffue with me upon this occafion has, in a great meafure, deprived me of the benefit of a reply, properly fo called, because he has produced no defence. His Lordfhip certainly has been accufed by me in many inftances of a very ferious nature. If he is really willing that his political, and my military conduct fhould be tried by facts alone, I certainly have not fhewn lefs inclination than his Lordfhip for that teft; but, taxed as I avow he has been by me, with proceedings derogatory to the obligations which ought to fubfift between man and man, I really expected, as I believe did the Houfe of Commons and the public, to have heard from him fome juftification in thofe refpects. Inftead of that, the noble Lord, in opening the fubjects to which he propofed to call evidence, touched fo flightly upon the branch of the enquiry in which we are parties, that a ftranger would hardly have thought there fubfifted a difpute between us. His Lordfhip contradicted nothing that I have alledged refpecting his conduct or my own; he ftated no circumftance of blame againft me, except he meant as fuch the enterprize of Bennington, which he qualified with the epithet " fatal, " and pronounced to be the caufe of all the fubfequent misfortunes. He paffed entirely over the tranfactions at Saratoga. Of forty officers or more, belonging to the Convention troops,

The conduct of Ld. G. Germain during the enquiry.

troops, then in England, one only was propofed to be called on his Lordfhip's part, *viz.* Lieutenant Colonel Sutherland, of the 47th regiment, upon parole from the Congrefs, and acting with a corps of the Fencible Men in North Britain; but, upon further reflection, his Lordfhip thought proper to difpenfe with the attendance of this officer; and the only witnefs under order of the Houfe was Mr. Skene. No man was better qualified to give an account of the proceedings at Bennington; and I heartily lament that the public is deprived of his teftimony.

But although I am thus left in poffeffion of the evidence, uncontroverted by the noble Lord, I avail myfelf of my right of clofing the caufe, for the following purpofes: firft, to collect from the minutes (which, in an enquiry of this nature, are unavoidably prolix and difarranged) the fcattered parts, and apply them to facts, under diftinct and feparate heads. Next, to examine whether the facts (which, from the filence of the noble Lord, I am to affure as admitted by him) are in any refpect invalidated by the crofs examination of the witneffes by other gentlemen. And laftly, to explain fuch circumftances, and anfwer fuch new and collateral objections, as have been pointed at in the fame crofs examination, and were omitted, or only flightly noticed in my opening, becaufe they did not exift, or were not deemed poffible objects of blame or cavil. In purfuing thefe purpofes, I fhall confider the proofs precifely in the order of the facts to which they are produced. *[margin: Claim of Gen. Burgoyne to clofe the caufe. Mode of proceeding.]*

Though the firft circumftance I took notice of in my opening, *viz.* my conduct refpecting Sir Guy Carleton, was rather an infinuation than an allegation againft me, I thought it right that it fhould be the firft overthrown by evidence; for while it remained in any degree of force, it gave a general tinge, as it was meant to do, to my whole caufe. I could not but expect even the virtuous prejudices of the human heart to be againft me, whilft it was poffible to be conceived that in abfence of the commander in chief, to whom I had acted *[margin: Infinuation of having acted unfairly by Sir G. Carleton overthrown by his own evidence.]*

second;

fecond; whofe attention I had conftantly experienced ;
and with whofe confidence I was then honoured ; I had
practifed unmanly and adulatory intrigue to fuperfede
him in a favourite object of command.—There are
few worfe modes of betraying a fuperior officer to be
found upon the records of difhonour; and whoever
reflects upon the degree of odium with which the moft
palliated acts of that fpecies have been received by
mankind, will not wonder at, or condemn my impatience, in applying my firft queftions to Sir Guy Carleton to that particular object.   Clear as my juftification
stood by the letter formerly referred to [No. II.] I fhall
be forgiven for obtaining, though with fome redundan-
cy, a full and fatisfactory confirmation of my inno-
cence, from the verbal teftimony of the party whom I
was fuppofed to have injured.

Carleton's evidence, qu. 1, 2, 3.

It may be proper here to obferve, that the abovemen-
tioned afperfion, to which I have fo often adverted, and
at which I have ftrove in vain for due terms to exprefs
my indignation, was not the only one caft upon me refpecting Sir Guy Carleton.   When impartial and candid men revolted at the infinuation of my treachery,
my prefumption and infolence (a leffer but ftill a ca-
lumnious charge) was pointed out in that part of the
paper [No. III.] that treats of the force to be left in Canada, and the difpofition of it.   I am pleafed with the
queftions in the crofs examination of Sir Guy Carleton, marking the prefcribed diftribution of the troops,
&c. (38, 39, 40, 41, 42, 43.) becaufe that enquiry affords me an opportunity of juftifying myfelf in a point
which I have not taken notice of before.   The pofts,
and the troops which I imagined would be neceffary to
occupy them, were fpecified merely to fhew that the
number of 3000 was indifpenfibly requifite for the defence of the province.   The whole of that detail concurred with General Carleton's requifitions for reinforcement, and with my reafoning upon thofe requifitions ;
and when I affert, as I now do, that I never prefumed
to fuggeft the neceffity or propriety of forming a detail
of

Afperfion from the paper, No. III.

refuted.

of posts (thus given for information) into precise orders for the general upon the spot, I am sure the secretary of state will no more contradict that assertion than he has done any other I have made.

When in the same paper I confidentially communicated my reasons for preferring certain corps to others, I was actuated by the same principle of offering every opinion that could conduce to make the intended service effectual. I thought it a just claim in an arduous undertaking, to have my own choice of the troops; and I am persuaded Sir Guy Carleton never took ill of me, either that claim, or a subsequent one in the same paper, of being held free from any imputation of delay, till I should be clear of the province of Quebec. With an unfeigned confidence in Sir Guy Carleton, I thought it a precaution fully justifiable, to secure myself against others, in the numerous and complicated departments under him, who might be found less equitable than he is.

No. III.

Apology for specifying corps.

I know I have before complained of the production of these secret communications; but after so many precedents as the last Session furnished, of withholding parts of correspondences from Parliament, upon the plea that they might affect individuals, the noble Lord's silence upon those complaints, gives me a right still to comment upon the sinister purposes that are to be ascribed to the production of that paper at length, rather than by extract. Those purposes were various; but it must be confessed one, and only one, good effect may result from a review of them, viz. It may serve as a salutary caution to any officer, who shall for the future be admitted into consultation with the same minister, how he commits himself by an opinion of men and things.

The next point that I entered upon previously to my narrative, was the tenor of my orders, and I believe it was generally expected that the noble Lord would have taken some notice of the fact I alledged, *that every discretionary latitude which I had proposed was erased,*
while

Remarkable circumftance refpecting the conftruction to be put on my orders.

while the plan was in his hand. As his Lordfhip had fo much commented upon the nature of peremptory orders, as a *general* queftion, in my abfence, it would have been fair in him to have reafoned upon them after that important and decifive circumftance was laid open.

The general opinion of the army upon forcing a way to Albany.

The general idea *of forcing a way to Albany*, which the army at its outfet conceived, by reafoning upon the apparent principles of the campaign, without participation of the letter of the orders is clear, from the general tenor of the evidence. I wifhed, it is true, to have heard more copioufly the fentiments of Sir Guy Carleton, becaufe he had full participation of the orders. From the temper and judgment that always direct his conduct, he declined giving an opinion at the bar upon what might become a queftion in the Houfe. But I have fince (upon requeft) received his permiffion to publifh a letter from him to me, dated foon after the Convention of Saratoga, which is in the Appendix No. X. and with this reference I clofe my review of the prefatory matter which I laid before the Committee.

Review of the firft Period.

Moft of the circumftances ftated in my Narrative refpecting the firft period of the campaign, were, from their nature, to be eftablifhed by written teftimony ; and the papers No. VII. and VIII. in the Appendix, were added to thofe before produced for that purpofe ;

Strength of the army.

but the returns of the troops, No. XI. are moreover authenticated by the proper official authority, the adjutant general, and the detail of the artillery, by the major of brigade in that department.

Proportion of artillery. Evidence of C. Bloomfield from qu. 4 to 9.

From the evidence of the latter, is alfo confirmed all that I advanced refpecting the opinion and recommendation of Major General Phillips, for the proportion of artillery employed ; for the moderate quantity of it, comparatively with the principles and practice of

other

other fervices, and for the great expected ufe of artillery in the country where we were to act.

Had thefe opinions been merely fpeculative, the intelligence of the perf ns from whom they came would have given them fufficient authority. But fortunately they are verified by facts ; for it appears from a multitude of evidence, that the enemy made the true ufe of local advantages : they fortified every pafs or proper poft : the nature of the country, and the neceffity of keeping the banks of rivers, made it impoffible to turn thofe pofts : had I wanted therefore artillery, I could not have proceeded any given ten miles, but at a heavy expence of my beft troops. When it was found that I was provided with that forcible arm, the enemy invariably quitted their entrenchments, either to retreat, or fight upon ground where they fuppofed artillery could be leaft effectually employed. I am to thank the honourable member, whatever his intentions might have been, who by his crofs examination placed the expediency of carrying the train I did, in fo clear a view.

The uses of it. Captain Blomfield, from queft. 10 to 17.

Evidence of Ld. Balcarras, from q. 14 to 19.

Ld. Balcarras's crofs examination, quef. 93, 94.

The only remaining fact of the firft period to which verbal evidence is applicable, viz. The impoffibility of following the enemy further than they were followed in their precipitate retreat from Ticonderoga, is eftablifhed by Lord Balcarras and by Lord Harrington.

Ld. Balcarras, quef. 8. Lord Harrington, quef. 4.

Review of the fecond Period.

In entering upon the evidence which refpects the firft tranfaction of the fecond period, viz. the march from Skenefborough to Fort Edward, I cannot help obferving how much of the blame imputed to me has been occafioned by mifreprefentation from perfons whofe bufinefs it was to decry my actions ; and by uncommon miftakes in the geography of the country by thofe to whom my actions were mifreprefented. By the crofs examination of Lord Balcarras it muft be fuppofed, that the perfons who fufpected I erred in not taking the route by *South Bay* after the fuccefs at Ticonderoga,

March from Skenefborough to Fort Edward.

Miftakes in geography. Ld. Balcarras, qu. 90.

did

did not know where *South Bay* was. They feem
equally ignorant of the fituation of *Pitch-pine Plains*,
by the queftion immediately following the former one ;
and it muft have been a furprife to the enquirers to find
that the route which they were inclined to approve,
was precifely that which the main body of the army
took under me in perfon, and with fuch effect, as to
come up with the rear of the enemy, and drive them
from their fortified poft at Skenefborough, with the
lofs on their part of five armed veffels and all the reft
of their water-craft.

But it may be faid, this part of the crofs-examination, though incomprehenfible in point of geography,
ftill applied to the queftion taken notice of in my narrative, viz. " Whether it would not have been more
" expedient to return to Ticonderoga, and take the
" route by Lake George, than to proceed, as I did,
" by the Pitch Pine Plains to Fort Edward ?"

I fhall not recapitulate the various motives I have
before ftated in fupport of that preference, having pub-
lickly in my favour the opinion of an officer fo en-
lightened in military fcience, and fo well acquainted
with the country as Sir Guy Carleton ;* and never
having heard a difference of opinion in any other officer of a like defcription, to reft much more upon a
fubject fo fupported by reafoning and by fuccefs, might
be conftrued an attempt to divert the attention of my
examiners from points lefs defenfible. I therefore fhall
only add two fhort remarks ; the one, that the fact of
gaining confiderable time by allotting the whole fervice of the water-craft to the tranfport of provifions
and ftores over Lake George, inftead of employing
great part of it for the tranfport of the troops is inconteftibly proved by the evidence of Captain Money and
Lieutenant Colonel Kingfton : the other, that to have
reached Fort Edward with the troops fooner than the
29th of July (the day that the firft embarkation of

Marginal notes:
Queft. 91.

Sir G. Car-
leton, qu.
9, 10.

Confidera-
ble time
gained by
the army
taking the
route to
Fort Ed-
ward by
land.

Capt. Mo-
ney, queft.
4 to 11.
Lieut. Col.
Kingfton,
queft. 23.

* See alfo the Map of the Country.

provifions

provifions arrived at Fort George) would not only have been ufelefs, but alfo highly impolitic; becaufe the fubfiftence of the troops at Fort Edward, before the arrival of that embarkation, muft have been brought by land carriage through much difficult road all the way from Fort Anne, when, on the contrary, by remaining in the neighbourhood of Skenefborough till the paffage of Lake George was effected, exclufively of the confiderations of covering the removal of the hofpital of Huberton, and alarming the Connecticut by the pofition of General Reidefel's corps, the army was commodioufly fupplied by water-carriage.

The next circumftance for examination, according to the order of the Narrative, is the tranfport of the magazines of provifions, &c. from Fort George; and it is highly incumbent upon me to fhew the difficulties of that operation, becaufe, if they were avoidable, it muft be acknowledged one of the principal grounds upon which I vindicate the plan of the expedition to Bennington will fail me.

But I am perfuaded, every candid examiner will firft indulge me in a fhort paufe. It will be recollected, that this is the only part of the campaign upon which the noble Lord has laid his finger, as judging it productive of the fubfequent events. The crofs-examination had already been preffed upon the fame ideas. Such want of knowledge of the nature of tranfport in that country has been betrayed; fo much prepoffeffion of unneceffary delays has appeared; fuch emphafis of queftion has attended every circumftance of my conduct at this period, that I fhall ftand acquitted of prolixity if I preface the application of the fubfequent evidence by a more comprehenfive and complete furvey of the difficulties and anxieties of my fituation than I thought was neceffary before. *The charges brought againft the Lt. General's conduct at this part of the campaign.*

Survey of his difficulties and anxieties.

The combination of arrangement for feeding the army might, in fact, be ftated to have extended even to Ireland; for fome part of the fupply depended upon the victualling fleet which was prepared in that country, *Feeding the army.*

according

concerned at no effects of his comments or communications, in the minister's closet or in the news-papers,* except as they may have tended to support the general system of deception which has so long and so fatally influenced his Majesty's advisers. The Indian principle of war is at once odious and unavailing; and if encouraged, I will venture to pronounce, its consequences will be severely repented by the present age, and universally abhorred by posterity.

German troops.

But to proceed to the survey of other difficulties of the time. Great attention was due to the management of the German troops.

The mode of war in which they were engaged was entirely new to them; temptations to desert were in themselves great, and had been enhanced and circulated among them by emissaries of the enemy with much art and industry. Jealousy of predilection in the allotment of posts and separate commands ever subsists among troops of different states; and a solid preference of judgment in the commander in chief often appears a narrow national partiality.

Character of M. G. Reidesel.

I confess I was much assisted in maintaining cordiality in an army thus composed, by the frank, spirited, and honourable character I had to deal with in Major General Reidesel;—a character which was very early impressed upon my mind, and which no trials of intricacy, danger, and distress, has since effaced; but address was still requisite to second his zeal, and to diffuse it through the German ranks; and I studied to throw them into situations that might give them con-

---

One of those comments Lord George Germain thought proper to state, in a speech in the House of Commons. His Lordship gave me a character in the words used by Mr. St. Luc, in a conversation between them.—" Il est brave, mais lourd comme un " Allemand."

The letter alluded to was addressed to me from Canada, after Mr. St. Luc's voyage from England. I do not know to whom the duplicate was addressed, but he certainly was a person of diligence; for it appeared in the news-papers the same day I received the original.

fidence

civilization : I mean with thofe called the domiciliated
nations near Montreal. I had been taught to look upon
the remote tribes who joined me at Skenefborough as
more warlike ; but a very little time proved that, with
equal depravity in general principle, their only pre-
eminence confifted in ferocity. The hopes I had placed
in their wild honour, and in the controul of their conductors, which, as I ftated before, at firft had been
promifing, were foon at an end ; and their ill humour
and mutinous difpofition were manifeft foon after my Lord Har-
arrival at Fort Edward.   The apparent caufes of their rington
change of temper were the refentment I had fhewn 6 to 23.
upon the murder of Mifs Macrea, and the reftraints I
had laid on their difpofition to commit other enormi-
mities ; but I never doubted that their evil paffions
were fomented, and their defection completed by the
cabals of the Canadian interpreters. Rapacity, felf-in-
tereft, and prefumption, are the characteriftics of thefe
men, with fome few exceptions. The acquifition of
the Indian language has ufually been a certain fortune
to a man with an artful head and a convenient con-
fcience.

To check the old practices of peculation in thefe
men, Sir Guy Carleton, with great judgment, had given
the fuperintendency of the Indian department to Major
Campbell and Captain Frazer, gentlemen of the higheft
integrity. The Britifh officers employed folely in the
military conduct of that department, were alfo felected
with equal propriety. The interpreters had from the
firft regarded with a jealous eye a fyftem which took
out of their hands the diftribution of Indian neceffaries
and prefents ; but when they found the plunder of the
country, as well as that of the government, was controuled, the profligate policy of many was employed to
promote diffention, revolt, and defertion.

I take this occafion to acquit Monfieur St. Luc of St. Luc.
any fufpicion of his being concerned in thefe factions ;
but I believe he difcerned them. He certainly knew
that the Indians pined after a renewal of their accu-

K   ftomed

ftomed horrors; and that they were become as impatient of his controul as of all other, though the pride and intereft of authority, and the affection he bore to his old affociates, induced him to cover the real caufes under various frivolous pretences of difcontent, with which I was daily tormented, but to which I conftantly attended: and though I differed totally with Saint Luc in opinion upon the efficacy of thefe allies, I invariably took his advice in the management of them, even to an indulgence of their moft capricious fancies, when they did not involve the difhonour of the King's fervice and the difgrace of humanity. The council of the 4th of Auguft was held at his preffing inftance; and in that council, to my great aftonifhment (for he had given me no intimation of the defign) the tribes with which he was moft particularly connected, and for whom he interpreted, declared their intention of returning home, and demanded my concurrence and affiftance. The embarraffment of this event was extreme. By acquiefcing, I voluntarily relinquifhed part of my force that had been obtained with immenfe charge to government, that had created high expectation at home and abroad, and that indeed my own army was by no means in condition to difpenfe with; becaufe, depending upon the fuppofed affiftance of this much over-valued race for fcouts and out-pofts, and all the leffer, but neceffary fervices, for giving due repofe to the camp, the Britifh light-infantry had been trained to higher purpofes: they were deftined to lead in the general and decifive combats I expected in the woods, and could not be fpared, or rifked, or harraffed, without palpable confequences of the moft difagreeable kind.

On the contrary, I was convinced a cordial reconciliation with the Indians was only to be effected by a renunciation of all my former prohibitions, and an indulgence in blood and rapine; I had not a friend in the department in whom I could confide except Major Campbell, Captain Frazer, and the other Britifh officers:

Lord Harrington's qu. laft. referred to.

2

cers:

cers: their ignorance of the languages, and the very probity of their characters, rendered them of no weight in Indian councils. An answer, nevertheless, was to be made upon the moment; and the part I took was to give a firm refusal to their proposition, and to adhere to the controuls I had before established; but, with a temperate reprefentation of the ties of faith, of generosity, and honour, to join every other argument confistent with those principles which I could devise, to persuade and encourage them to continue their services.

This speech appeared to have the desired effect. The tribes nearest home affected to separate from the others, and only pressed for permission to return in parties to gather in their harvest, proposing to relieve each other; which was granted. Some of the remote tribes also seemed to retract their propositions, and professed a zeal for the service; but the desertion took place the next day by scores, loaded with such plunder as they had collected; and it continued from day to day, till scarce a man that had joined at Skenesborough remained. This whole transaction, I aver, was before the plan of Bennington was formed. It appears so from the evidence produced upon the cross examination by the gentlemen to whom I am obliged upon so many occasions, for elucidating different subjects; and the precise date could have been further supported by a memorandum of Sir Francis Clarke; but I thought that reference superfluous in a matter so notorious.

That Monsieur St. Luc, anxious for the credit of his favourite troops, and invited by the propensity he found in the minister to listen to any whispered intelligence, in contradiction to that he received from the General himself; that, under these temptations, that wily partizan should misplace dates, and confound causes, neither surprises nor offends me. With this exposition of fact, I leave him in full possession of his petulancy respecting my military talents; and am

Lord Harrington's qu. laft referred to. ib. qu. 87.

K 2　　　concerned

concerned at no effects of his comments or communications, in the minister's closet or in the news-papers,* except as they may have tended to support the general system of deception which has so long and so fatally influenced his Majesty's advisers. The Indian principle of war is at once odious and unavailing; and if encouraged, I will venture to pronounce, its consequences will be severely repented by the present age, and universally abhorred by posterity.

German troops.

But to proceed to the survey of other difficulties of the time. Great attention was due to the management of the German troops.

The mode of war in which they were engaged was entirely new to them; temptations to defert were in themselves great, and had been enhanced and circulated among them by emissaries of the enemy with much art and industry. Jealousy of predilection in the allotment of posts and separate commands ever subsists among troops of different states; and a solid preference of judgment in the commander in chief often appears a narrow national partiality.

Character of M. G. Reidesel.

I confess I was much assisted in maintaining cordiality in an army thus composed, by the frank, spirited, and honourable character I had to deal with in Major General Reidesel;—a character which was very early impressed upon my mind, and which no trials of intricacy, danger, and distress, has since effaced; but address was still requisite to second his zeal, and to diffuse it through the German ranks; and I studied to throw them into situations that might give them con-

---

* One of those comments Lord George Germain thought proper to state, in a speech in the House of Commons. His Lordship gave me a character in the words used by Mr. St. Luc, in a conversation between them.—" Il est brave, mais lourd comme un " Allemand."

The letter alluded to was addressed to me from Canada, after Mr. St. Luc's voyage from England. I do not know to whom the duplicate was addressed, but he certainly was a person of diligence; for it appeared in the news-papers the same day I received the ginal.

fidence

fidence in themfelves, credit with their prince, and alacrity in the purfuit of an enterprife, which, when its difficulties were confidered, in fact required enthufiafm.

Other parts of the alliance, though not liable to fufpicion of treachery, like the Indians, nor of confequence to be fo much attended to as the Germans, neverthelefs had their perplexities. The Canadians, were officered by gentlemen of great condition in their country, but were not to be depended upon. Inftead of the enterprifing and daring fpirit which diftinguifhed the character of that people under the French government, was fubftituted a longing after home, the effect of difufe of arms and long habits of domeftic enjoyments; and this difeafe *(mal de payz)* is carried in them to a greater proverbial extreme than in any other people to whom the term is more commonly applied. *The Canadian troops.*

It was neither eafy to keep thefe people together, nor to fupport the ideas of refpect which the enemy entertained of them from the remembrance of the former war. The only manner of effecting the latter purpofe was to fhew them occafionally at a diftance, but rarely to commit them upon parties where they were likely to fall in with the beft claffes of the Rangers oppofed to us: perhaps there are few better in the world than the corps of Virginia Riflemen, which acted under Colonel Morgan.

The Provincial Corps, of which I had two in embryo, and feveral detached parties, were yet a heavier tax upon time and patience. They were compofed of profeffed Loyalifts, many of whom had taken refuge in Canada the preceding winter, and others had joined as we advanced. The various interefts which influenced their actions rendered all arrangement of them impracticable. One man's views went to the profit which he was to enjoy when his corps fhould be complete; another's, to the protection of the diftrict in which he refided; a third was wholly intent upon revenge againft his perfonal enemies; and all of them *Provincial corps.*

were

were repugnant even to an idea of fubordination. Hence the fettlement who fhould act as a private man, and who as an officer, or in whofe corps either fhould be, was feldom fatisfactorily made among themfelves ; and as furely as it failed, fucceeded a reference to the Commander in Chief, which could not be put by, or delegated to another hand, without diffatisfaction, encreafe of confufion, and generally a lofs of fuch fervices as they were really fit for, *viz.* fearching for cattle, afcertaining the practicability of routes, clearing roads, and guiding detachments or columns upon the march.*

Other critical embarraffments. Such were the embarraffments of my mind, added to the many neceffary avocations of command purely military. It will likewife be remembered that Lieutenant Colonel St. Ledger was, at this time, before Fort Stanwix : every hour was pregnant with critical events. The candid and unprejudiced, reflecting upon fuch a fituation, will check the readinefs of their cenfure : far be it from me to contend that I did not commit many errors : I only hope to have proved, that they are not thofe which have yet been fpecifically pointed at, and whatever blame may be imputable to me in other inftances, my late examiners are not juftly intitled to triumph on any of their difcoveries.

Expedition to Bennington. And now for the expedition to Bennington as it ftands upon evidence.

The queftions upon the crofs examination are fo explanatory of the hints which fell from the noble Lord afterwards, that one would almoft imagine the hints

---

* I would not be underftood to infer, that none of the Provincials with me were fincere in their loyalty; perhaps many were fo. A few were of diftinguifhed bravery, among which it would be unjuft not to particularize Mr. Fiftar, who fell at Bennington, and Capt. Sharwood, who was forward in every fervice of danger to the end of the campaign. I only maintain that the interefts and the paffions of the revolted Americans concenter in the caufe of the Congrefs ; and thofe of the Loyalifts break and fubdivide into various purfuits, with which the caufe of the King has little or nothing to do.

were

were originally defigned to precede. It will be regular for me, therefore, to confider them in that manner, and, from the whole I am to collect, that the faults meant to be eftablifhed are, that I employed Germans to found the difpofition of a country in which no Germans refided: that the mounting dragoons was unneceffary: that the range given to the expedition was too great: that it was not originally defigned for Bennington: that the force was inadequate.

In regard to the firft of thefe charges, relative to the employment of Germans, it would be wafte of time to add to the full anfwer given by Lord Harrington. Colonel Kingfton has anfwered the queftion refpecting the mounting the dragoons; and moreover it will be remembered, that the collecting horfes was by no means confined to that fervice. They were requifite for carrying the baggage of the army, as expreffed in the inftructions to Colonel Baume, to the amount of 1500. This circumftance may have ftruck fome gentlemen, as confirming the idea that the baggage attending the army was of enormous bulk. I requeft a fufpence of judgment upon this article, till I come to the proper place of explanation; and I revert to the part of the charge which feems of moft importance, viz. the extent of the march, as defcribed in the Inftructions, compared with the ftrength of the detachment, &c.

It can hardly efcape obfervation, what ftrength to my defence upon this point may be derived from advocates who were not expected to appear in my behalf. For I take fupport from the noble Lord himfelf, and all who have believed in his late affertions, or adhered to his favourite doctrines, by pleading that I undertook the expedition to Bennington upon report, ftrengthened by the fuggeftion of *perfons of long experience and refidence in America; who had been prefent on the fpot when the rebellion broke out*; and whofe information had been much refpected by the adminiftration in England; *that the friends to the Britifh caufe were as five to one,* and that they *wanted only the appearance of a protecting*

Marginal notes:
Faults fuppofed.

Fault of employing Germans, Lord Harrington, queft. 90. 91. Lieut. Col. Kingfton, queft. 134 to 137.

See the Inftructions and all other papers refpecting Bennington No. XII.

K 4 *force*

force to shew themselves. Some criticisers upon the adequacy of the force I employed, may desert the cause of the noble Lord ; but will *He* maintain, that a recruit of force from the enemy's country was a wild expectation, when the recruiters, provincial colonels, governors, land proprietors, and popular leaders of the party who glory in the designation of Tory, were upon the spot, and personally interested in the levies ? *He* must surely stand forth my advocate in this point, or entirely forget the reasoning he held to Sir William Howe, when without the advantages of such recruiters ; against the belief of the General himself ; unprepared to repair the disappointment, if disappointment ensued, in a measure of so much more magnitude, and so much less real encouragement, *He* referred to that expedient of recruiting from the enemy, what he had not strength to supply from the national troops.*

The ground of the undertaking to Bennington supported by the doctrine of Lord G. Germain.

This I must insist is an unanswerable defence, with respect to the noble Lord, and those who think with him ; for it is strict and positive coincidence with their opinions, past and present—and if I said it will be so with those to come, my prophecy would be authorized by the conviction and triumph which Mr. Galway's evidence, respecting the loyalty of the Americans, seemed to produce in the parties to whom I allude.

But in due respect to other judges, it is incumbent upon me to state a more serious defence.

As Lieutenant Colonel Kingston cannot prove juridically that the rough draft of the design which ended

* In a letter from Lord George Germain to Sir William Howe, dated May 28, 1777, after acknowledging that the force for the campaign would be short of the General's requisitions, is the following paragraph :
  " If we may credit the accounts which arrive from all quarters, " relative to the good inclinations of the inhabitants, there is " every reason to expect that your success in Pensylvania will " enable you to raise from among them such a force as may be " sufficient for the interior defence of the province, and leave the " army at liberty to proceed to offensive operations."
  The whole of the letter, from which the above is an extract, is curious, and may be seen in the Parliamentary Register, No. 68.

in

in the affair of Bennington was the fame which was delivered by General Reidefel, and I am unwilling upon memory to incur a poſſibility of miſtake, even in an immaterial circumſtance that reſpects an abſent friend, I am content it ſhould be conſidered as an uncertainty, and I drop all uſe that could be drawn from the original compoſition. It will fully anſwer my purpoſe to adhere to the bare aſſertion which I am ſure will never be contradicted, that Major General Reidefel originally conceived an expedition for the purpoſe of mounting his dragoons, and ſupplying the troops in general with baggage-horſes; that I thought his idea might be extended to much greater uſe, and that the plan was conſidered, amended, and enlarged, in concert with him. Therefore upon the abſtract ground and reaſon of the meaſure, I might urge, that it was ſupported by naked military principle, according to the ſentiments of a general of great natural talents, and long ſervice under the firſt maſters of the age. It is proved, that the fame ſentiments were ratified by the full approbation of Major General Phillips, an officer of ſimilar deſcription, to whom the plan was communicated; and if a ſingle part of the ſame plan, mentioned to be at firſt diſapproved by Brigadier General Fraſer, continued to be ſo after explanation, that diſapprobation did not appear. Indeed the utmoſt that can be drawn from the evidence of Lieutenant Colonel Kingſton, or any other witneſs, amounts to no more than an implied wiſh in the Brigadier to have conducted the expedition at the head of his diſtinct corps. It was the fact. Devoted to glory, and prodigal of life; earneſt for the general ſucceſs of the campaign, and particularly anxious for every plan adopted by the man he loved, he grudged a danger or care in other hands than his own. It was not envy or diſparagement of the German troops, but zeal and impatient for employment, that influenced his predilection for the Britiſh. I honoured the principle, while I reſtrained it; and I reſerved his ardour and judgment for a ſecond movement.

Lieut. Col. Kingſton's queſt.

ment, which required thofe qualities much more than the expedition to Bennington did, according to any intelligence or appearance of things at the time. It will be obferved from the evidence, that the whole of Brigadier Frafer's corps was thrown over the river, and actually pofted at the opening of the plain near Saratoga, when Colonel Baume marched ; and the defign was, upon the firft news of Baume's fuccefs, to have pufhed that corps to take poffeffion of the heights near Stillwater, and to have intrenched there, till the army and the provifion could have joined, by which means the whole country on the weft fide the river, to the banks of the Mohawk, would have been our own.

But moreover it is to be obferved, that Major General Reidefel was far from being ignorant, as has been fuggefted, of the nature of the country, or the profeffions of the inhabitants. He was juft returned from commanding a detached corps at a confiderable diftance from the main army, in the very heart of the country from wh ch the enemy's force at Bennington was afterwards fupplied. He fpoke the Englifh language well ; he was affifted by many natives of the beft information.

It is evident, that the brave but deceived officer who commanded the detachment, was induced to deviate from the cautions prefcribed in the inftructions. A plan, drawn by an engineer upon the fpot, is added to the evidence produced to the committee, to fhew more clearly where that deviation happened. It appears alfo in proof, that the meafures taken to relieve Colonel Baume, upon the news of his difficulty, were the moft speedy that could be ufed, and would have been timely, had not Colonel Brieman's march been more tardy than could have been fuppofed poffible. I take the fact as ftated in his own account, without impeaching his credit with regard to the obftacles he defcribes. But as a farther vindication of the intelligence and principle upon which the original ftrength of the detachment was framed, and the mere accident which made even

error

Lord Harrington, q 28 to 31.

error póffible, I requeft admiffion for the proof of a
new fact which I did not know it was in my power to
bring, till after Captain Money had left the bar of the
Houfe of Commons ; and as I was precluded from
calling him a fecond time, by the abrupt clofe of the
proceedings, I had no other way of laying it before the
public, than by ftating the queftion in writing, and re-
quiring his authority to publifh the anfwer, which I obtained, and they are as follows :

Q. Do you know any circumftance refpecting an unexpected reinforcement received by the rebels at Bennington near the time of the action ?

A. " A few days after I was prifoner in the rebel
" camp, fome of their officers told me, that it was a
" providential circumftance, that General Starks was
" coming through Bennington with 1200 militia of the
" New-Hampfhire Grants, to join their main army
" near Albany, for the guard on the provifion at Ben-
" nington did not amount to more than 400 men ; and
" that on his hearing of a detachment of our army being
" only four or five miles from him, he with the guard,
" and what militia could be collected in the neighbour-
" hood, attacked and defeated the detatchment, as
" well as the reinforcement that were on their march
" to join them. The rebel officers alfo informed me,
" and I have feen accounts that agree with what I then
" heard, that during the action General Starks was
" ' luckily' joined by Colonel Warner with a confi-
" derable body of men. I have frequently heard our
" officers fay that were in this action, that had Colonel
" Baume retreated four miles, and recroffed the river
" he paffed the day before, and taken poft there, when
" he found by information he could not proceed, and
" had wrote for a reinforcement, he would have met
" Colonel Brieman coming to his affiftance, and would
" not have rifqued the lofs of his corps, which by his
" inftructions were fo ftrongly recommended, as not
" even to rifque a confiderable lofs. This, Sir, is as
" nearly as poffible the anfwer I fhould have given had
                                        " the

" the queſtion been aſked me in the Houſe of Com-
" mons.—J. Money."

This piece of evidence will ſerve to ſhew that it was not
the ſucceſs of the rebels at Bennington that animated the
militia to aſſemble, and march in the cauſe of the Congreſs ; and he muſt be of ſteady faith indeed in American loyalty who can ſuppoſe much of it really exiſted
in the country of the Hampſhire Grants (howſoever it
had been affected and profeſſed) when he reflects, not
only that General Starks and Colonel Warner were not
oppoſed in collecting their men, though my army, then
in a tide of ſucceſs, were near at hand ; but alſo that
not a loyaliſt was found earneſt enough to convey me
intelligence.

It will likewiſe appear, from this piece of evidence,
when compared with the map of the country and the
diſpoſition of the troops, that had not the accidental
paſſage of the detachments under Starks and Warner
been exceedingly critical, it could not have availed.—
Forty-eight hours ſooner, they would have joined General Gates ; and he would hardly have detached them,
or any other part of his force, back to Bennington,
even though he had heard of a movement to my left ;
becauſe he muſt have known that the whole of Fraſer's
corps lay ready to march rapidly upon him from my
right.—Forty-eight hours later, the blow would have
been ſtruck ; and the ſtores, conſiſting of live cattle,
and flower, with abundant carriages to convey it, would
have been out of reach.

Another reflection will be apt to ariſe in ſpeculative
minds upon this ſubject, viz. on what nice chances depends the reputation of an officer who acts under ſelfiſh
and ungenerous employers ! Such men not only withhold the fair protection that would ariſe from an explanation of his motives, but are the firſt to join the cry
of the uninformed multitude, who always judge by
events. Thus every plan receives a colouring in the
extreme ; and is denominated (often with equal inju-
ſtice) a fatal error or a brilliant enterprize.

But

But it ftill may be faid, the expedition was not ori-Crofs exa-
ginally defigned againft Bennington. I really do notmination of
Lord Har-
fee to what it could tend againft me, if that fuppofitionrington, q.
were in a great degree admitted. That fome part of[89]
the force was defigned to act there, will not be difputed
by any who read Colonel Baume's inftructions, and con-
fult the map. The blame or merit of the defign altogether, muft reft upon the motives of expediency ; and
it is of little confequence whether the firft and principal direction was againft Bennington, or Arlington, or
any other diftrict, as my intelligence might have varied
refpecting the depofits of corn and cattle of the enemy.
At the fame time I muft obferve it is begging the queftion, to argue that Bennington was not the real, original object, becaufe Bennington was not mentioned in the
draft of inftructions. A man muft indeed be void of
military and political addrefs, to put upon a paper a
critical defign, where furprize was in queftion, and every thing depended upon fecrecy. Though it were true,
that I meant only Bennington, and thought of nothing
lefs than the progrefs of the expedition, in the extent
of the order, I certainly would not now affirm it, becaufe I could not prove it ; and becaufe it would feem,
that I fearched for remote and obfcure juftification, not
relying upon that which was manifeft ; but furely there
is nothing new or improbable in the idea, that a general
fhould difguife his real intentions at the outfet of an expedition, even from the officer whom he appointed to
execute them, provided a communication with that officer was certain and not remote.

This review of the affair of Bennington, tho' long,
I truft will not be deemed mifplaced ; and from the different parts of it, I think, will clearly be eftablifhed the
few following affertions :

1ft. That the defign upon Bennington was juftified
by the circumftances of the time.

2d. That there was no reafon to fuppofe the force of
the enemy there greater than what the detachment was
adequate to defeat.

3d. That

3d. That when the force was difcovered to be greater, the ill confequences would have been avoided had not Colonel Baume deviated from his inftructions, by committing his regular force in the woods inftead of fortifying a poft in the open country, and exploring the woods only with the Indians, Canadians, and Provincials, fupported by Captain Frafer's corps, who were complete mafters of fuch bufinefs.

4th. That after Colonel Baume had committed that error, it would have been retrieved had Colonel Brieman's reinforcement accomplifhed their march in the time they ought to have done.

5th. That the ftrength of the enemy was merely accidental.

And, as a final obfervation, I will add, that when a minifter ftates a common accident of war, independent of any general action, unattended with any lofs that could affect the main ftrength of the army, and little more than the mifcarriage of a foraging party, to have been fatal to a whole campaign, of which he had directed the progrefs and apportioned the force, he makes but an ill compliment to his own judgment.

Difficulty of forming a magazine after the difappointment at Bennington Lieut. Col. Kingfton, q. 24 to 31. The next clafs of proofs in regular progreffion, applies to the difficulty of bringing forward a magazine of provifion, after the difappointment of obtaining live ftock and flower at Bennington. It has been fhewn, by the evidence of Captain Money, Lieutenant Colonel Kingfton, and the authentic memorandums of Sir Francis Clarke, that early in the month of Auguft it was no eafy tafk to fupply the daily confumption of the army. Our powers were afterwards, in fome degree, encreafed by the arrival of more contract horfes, acquifitions of more ox-teams from the country, and the great vigilance exerted in the departments of the quarter-mafter-general and infpector, whofe affiftants had been augmented.

A minute inveftigation of this operation, I am fenfible, will be thought dry, and perhaps unneceffary, by general readers—they will pafs it over—but there are thofe
who

who have laid much ſtreſs upon a waſte of time, and
who take delight in tracing the ſmall parts of a ſubject with ſcrupulous exactneſs. With ſuch it is my duty, as a perſon on my defence, to enter into detail, and
I will lay my ground in the queſtion put to Captain Money in his croſs-examination and his anſwer.

Q. " Why did the army remain from the 16th of
" Auguſt to the 13th of September before they croſſed
" the Hudſon's-River to engage the rebels at Still-
" water ? "

A. " To bring forward a ſufficient quantity of pro-
" viſions and artillery, to enable the General to give up
" his communication."

With all the powers of conveyance poſſible to be
muſtered, Captain Money computes (and his computation tallies nearly with the table formed by the commiſſary-general) that five days proviſion, viz. four for
forming the magazine, and one for daily conſumption,
was the moſt that could be conveyed at once.

Capt. Money, q. 20; and for the general account of the efforts uſed ſee the ſame evidence from queſt. 12 to 25.

To bring this to an average I will aſſume only two
days for accidents of weather, roads, fatigue of cattle,
breaking of carriages, and other common diſappoint-
ments : this is much leſs time than according to the
evidence might be allowed, and upon This computation
it would take ten days to convey the magazine to Fort
Edward only. The ſtage from thence to the encampment and intended depoſitary muſt not be computed by
diſtance but by impediments. The rapids of the river
and the different carrying-places have been deſcribed by
the witneſſes, and it reſults that this ſtage was much
longer in point of time than the former one. It was
not poſſible to keep the tranſports going at both ſtages
together for the ten days mentioned, becauſe there were
not boats in the river ſufficient for more than the daily
ſupply ; nor could they have been conveyed there in
that time by any poſſible means, for theſe reaſons ; the
boat carriages, which were of a conſtruction ſimilar to
timber carriages uſed in England, were only twelve in
number, and each carriage employed ſix horſes or four
oxen

oxen to draw it; and could any other means of draft for boats over land have been contrived, or cattle have been supplied from the artillery, or any other department, all would have been useless; because the boats themselves, to a greater amount than those above specified, were wanting till after the whole of the provision transport between Ticonderoga and Fort George, upon which they were employed, was finished, and it had barely kept pace so as to supply the land transport between Fort George and Fort Edward.

I desire only an allowance of fifteen days for the carriage over the second stage, and it will thus take, in the whole, twenty-five days to form the magazine alone.

I claim no additional allowance of time for conveying one hundred boats, at least, through the difficulties of land and water, in the two stages, but comprise that labour among the rest of the last fifteen days. It must be nevertheless observed, that even this number was short of what was wanting, and, to save time, all the artificers were employed in building scouls (fourteen of which were finished during the transport) to make water craft, in the whole sufficient to carry the magazine forward, after the communication should be at an end. The new caulking the boats, though indispensibly neceffary to great part of them, after paffing the lakes loaded, and afterwards being shaken and damaged by land carriage, is another work which I throw into the last fifteen days of the transport, or into the subsequent four days, which must at the least be allotted for loading the magazines, and arranging the order of its proceeding both in respect to navigation and defence. This was committed to very expert naval officers, and was matter of no trivial concern, or easy execution.

The whole business, according to the above representation and calculation, both which are founded upon evidence, would have taken twenty-nine days: twenty-seven only were employed, viz. from August

the

the 16th to September the 13th. The exertions in fact outwent the calculation; and I challenge the moſt minute ſpeculatiſts to try the time and the powers we poſſeſſed, by every poſſible diſtribution of carriages and cattle, different from that which was practiſed, and I will venture to ſay none will be found leſs dilatory.

It appears clearly in proof, that no impediment to this tranſport was occaſioned by the interference of the artillery; but it has been implied by ſome queſtions in the croſs examinations, that if the artillery did not interfere with the tranſport, the tranſport ought to have interfered with the artillery, and that by appropriating their horſes to the proviſion train, much time might have been ſaved.

It might be a ſufficient anſwer, that the artillery, for the reaſons I have before aſſigned, was not to be diſpenſed with, and conſequently the horſes were to be preſerved; but I beſides have ſhewn, that they could not have been of uſe to the tranſport of the boats; and to ſatisfy every ſcruple, and to ſhew how miſtaken they are who ſuppoſe an advantage was to be obtained by the employment of artillery-horſes to convey proviſions, I now offer to their reflection the additional fact, that they could have been of no avail, becauſe we had neither carts nor pack-ſaddles, more than were in uſe already.

That the baggage of the army was an impediment to the tranſport, is another accuſation clearly confuted by the united evidence of Lieutenant Colonel Kingſton and Captain Money *. Lieut. Col. Kingſton, q. 5 to 8 incluſive, and from 122 to 130.

Having

* In juſtice to the officers who are ſuppoſed to have diſobeyed orders, in reſpect to the bulk of it, it may be neceſſary to take ſome notice (and this is the proper place) of the error of making that ſuppoſition upon the directions given to Col. Baume for procuring 1300 horſes for that ſpecific uſe.

I believe the loweſt allowance of bat horſes ever made to an army was as follows:

L

To

Having thus shewn that the transport of provisions and other stores, for about thirty days, was effected in the shortest time possible, it now becomes necessary to examine the question, which has been very much canvassed in print, and by the cross examination appears to have made impression upon some gentlemen; whether this preparation might not have been dispensed with, and the army have reached Albany by a rapid march, the soldiers carrying upon their backs a sufficiency of provision to support them during the time?

Question made, whether the army might not have proceeded to Albany without stores?

To a field officer	-	3 per battalion	6
A captain	-	2 do.	12
A subaltern	-	1 do.	16
A surgeon and mate	-	2 do.	2
A chaplain	-	1 do.	1
A quartermaster	-	1 do.	1
For carrying the company's tents, 2 horses to each company	-	do.	16

Total per battalion   54

N. B. This calculation was made upon eight companies to a battalion, in which two field officers companies are included.

The horses for the five British battalions of the line, upon calculation, amount to	270
General Fraser's corps, reckoned to be equal to four battalions	216
Five German battalions, at 70 horses per battalion, that being the difference in proportion to their strength	350
Breyman's corps	100

Total for the regiments of the regulars   936

S T A F F.

Two major generals	12
Four brigadiers	16
British quartermaster general, and his assistants	12
German ditto	12
The hospital	30

Total of staff   82

I R R E G U L A R S.

Canadians, Indians, and Provincials	200
Artificers	50

Total of irregulars   250

Recapitulation of the whole distribution   1268

It

It is very natural for men of all defcriptions, to apply the idea of a rapid march to a diftance of fifty miles, for it is not more meafuring in a ftreight line from Fort Edward to Albany, and it will be proper to confider the principle and practicability of fuch march, with refpect to two diftinct periods, the one before, the other after the attempt upon Bennington.

With refpect to the firft, it will be remembered, that in the ftate the roads then were, and with the re- fources then to be employed, no provifion before-hand was attainable. Therefore, to have brought the plan of a rapid advance within the compafs of a poffibility, the operation muft have begun by marching the whole rapidly backward, in order to load the men with their packs of provifions. How the troops, zealous as they were, would have relifhed a ftep fo uncommon in its nature, and productive of fo much unexpected fatigue, particularly how the Germans would have been fo perfuaded of the neceffity as to have under- taken it with good will, cannot be afcertained.

But thefe doubts apart, it remains to be confidered, how the troops were to pafs two very large rivers, the Hudfon and the Mohawk, without previous pro- vifion for a bridge, or water-craft for conveying large bodies at once. Every conceffion a fanguine projector can defire fhall be made upon this point alfo ; the con- trivance of rafts, bound together by twigs and ftrips of bark, as in fact was practifed at this very period for the paffage of Frafer's corps over Hudfon's River, fhall be admitted equally practicable for the whole army ; and in argument be it trufted to chance to pafs the Mohawk in the fame way ; or fhould it fail, let re- courfe be had to the ford, which is known to be prac- ticable, *except after heavy rains*, near Schenectady, about fifteen miles from the mouth of the river.

Thefe conceffions granted, we will fuppofe the army on the bank of the Hudfon's River, where they after- wards paffed it.

The

The idea of a rapid march will of courfe be exempt
from all thought of perfonal incumbrances (provifion
exempted) and the foldier will ftand reprefented in the
imagination, trim and nimble as he is feen at an exer-
cife in an Englifh encampment—Indeed it is neceffary
he fhould be confidered in that form ; for nothing can
be more repugnant to a project of rapidity, than the
foldier's load, were he to carry all the articles belonging
to him in a campaign.*

But it may be faid, and with truth, that troops are
ufually relieved from a confiderable part of this burthen,
and many examples of this relief may be brought from
the general cuftom of fervice, and from many movements of General Howe's army in particular—nay
more, it was a frequent practice of the very army in
queftion, to march free from knapfacks and camp equipage. The Wigwam, or hut conftructed of boughs,
may be made a very wholfome fubftitute for a tent ;
and when victual can be cooked before hand, even the
camp kettle for an expeditious march may be laid afide.
All thefe examples are admitted : but they all imply
conveniencies for the feveral articles to follow, and
to be brought up in due time.   In our cafe they muft
have been loft irrecoverably.

Will it be argued, that fome medium might have
been devifed ? And although it were impoffible, con-
fiftently with the idea of rapidity, to carry forward
more provifion than for bare fuftenance during the
march, yet carts might have been found fufficient to
carry the men's knapfacks, and camp kettles, and
other indifpenfible articles ? This fuppofition would
betray a great ignorance of the country.   From Sara-

---

* They confift of a knapfack, containing his bodily neceffaries,
a blanket, a haverfack with provifions, a carteen, a hatchet, and
a fifth fhare of the general camp equipage belonging to his tent.
Thefe articles (reckoning the provifion to be for four days) added
to his accoutrements, arms, and fixty rounds of ammunition, make
a bulk totally incompatible with combat, and a weight of about
fixty pounds.

toga to Albany there is only one road practicable for wheel carriage. There are many places where by deftroying the bridges over deep gullies which difcharge themfelves into the main river, a paffage would be rendered impaffable, not only for a wheel carriage, but a horfe. There are others where the road is bounded by the river on one fide, and by almoft perpendicular afcents covered with wood on the other. Here the very fhort work of felling a few trees would ftop all paffage. The expence of time to remove thefe obftructions, or to make new roads, would have brought famine. All notion, therefore, of conveying any articles more than could be carried upon men's fhoulders muft ceafe. ˌThe notion of artillery, even the fmalleft pieces, muft alfo ceafe of courfe, not even a little ammunition-tumbril could have found its way.—An eafy facrifice to the theorifts, who have maintained the inutility of artillery : but any officer who has feen the ground of this fuppofed march, would point out a dozen paffes, not to fpeak of the paffage of the Mohawk, where, ftrengthened with abattis and fuch other works as the rebels are expert in making in a few hours, five hundred militia would ftop for a time, ten times their number of the beft troops in the world who had not artillery to affift them.

Having ftated thefe objections to the principle of a rapid march, let us now, from the knowledge that has been fince obtained of circumftances, confider what would have been the certain confequences of the attempt.

Thofe who are acquainted with the capricious workings of the tempers of men, will not wonder at the difficulty of prevailing upon a common folder in any exigency to hufband his provifions. In a fettled camp, the young foldier has very fhort fare on the fourth day after delivery : but upon a march in bad weather and bad roads, when the weary foot flips back at every ftep, and a general curfe is provoked at the weight that caufes the retardment, he muft be a patient veteran, and of

much

much experience in fcarcity, who is not temped to throw the whole contents of the haverfack into the mire. He feels the prefent incumbrance grievous— Want is a day remote.—" Let the General find a fupply: it is the King's caufe and the General's intereft —he will never let the foldier be ftarved."

This is common reafoning in the ranks. I ftate it for thofe who have not feen fatiguing fervice, and may have a judgment to form upon it. It need not be applied to the prefent confideration ; for had the march taken place at the time it ought to have done, upon the principle of the defenders of that fcheme, the time that Frafer's corps firft paft the river upon the bridge of rafts, wafte would only have confpired to accomplifh in *three days* a ruin that with the beft hufbandry would have been inevitable in *fix* : for the fame fall of rain which it has been fhewn in evidence actually carried away the bridge a very few days after it was conftructed, neceffarily made the ford of the Mohawk for an advance, and every ford of the Hudfon's River for a return, impaffable. It hardly need be noticed, that a flood muft have made any ufe of rafts, could they have been timely obtained, equally impracticable. The army, therefore would have become victims to famine, without a blow, or a fingle effort of the enemy. Saratoga muft have been the anticipated fcene of furrender, without other conditions than the mercy of fuftenance ; the whole force of Mr. Gates would have been loofe to co-operate with Mr. Wafhington, with the fineft feafon of the campaign before them ; and the General of the northern army, without a fhadow of profeffional defence, and precluded from the plea ufually fo perfuafive, that he fought hard before he failed, muft have met the cenfure of his Sovereign and a juftly offended country, with none to fupport him but the prefent advocates of a rapid march. Could his dependence have been fure even upon them ? Would they not rather have adhered to their oppofite and original fyftem (for ftrange as it

4

is, the fame men have fupported both) and have afferted,
that it was extreme rafhnefs to crofs the Hudfon's
River at all ?

If what I have faid in objection to the principle and
practicability of a rapid march to Albany, previous to
the attempt upon Bennington, has weight, very little
need be added on the fubject afterwards, becaufe every
objection will multiply upon the mind of the moft
curfory obferver. I fhall only call the attention to a
very few effential circumftances. The enemy was in
force ; a proof of his being fo is, that Mr. Gates
quitted his pofition behind the Mohawk, which was
his ftrongeft, and advanced to Stillwater. The force
found at Bennington upon the march from the Hampfhire Grants to the main army, proved the vigour and
alacrity of the enemy in that country. The circumftances of the action at Bennington eftablifhed a yet
more melancholy conviction of the fallacy of any dependence upon fuppofed friends. The noble Lord has
faid, that " I never defpaired of the campaign before
the affair of Bennington ; that I had no doubt of gaining Albany in as fhort a time as the army (in due condition of fupply) could accomplifh the march." I
acknowledge the truth of the affertions in their fulleft
extent ; all my letters at the time fhew it. I will go
further, and in one fenfe apply with the noble Lord
the epithet " fatal" to the affair of Bennington. The
knowledge I acquired of the profeffors of loyalty was
" fatal," and put an end to every expectation from enterprize unfuftained by dint of force. It would have
been excefs of frenzy to have trufted for fuftenance to
the plentiful region of Albany. Had the march thither
been practicable in all refpects, and even unoppofed,
(which nobody will think would have been the cafe)
the enemy finding the Britifh army unfupplied, would
only have had to compel the Tories to drive the cattle
and deftroy the corn or the corn mills, and the convention of Albany inftead of Saratoga muft have followed.
Would the Tories have rifen ? Why did they not rife

round Albany and below it, at the time they found Mr. Gates's army increasing by separate and distinct parties from remote distances? They were better qualified by their situation to catch the favourable moment than I was to advise it. Why did they not rise in that populous and as supposed well affected district, the German Flats, at the time St. Leger was before Fort Stanwix? A critical insurrection from any one point of the compass within distance to create diversion, would probably have secured the success of the campaign.

Col. St. Leger's letter, No. XIII. But to revert to the increase of reasons against a rapid march after the affair of Bennington. It was then also known, that by the false intelligence respecting the strength of Fort Stanwix, the infamous behaviour of the Indians, and the want of the promised co-operation of the loyal inhabitants, Lieut. Col. St. Leger had been obliged to retreat. The first plausible motive in favour of hazardous haste, the facilitating his descent of the Mohawk, was thus at an end. The prospect of finding the enemy dispersed, it has before been shewn, was over.

The impossibility of preserving a communication was also evident. Was the army to have proceeded to action without hospital stores, as well as without victual? The general who carries troops into fire without precautions to alleviate the certain consequences, takes a sure step to alienate affections, and destroy the ardour of the soldier—he exacts more than human spirit can furnish. Men need not be habituated to fields of battle to be convinced of this truth. Let the mind rest for a moment on the objects which will rise within it after the mention of action, and then reflect, there is not a mattrass for broken bones, nor a cordial for agony and faintness. They who talk of these rapid marches, suppose no opposition, or no suffering in consequence of opposition. The hundreds of wounded men to be cruelly abandoned (if the rest could be prevailed upon to abandon those whose case might the next day be their own) make no part of the

2   con-

confideration of thefe gentlemen of precipitate imagi-
nations. But officers who are refponfible to God and
their country for the armies they conduct, cannot eafily
overlook fuch objects; and muft be patient at leaft till
a few hundred beds, and a proper proportion of me-
dicine and chirurgical materials, can be brought up
for troops that are to fight as well as to march.

The confideration of rapid movement has run into
much length : the ftrefs laid upon it in the crofs-examination, was the caufe. I beg leave very fhortly to recapitulate the principal points, and fhall then difmifs
it to the public judgment, without great apprehenfion
of having it renewed even in fpeculation.

Had a proper ftore of live cattle been obtained by
the expedition to Bennington, (and by the bye it will
be remembered, that had the loyalifts of the country
been really of the number and defcription reprefented,
that acquifition might have been made without an
action) all the carriages might have been appropriated
folely to the conveyance of flour, hofpital accommodations, entrenching tools, and other abfolute neceffaries;
and a rapid march to Albany might have been hazarded.

After the expedition to Bennington had failed of
that great purpofe, had a garrifon for Ticonderoga
been attainable from Canada, and the force then at
Ticonderoga been brought forward, to eftablifh a poft
of communication, and fecure a paffage of the river
by a fortified bridge, and redoubts upon the heights
which every where command the river, on one fhore
or the other, a forced march might ftill have been
juftifiable, becaufe a retreat was fecure : but, divefted
of both thefe refources, a rapid movement muft inevitably have led to rapid ruin.

Having gone through all the material points previous to the 13th of September, and fhewn, I truft, by
diftinct evidence, as well as reafoning, the expediency
of the march from Skenefborough to Fort Edward;
the principle of the expedition to Bennington; the
caufe of its failure; the efforts ufed to bring forward

the

Review of the meafure of the paffing the Hudfon's River. the provifion and neceffary ftores, and the impractica-bility of proceeding without thofe ftores; the attention of the reader will now be carried to a review of the meafure of paffing the Hudfon's River on that day.

I entered pretty fully, in my Narrative, into the principles which then actuated me; and I fhall not enlarge upon them. I have only to requeft every man who has been led to doubt whether I was required by duty, fituation, the voice of the army, and the voice of reafon, to advance and fight, to follow the confi-Lord Bal-carras's queft. 3 and 4, 21 to 28, 30 to 32. Lord Har-rington's, 32 to 37. Capt. Mo-ney, 56, 61, and 65 to 68. deration of thofe principles, with a revifal of the ap-plicable part of the verbal evidence, and I will then venture further to appeal to their judgment, whether, inftead of being required, I was not compelled, by the ftate of things, to act as I did; even independently of the peremptory tenor of my orders, which, confi-dent in the ftrength of my cafe, I have purpofely omit-ted, upon this occafion, to reconfider.

In regard to the point fo much agitated in this coun-try, though with no foundation whatever from any thing that happened in America, Brigadier Frafer's Brigadier Frafer's fentiments. fentiments upon this meafure of paffing the Hudfon's River, it would be trifling with the patience of the reader to recapitulate and point the evidence to a matter which I do not believe there is a man fo prejudiced as now to difpute, viz. that that officer joined in opinion and impatience with the reft of the army. But though the falfehoods fo grofsly and fo long impofed upon the public, refpecting this matter, are no more, it may not be unworthy curiofity to explore their origin and trace their progrefs.

Progrefs of the falfe-hoods pro-pagated. It is not difficult to difcern that the fufpicion of dif-ference of opinion in the army, upon the meafure of paffing the Hudfon's River, arofe from the paragraph in my public letter from Albany to the Secretary of State, wherein I fay that I had called no council upon that fubject, but had acted upon my own judgment of the peremptory tenor of my orders.

That

That a man, chief in authority, fhould take intirely upon himfelf a meafure of doubtful confequence, and upon mere principle preclude himfelf from any future means of fhifting or dividing the blame that might enfue, appeared incredible at Whitehall: the greater part of that political fchool concluded the profeffion of fuch candour muft be a fineffe, and that, in fact, the General had not communicated with his officers, becaufe he knew opinions would have been againft him.

When little minds think they have got a clue of littlenefs, it is wonderful with what zeal and dexterity they purfue and improve it. Correfpondence and intelligence were not wanting; difappointed jobbers, difcarded fervants, diffatisfied fugitives of every fort, fpies, tale-bearers, and fycophants, whom it is to the honour of a General to have his enemies, and a difgrace to office to encourage, abounded in town; and the primary idea once given, it was carried forward by very ready affiftance, and even logical deduction.——— As thus:

The General declares in his difpatch, he called no man into council upon the meafure of paffing the Hudfon's River: *Therefore*, his officers differed in opinion upon the expediency of advancing.

To differ in opinion upon that expediency, they muft conftrue his orders not to be peremptory: *Therefore*, he ftands fingle in the interpretation he put upon his orders.

If his officers faw that he was unadvifedly and defperately leading his army to death, they would certainly remonftrate: *Therefore*, they remonftrated.

The remonftrance would naturally be made to him by fuperior officers: *Therefore*, the conclufion follows; Major General Phillips and Brigadier General Frafer actually made a remonftrance againft paffing the Hudfon's River.

General Reidefel, who was next in rank to General Phillips, feems to have been forgotten. He was probably

bably overlooked in the eagernefs to get at General Frafer, on whofe name the important ftrefs was laid, and for two palpable reafons ; the one, that his name ftood high in the public eftimation, and greatly as it deferved fo to ftand, perhaps it acquired, upon this intended ufe, more juftice from fome quarters than it would otherwife have received.

The fecond and more prevalent reafon was, that Brigadier General Frafer was dead.

Thus then ftood the affertion when I arrived in England : " *Major General Phillips and Brigadier General Frafer remonftrated againft paffing the Hudfon's River, which movement was the caufe of all the fubfequent misfortunes.*" And having traced this falfehood to its maturity, it now may be equally curious to follow its decline.

After my arrival in England, the friendfhip, and general conformity of fentiment between General Phillips and me became more known. He was alive, and might poffibly foon return. His name was therefore withdrawn from the remonftrance, and referved, in eafe he did not return, to give colour to a fecond falfehood,* then kept back, but fince produced as one of the laft efforts of malignity in the courfe of the late enquiry.

The firft public occafion that offered was feized by me to pledge my honour upon the whole ftory of difagreement of opinion being falfe ; and I dared any man to produce a letter or a fentence, from Brigadier Frafer or any other officer, to authorife a fufpicion of its being true. Lieutenant General Frafer, upon the fame occafion in the Houfe of Commons, voluntarily and generoufly entered into my juftification, upon the authority of his correfpondence with his late relation, and the knowledge of his general fentiments.

---

* That General Phillips offered to conduct a part of the army from Saratoga to Ticonderoga. See this falfehood refuted, in the evidence of Lord Balcarras, Col. Kingfton, &c.

The

The falsehood was immediately so far weakened, that the word *Remonstrance* was changed into *Opinion.* " *Brigadier Fraser's opinion was against passing the Hudson's River* ;" and thus it remained, now and then assisted and cherished, when it was very languid, by a whisper, " *that there were still letters to be produced,*" till the late enquiry took place ; and the evidence of Lord Balcarras, Lord Harrington, Colonel Kingston, &c. gave the death blow to the last struggling efforts of that calumny. The rashness of passing the Hudson's River was obliterated ; every comment upon that *fatal* step was suddenly dropt, as if the river had sunk under ground ; the charge, with the full accompaniment of General Fraser's disapprobation, remonstrance, &c. &c. was shifted ; the minister was as nimble as his confederates, and exclaimed upon the *fatality* of the expedition to Bennington.

And here I shall finally rest the support I have been so anxious to derive from that grave which has been ransacked by my adversaries for evidence against me. As a soldier I avow a pride in having possessed Brigadier Fraser's esteem. As a defendant I am sensible I have dwelt upon it to a fault. The precedent of a Chief in Command suffering the comments of an inferior to be a test of his actions, requires an apology to my profession. It lies in the eminence of my friend's character. His approbation gave a grace to my defence, and I was impatient to confute the calumny that would have robbed me of it ; but to admit that it was necessary for my acquittal would be to countenance and forward the most pernicious and preposterous doctrine that ever was practised to mislead the public, and to betray the service.

The comments of an inferior officer no proper test of a superior's conduct.

When a minister or his confederates lean upon private report, table talk, and half sentences, to depreciate an officer they dare not themselves accuse, it is a feebleness of vengeance that, in its first aspect, is contemptible in the extreme ; but it calls for our indignation when we extend our view to its principle and effects.

effects. They operate to the very inverfion of due patronage, and the abfolute extinction of every idea upon which command ought to be beftowed, or can efficacioufly be exercifed; they tend to encourage officers to be fpies and informers; to render camps and fleets, properly the refidence of harmony and honour, the feats of fufpicion, difcord, faction, treachery, and mutiny.

The diverfity and importance of the matter brought to review in the period of the campaign I am now clofing, has led to greater length than I was aware of; but I cannot difmifs it without one reference, addreffed to fuch of the examiners of my conduct as have infifted upon the tardinefs of the northern army.

Compara-
tive view of
the cam-
paigns in
1759 and
1777. The reference I would plead is to a campaign in the fame country, memorable for having been conducted by an officer whofe example muft be acknowledged, at this juncture, to be of fplendid and peculiar authority; I mean the campaign of Lord Amherft, in the year 1759.

The great points of the war in America that year were to divide the enemy's force, and at the fame time to direct the feveral operations with fuch concurrence, that, though feparate and remote, they fhould affift each other. The firft objects of the army to which I allude were to reduce Ticonderoga and Crown Point, and the ultimate and moft important one was to effect a junction with Mr. Wolfe before Quebec.

Thus far there is great fimilarity between the plans of the two campaigns, except that the points from which the armies marched, and to which they were deftined, were exactly reverfed.

In the Spring, 1759, the army, then affembled at Albany, took the field as early as the feafon would admit: but fuch were the natural impediments of the country, that though fupported by the unanimous zeal of the inhabitants, and furnifhed with abundant fupplies of draft cattle, carriages, water-craft, and every other neceffary; the feveral departments well directed,

and

and no enemy to oppofe the march, the General (Lord Amherft) was not able to commence the attack of Ticonderoga till the 7th of July, when the enemy abandoned that poft, and retreated to Crown Point.

The diftance from Albany to Fort George is between fixty and feventy miles, the paffage over Lake George to Ticonderoga about forty miles.

The General had reafon to believe that Crown Point would be given up at his approach as precipitately as Ticonderoga had been. He did not, however, reach it, a diftance of thirteen miles, and water-carriage at will, till the 14th of Auguft.

Was it at that time afked by the minifter or his adherents, what was the army doing not to purfue a flying enemy?——Not to purfue when the whole country behind was their own, and magazines, baggage, hofpitals, and every other neceffary, might follow at leifure, and in fecurity! When it was forefeen an encreafe of fleet was to be conftructed at Crown Point, to obtain the fuperiority over the enemy upon Lake Champlain, and confequently that every day's delay, in becoming mafter of that poft, rifked the campaign!

Although thefe enquiries were not then fuggefted to the public, an anfwer to them has been given, greatly to the honour of the General, in a very impartial hiftory of that time. " The army was em-" ployed in repairing the fortifications at Ticondero-" ga; and the General took his meafures with the " fame care as if he had expected an obftinate defence, " and attempt to furprife him on his march."

The enemy actually did abandon Crown Point on the approach of the General, the 14th of Auguft; and, as foon as in poffeffion of that poft, he fet about fortifying it as he had done Ticonderoga. The time confumed in that operation, and in building new veffels, brought it to the middle of October before the General could embark upon the Lake. A fufpence, undoubtedly, of great anxiety; for the great end of the

the campaign, the junction of the two armies, upon which the reduction of all Canada was thought to depend, was unattained.

But did the minifter or his adherents *then* cavil at the tardinefs of that army?—Enterprifing, fanguine, and impetuous, as was the character of that minifter's councils, there was not lefs energy in his protection. The nation, not a party, were his adherents; and his word was a *fiat* of fame. He beftowed emphatic praifes on his general; and a failing campaign became part of that bafis, from which he has afcended to the high honours he now defervedly poffeffes.

It would be great prefumption, and it is far from being intended, to draw any parallels or inferences from the campaigns of 1759 and 1777, except fuch as merely apply to confumption of time under fimilar circumftances. In other points the pretenfions of the refpective Generals may be as different as their fortunes; or, to make a much clearer diftinction, and a yet ftronger contraft, as wide afunder as the aufpices under which they ferved, thofe of Mr. Pitt and of Lord George Germain.

Obfervations, &c. refpecting the third Period.

" A feries of hard toil, inceffant effort, ftubborn
" action, till difabled in the collateral branches of the
" army, by the total defection of the Indians, and the
" defertion or timidity of the Canadians and Provincials,
" fome individuals excepted; difappointed in the laft
" hope of any timely co-operation from other armies;
" the regular troops reduced, by loffes from the beft
" parts, to 3500 fighting men, not 2000 of which
" were Britifh; only three days provifions, upon fhort
" allowance, in ftore; invefted by an army of 16,000
" men, and no apparent means of retreat remaining,
" I called into council all the generals, field officers,
" and captains commanding corps, and by their una-
" nimous concurrence and advice, I was induced to
" open a treaty with Major General Gates, &c."

Such

Such was the fummary of affairs given in my let- Appendix No. XIV.
ter from Albany to the fecretary of ftate.   At the time
it was written, I little expected to have occafion for
any other teftimony of my actions ; and it has therefore been fuppofed, that I gave them a colouring more
fpecious than exact.   This is the ftage of my defence
in which I am defirous to bring that matter to judgment ; and I have quoted the above paffage, exprefsly
to lead the attention of every examiner to the whole
of that letter.   Let it now be confidered, unitedly
with my late Narrative, and both be compared in detail with the evidence—I am bold to ftake my caufe
upon the iffue—And refting upon thefe references, my
comments upon this period, though it is the moft important, will be fhorter than upon either of the former : the proofs alfo are more collected, and the
matters controverted or ftarted in crofs-examination
are fewer.

The firft remark I have to make is, that while the
managers of the minifter's caufe have never admitted
a doubt of the reality of thofe movements in the
campaign, with the propriety of which their ingenuity promifed them even a colourable caufe of cavil,
they have had the addrefs, when any little fkill and
conduct were generally acknowledged, to call the exiftence of fuch movements into queftion.   I cannot
make this remark more pertinently than at prefent,
when the march of the army, preceding the action of
the 19th of September, is in its due place the object of
notice—" A pretty combination of columns and de-
" ployments compofed at Albany, and very fit for a
" Gazette."   This fort of language I believe moft perfons have heard, who have converfed with the de-
pendents or runners of office, and it will be my excufe for fubmitting to the judgment of my profeffion
a plan of the movement.   It will fhew in fome degree
the difficulties that the nature of the country oppofed March to the enemy on the 19th of Sept. Plan IV
to a combined march of columns ; and at the fame
time the difadvantage (I might fay, the certain defeat)

M   that

that muft have been fuftained, had the army been only
in one column upon the ground where it was attacked,
or had the combination of the other columns, thofe
of General Frafer in particular, been lefs exact to the
point of time in which it was expedient they fhould
arrive and form.

To prove that this march was not *compofed* at Albany, I refer to feveral witneffes, but particularly to the
Earl of Harrington. His fituation, as my aid-de-
camp, gave him a general knowledge of a movement,
that an officer employed in the execution of a fingle
part of it could not have acquired. It will be confidered by all who know the qualities of my noble
friend, as very honourable to the difpofitions of that
day, that they are fo circumftantially retained in fo
diftinguifhing a mind ; and for my own part, I cannot
commit them to military judgment under a better truft
than the accuracy of his defcription.

I fhall not therefore detain the reader an inftant
longer from a fubject fo worthy his attention, as the
evidence refpecting the behaviour of the troops in the
enfuing events of that day.

Few actions have been characterized by more obftinacy in attack or defence. The Britifh bayonet was
repeatedly tried ineffectually. Eleven hundred Britifh
foldiers, foiled in thefe trials, bore inceffant fire from
a fucceffion of frefh troops in fuperior numbers, for
above four hours ; and after a lofs of above a third
of their numbers, (and in one of the regiments above
two thirds) forced the enemy at laft. Of a detachment of a captain and forty-eight artillery men, the
captain and thirty-fix were killed or wounded. Thefe
facts are marked by a concurrence of evidence that
no man will difpute. The tribute of praife due to
fuch troops will not be wanting in this generous nation ; and it will as certainly be accompanied with a
juft portion of fhame to thofe who have dared to depreciate or fully valour fo confpicuous—who have their
ears open only to the prejudice of American cowardice ;

ears

Marginal notes:

Lord Bal-
carras, q.
33, 34,
Maj. For-
bes, q. 3 to
7, Lord
Harring-
ton's q. 38
to 42 inclu-
five.

Action of
19th Sept.

Lord Har-
rington's q.
43, to 49
inclufive.
Lord Balcar-
ras, 35 to 39.
Capt. Mo-
ney, 26 to
30.
Maj. For-
bes, 8 to 10.
Lieut. Col.
Kingfton,
57 to 67.

and having been always loud upon that courtly topic, ftifle the glory of their countrymen to maintain a bafe confiftency.

It will be obfervable from the accounts of the killed and wounded, that the lofs of officers in all the actions of the campaign was proportionably much greater than that of the private men : and as this obfervation applies particularly to the action we are confidering, it may not be improper to account for it in this place.

The enemy had with their army great numbers of markfmen, armed with rifle-barrel pieces : thefe, during an engagement, hovered upon the flanks in fmall detachments, and were very expert in fecuring themfelves, and in fhifting their ground. In this action, many placed themfelves in high trees in the rear of their own line, and there was feldom a minute's interval of fmoke, in any part of our line without officers being taken off by fingle fhot.*

Reafon of the difproportion of killed and wounded.

It will naturally be fuppofed, that the Indians would be of great ufe againft this mode of fighting. The example of thofe that remained after the great defertion proved the contrary, for not a man of them was to be brought within the found of a rifle fhot. The Canadians were formerly very expert in fervice of this nature ; but befides the change in their military character, which I noticed before, their beft officer was killed early in the action, which event caft a general damp upon the corps. A few of the Provincials were ferviceable : but the beft men I had to oppofe as markfmen were the German chaffeurs, though their

---

* Captain Green, aid-de-camp to Major General Phillips, was fhot through the arm by one of thefe markfmen as he was delivering me a meffage. I learned, after the convention, from the commanding officer of the riflemen, that the fhot was meant for me ; and as the captain was feen to fall from his horfe, it was for fome hours believed in the enemy's army that I was killed. My efcape was owing to the captain happening to have a laced furniture to his faddle, which made him miftaken for the general.

number

number was fo fmall, as not to be one to twenty of the enemy.

The crofs-examination upon the proceedings of the army after this action will fhew the folly there would be in bringing a military caufe to a parliamentary enquiry, upon the prefumption that any parts of it would be left unexamined. The very want of practical knowledge in the enquierries renders them more inquifitive, and much more tenacious of doubts and furmifes, than

they would otherwife be: for inftance; I do not believe that with an army exhaufted by a long and fevere action, and deprived of an uncommon portion of officers, the queftion of attacking the enemy next morning would have occurred to any man of profeffional judgment: that enemy too in a pofition of which no further knowledge could be obtained than that it was covered by an intrenchment and abattis, and the approach to be made through a thick wood, without any avenue cut, or a fingle poft fortified to fecure a retreat, or to eover the magazine, which afforded the only poffible means of fubfiftence.

Equally remote would be the thoughts of military men from attacking a few days after, when it appeared I had received a letter from Sir Henry Clinton, informing me of a diverfion fo powerful as an attack upon Fort Montgomery to be undertaken as at that very time.

The queftions relating to the enemy having their baggage packed, if that circumftance was meant as an indication that they meant to retreat, is another proof how little the queftioners knew of fervice. It does not appear in evidence how the fact was: but no officer will difpute, that if the enemy had not only packed their baggage, but actually conveyed it to the other fide the river, they would have acted conformably to the general practice of fervice when action is expected; and to no circumftance of fervice more than to that when it is refolved to difpute a poft to the laft extremity.

Upon

Upon the whole of my fituation at that time, I am fo confident that it was the part of an officer to fortify and wait events, that I am only further intent to prove that I fortified properly, the nature of the ground and my feveral purpofes confidered. Upon this principle I fubmit the plan annexed. It will alfo fhew the na- Plan No. V. ture of the ground between the two armies, and ferve to explain the difficulties the witneffes exprefs of taking a view of the enemy's left: but it will be confidered, that befides thefe apparent obftacles to a near approach, the enemy abounded in militia, which fupplied out-pofts and fcouts, that could by no means be driven in without making the army liable to a general action.

As for any other intelligence than what could be obtained by eye-fight it was generally contradictory, always imperfect; the deferters were often fufpicious, the prifoners very few. I never faw any inftance of fervice where it was fo difficult to obtain information. Among people fpeaking the fame language with ourfelves, and many of them profeffing the moft favourable difpofitions, fcarcely any could be prevailed upon, by rewards or principle, to rifk his perfon for the purpofe of intelligence.

In regard to the crofs-examination, refpecting the time neceffary for the conftruction of the redoubts and other works, I neither thought it worth while to conteft it at the time, nor fhall I conteft it now, though nothing would be more eafy than to fhew that there was a great deal of neceffary labour which the queftions did not lead to, and confequently the witneffes could not with propriety enter into the explanation of them. But what makes the confumption of time to me immaterial is, that I place my juftification upon the expediency of waiting the co-operation from Sir Henry Clinton. It is in proof, that I received a letter from him the day after the action of the 19th,* informing

* The original letter is in my poffeffion, but could not be produced without difcovering a fecret mode of conveying intelligence that it might be improper to make public.

M 3

me

me that he meditated an attack upon Fort Montgomery as at that very time. And as I have already faid, that I fhould have thought it the part of madnefs to have rifked an attack upon the enemy, in the weak ftate of my army, for fome time after the late action, and under the expectation of fo powerful a diverfion; fo fhould I have deferred it longer, even after being recruited from the hofpital, on account of the fame expectation, and the further chance of the reinforcement of Colonel St. Leger's corps, and perhaps a convoy of provifions from Ticonderoga: fo far am I from conceiving the paft delay blameable, that I acknowledge the meafure of the 7th of October was precipitated by fome days, by the forage being become fo fcarce, that a fupply could only be obtained by a movement of the army.

If any perfons have fuppofed, that what has been called the inactive ftate of the army at this period was a ftate of reft, they are as much miftaken as they would be if they fuppofed it in any other circumftance comfortable. From the 20th of September to the 7th of October, the armies were fo near, that not a night paffed without firing, and fometimes concerted attacks upon our advanced picquets; no foraging party could be made without great detachments to cover it; it was the plan of the enemy to harrafs the army by conftant alarms, and their fuperiority of numbers enabled them to attempt it without fatigue to themfelves.

By being habituated to fire, our foldiers became indifferent to it, and were capable of eating or fleeping when it was very near them: but I do not believe either officer or foldier ever flept during that interval without his cloaths, or that any general officer, or commander of a regiment, paffed a fingle night without being upon his legs occafionally at different hours, and conftantly an hour before day-light.

The circumftances in general of the action of the 7th of October ftand in that arrangement in the evidence

evidence of the Earl of Balcarras, Earl of Harrington, Lieut. Col. Kingston, and Captain Money, and have been so little controverted by cross-examination, that any length of comment upon them is unneceffary. I will only obferve, that the movement of the enemy under General Arnold, mentioned in my Narrative, is confirmed as far as circumftantial teftimony can confirm it, by Captain Money. And if there can be any perfons, who, after confidering that circumftance, and the pofitive proof of the fubfequent obftinacy, in the attack upon the poft of Lord Balcarras, and various other actions of that day, continue to doubt, that the Americans poffefs the *quality* and *faculty* of fighting (call it by whatever term they pleafe) they are of a prejudice that it would be very abfurd longer to contend with.

Lord Harrington, 57, &c.
Lieut. Col. Kingfton, 77, &c.
Capt. Money, 35 to 48.
See alfo Plan V.

But though comments upon this part of the evidence may be fpared, the remembrance of what I perfonally underwent cannot fo eafily be fuppreffed ; and I am fure I fhall not outgo the indulgence of the candid, if in delineating fituations fo affecting, I add feelings to juftification. The defence of military conduct is an interefting point of profeffiona! honour ; but to vindicate the heart, is a duty to God and to fociety at large.

Few conjunctures in the campaign I have been defcribing, few, perhaps, upon military record can be found fo diftinguifhed by exigencies, or productive of fuch critical and anxious calls upon public character, and private affection, as that which now took place.

In the firft place, the pofition of the army was untenable, and yet an immediate retreat was impoffible ; not only from the fatigue of the troops, but from the neceffity of delivering frefh ammunition and provifions.

Lord Balcarras, 52.

The loffes in the action were uncommonly fevere. Sir Francis Clarke, my aid-de-camp, had originally recommended himfelf to my attention by his talents

and

and diligence: as fervice and intimacy opened his character more, he became endeared to me by every quality that can create efteem. I loft in him an ufeful affiftant, an amiable companion, an attached friend: the ftate was deprived by his death, of one of the faireft promifes of an able general.

The fate of Colonel Ackland, taken prifoner, and then fuppofed to be mortally wounded, was a fecond fource of anxiety—General Frafer was expiring.

In the courfe of the action, a fhot had paffed through my hat, and another had torn my waiftcoat. I fhould be forry to be thought at any time infenfible to the protecting hand of Providence; but I ever more particularly confidered (and I hope not fuperftitioufly) a foldier's hair-breadth efcapes as incentives to duty, *a marked renewal of the truft of Being*, for the due purpofes of a public ftation; and under that reflection to lofe our fortitude, by giving way to our affections; to be diverted by any poffible felf-emotion from meeting a prefent exigency with our beft faculties, were at once difhonour and impiety.

Having therefore put afide for a time my private fenfations, it has been fhewn that I effected an entire change in the pofition of the army before day-light. The plan will fhew the new ground taken up. Early in the morning of the 8th, General Frafer breathed his laft—and with the kindeft expreffions of his affection, his laft requeft was brought me, that he might be carried without parade by the foldiers of his corps to the great redoubt, and buried there. The whole day of the 8th of October was correfpondent to this inaufpicious beginning. The hours were meafured by a fucceffion of immediate cares, encreafing doubts, and melancholy objects. The enemy were formed in two lines. Every part of their difpofition, as well as the repeated attacks upon Lord Balcarras's corps, and the cannonade from the plain, kept the troops in momentary expectation of a general action. During this fufpence, wounded officers, fome upon crutches, and others

Lord Balcarras, 53. Lord Harrington, 66. Plan, No. VI. State of things on the 8th.

Lord Harrington, 67, &c.

others even carried upon hand-barrows by their fervants, were occafionally afcending the hill from the hofpital tents, to take their fhare in the action, or follow the march of the army. The geenarls were employed in exhorting the troops.

About fun-fet the corpfe of General Frafer was brought up the hill, attended only by the officers who had lived in his family. To arrive at the redoubt, it paffed within view of the greateft part of both armies. General Phillips, General Reidefel, and myfelf, who were ftanding together, were ftruck with the humility of the proceffion: They who were ignorant that privacy had been requefted, might conftrue it neglect. We could neither endure that reflection, nor indeed reftrain our natural propenfity to pay our laft attention to his remains. The circumftances that enfued cannot be better defcribed than they have been by different witneffes. * The inceffant cannonade during the folemnity; the fteady attitude and unaltered voice with which the chaplain officiated, though frequently covered with duft, which the fhot threw upon all fides of him; the mute but expreffive mixture of fenfibility and indignation upon every countenance: thefe objects will remain to the laft of life upon the minds of every man who was prefent. The growing dufkinefs added to the fcenery, and the whole marked a character of that juncture that would make one of the fineft fubjects for the pencil of a mafter that the field ever exhibited—To the canvas and to the faithful page of a more important hiftorian, gallant friend! I confign thy memory. There may thy talents, thy manly virtues, their progrefs and their period, find due diftinction; and long may they furvive;——long after the frail record of my pen fhall be forgotten.

The reflections arifing from thefe fcenes gave place to the perplexities of the night. A defeated army was to retreat from an enemy flufhed with fuccefs, much fuperior in front, and occupying ftrong pofts in the country behind. We were equally liable upon that

Gen. Frafer's funeral.

Night march of the 8th.

march

* Particularly Lieut. Col. Kingfton, 85.

march to be attacked in front, in flank, or rear. The
difpofition of a march had been concerted as much as
circumftances would admit; and it was executed by
the officers and the troops in general with a precifion
that experience in critical fituations can only teach.
The baggage, which could only move in one column,
and in a narrow road, fell into the confufion which it is
impoffible for caution to guard againft in the dark,
becaufe a fingle accident of an overturn or a broken
wheel, or even the ftupidity or drunkennefs of a
driver, may ftop, and often confufe the motion of the

Lord Har-
rington 70,
and from
112 to 118. whole line. Care was taken that no fuch accident
fhould break the order of the troops: and orders were
fent to Major General Phillips, who commanded the
rear guard, in cafe he was attacked, to pay attention
only to the main object of covering the troops; or, if
occafion were, of taking a pofition to give them time
to form.

Continu-
ance of the
march on
the 9th. At day-break the next morning the army had reached very advantageous ground, and took a pofition in
which it would have been very defirable to receive
the enemy. A halt was neceffary to refrefh the troops,
and to give time to the bateaux, loaded with provifions, which had not been able to keep pace with the
troops, to come a-breaft. A portion of provifions
was delivered alfo from the bateaux, not without apprehenfion that that delivery might be the laft: for
there were parts of the river in which the boats might
be attacked from the other fide to great advantage,
notwithftanding the correfpondent movement of the
army.

The above purpofes being effected, the army proceeded in very fevere weather, and through exceeding
bad roads.

Befides the continuation of difficulties and general
fatigue, this day was remarkable for a circumftance
of private diftrefs too peculiar and affecting to be
omitted. The circumftance to which I allude is
Lady Harriet Ackland's paffage through the enemy's
                                                                army,

army, to attend her wounded hufband, then their prifoner.

The progrefs of this lady with the army could hardly be thought abruptly or fuperfluoufly introduced, were it only fo for the purpofe of authenticating a wonderful ftory.—It would exhibit, if well delineated, an interefting picture of the fpirit, the enterprize, and the diftrefs of romance, realized and regulated upon the chafte and fober principles of rational love and connubial duty.

Extraordinary occurrence of private diftrefs.

But I beg leave to obferve befides, that it has direct reference to my fubject, to fhew what the luxuries were with which (as the world has been taught to believe) the army was encumbered ; what were the accommodations prepared for the *two thoufand women* that are gravely fuppofed, in the crofs examination, to have followed with the baggage. An idea fo prepofterous, as well as falfe, would have been a fitter fubject for derifion than refutation, but that it was malicioufly intended; not, I am confident, by the member who afked the queftions, but by the perfons who impofed upon him, to effect by prejudice what they defpaired of effecting by fact.—Not content with cavilling at our pretenfions of having *fought* hard, they would not allow the army even the claim upon the good-nature of the nation, of having *fared* hard for its fervice.

Lieut. Col. Kingfton, from 131 to 133.

I fhall however confider part of this ftory as fo far unconnected with the immediate bufinefs I was upon (purfuing the line of evidence upon the retreat to Saratoga) as to give it in the margin. It may well ftand by itfelf; and I venture to think that this one example of patience, fuffering, and fortitude, will be permitted to pafs without cenfure or obloquy*.

When the army was upon the point of moving after

---

* Lady Harriet Ackland had accompanied her hufband to Canada in the beginning of the year 1776. In the courfe of that campaign fhe had traverfed a vaft fpace of country, in different

the

the halt defcribed, I received a meffage from Lady Harriet, fubmitting to my decifion a propofal (and expreffing an earneft folicitude to execute it, if not interfering with my defigns) of paffing to the camp of the enemy, and requefting General Gates's permiffion to attend her hufband.

Though I was ready to believe (for I had experienced) that patience and fortitude, in a fupreme de-gree

extremities of feafon, and with difficulties that an European traveller will not eafily conceive, to attend, in a poor hut at Chamblée, upon his fick bed.

In the opening of the campaign of 1777 fhe was reftrained from offering herfelf to a fhare of the fatigue and hazard expected before Ticonderoga, by the pofitive injunctions of her hufband. The day after the conqueft of that place, he was badly wounded, and fhe croffed the Lake Champlain to join him.

As foon as he recovered, Lady Harriet proceeded to follow his fortunes through the campaign, and at Fort Edward, or at the next camp, fhe acquired a two-wheel tumbril, which had been conftructed by the artificers of the artillery, fomething fimilar to the carriage ufed for the mail upon the great roads of England. Major Ackland commanded the Britifh grenadiers, which were attached to General Frafer's corps ; and confequently were always the moft advanced poft of the army. Their fituations were often fo alert, that no perfon flept out of their cloaths. In one of thefe fituations a tent, in which the major and Lady Harriet were afleep, fuddenly took fire. An orderly ferjeant of grenadiers, with great hazard of fuffocation, dragged out the firft perfon he caught hold of. It proved to be the major. It happened, that in the fame inftant fhe had, unknowing what fhe did, and perhaps not perfectly awake, providentially made her efcape, by creeping under the walls of the back part of the tent. The firft object fhe faw, upon the recovery of her fenfes, was the major on the other fide, and in the fame inftant again in the fire, in fearch of her. The ferjeant again faved him, but not without the major being very feverely burned in his face and different parts of the body. Every thing they had with them in the tent was confumed.

This accident happened a little time before the army paffed the Hudfon's River. It neither altered the refolution nor the chear-fulnefs of Lady Harriet; and fhe continued her progrefs, a partaker of the fatigues of the advanced corps. The next call upon her fortitude was of a different nature, and more diftrefs-ful, as of longer fufpenfe. On the march of the 19, the

grenadiers

gree, were to be found, as well as every other virtue, under the moft tender forms, I was aftonifhed at this propofal. After fo long an agitation of the fpirits, ex-haufted not only for want of reft, but abfolutely want of food, drenched in rains for twelve hours together, that a woman fhould be capable of fuch an under-taking as delivering herfelf to the enemy, probably in the night, and uncertain of what hands fhe might firft fall into, appeared an effort above human nature. The affiftance I was enabled to give was fmall indeed; I had not even a cup of wine to offer her; but I was told fhe had found, from fome kind and fortu-nate hand, a little rum and dirty water. All I could furnifh to her was an open boat and a few lines, written

grenadiers being liable to action at every ftep, fhe had been di-rected by the major to follow the route of the artillery and bag-gage, which was not expofed. At the time the action began fhe found herfelf near a fmall uninhabited hut, where fhe alighted. When it was found the action was becoming general and bloody, the furgeons of the hofpital took poffeffion of the fame place, as the moft convenient for the firft care of the wounded. Thus was this lady in hearing of one continued fire of cannon and mufketry, for four hours together, with the prefumption, from the poft of her hufband at the head of the grenadiers, that he was in the moft expofed part of the action. She had three female companions, the Baronefs of Reidefel and the wives of two Britifh officers, Major Harnage and Lieutenant Reynell; but in the event their prefence ferved but little for comfort. Major Harnage was foon brought to the furgeons, very badly wounded; and a little time after came intelligence that Lieute-nant Reynell was fhot dead. Imagination will want no helps to figure the ftate of the whole groupe.

From the date of that action to the 7th of October, Lady Harriet, with her ufual ferenity, ftood prepared for new trials! and it was her lot that their feverity encreafed with their num-bers. She was again expofed to the hearing of the whole action, and at laft received the fhock of her individual misfortune, mixed with the intelligence of the general calamity, the troops were defeated, and Major Ackland, defperately wounded, was a pri-foner.

The day of the 8th was paffed by Lady Harriet and her com-panions in common anxiety, not a tent, nor a fhed being ftand-ing, except what belonged to the Hofpital, their refuge was among the wounded and the dying.

upon

upon dirty wet paper, to General Gates, recommending her to his protection.

Mr. Brudenell, the chaplain to the artillery (the same gentleman who had officiated so signally at General Frazer's funeral) readily undertook to accompany her, and with one female servant, and the major's valet-de-chambre (who had a ball which he had received in the late action then in his shoulder) she rowed down the river to meet the enemy. But her distresses were not yet to end. The night was advanced before the boat reached the enemy's out-posts, and the centinel would not let it pass, nor even come on shore. In vain Mr. Brudenell offered the flag of truce, and represented the state of the extraordinary passenger. The guard, apprehensive of treachery, and punctilious to their orders, threatened to fire into the boat if it stirred before day-light. Her anxiety and suffering were thus protracted through seven or eight dark and cold hours; and her reflections upon that first reception could not give her very encouraging ideas of the treatment she was afterwards to expect. But it is due to justice at the close of this adventure to say, that she was received and accommodated by General Gates with all the humanity and respect that her rank, her merits and her fortunes deserved.

Let such as are affected by these circumstances of alarm, hardship and danger, recollect, that the subject of them was a woman; of the most tender and delicate frame; of the gentlest manners; habituated to all the soft elegancies, and refined enjoyments, that attend high birth and fortune; and far advanced in a state in which the tender cares, always due to the sex, become indispensibly necessary. Her mind alone was formed for such trials.

Arrival of the army at Saratoga. Lord Harrington, 71, &c.

Ld. Balcarras, 57, &c.

I now return to the army, which arrived in the night at Saratoga, in such state of fatigue, that the men for the most part had not strength or inclination to cut wood and make fires, but rather sought sleep in their wet cloaths upon the wet ground under the continuing rain, and it was not till after day-light that the artillery and the last of the troops past the Fish-Kill, and took a position upon the heights and in the redoubts formerly conftructed.

The interval between taking that pofition, and the conclufion of the treaty, is the folemn crifis in which I confider myfelf as peculiarly accountable to my country. And if all the circumftances mentioned by me, in my own vindication, in my Letters, or my Narrative, are not eftablifhed, and many of them ftrengthened by pofitive proof ; if every furmife of a furrender on my part, while there was a poffibility of avoiding it by fight, by manœuvre, or by retreat, is not done away ; if even in the laft extremity, it does not appear I was ready and forward to prefer death to difhonour; if the evidence I have adduced is not clear, diftinct, and direct to thefe points, the public odium, piercingly as it affects a fenfible breaft, would be far fhort of the punifhment I deferve.

Interval between the arrival at Saratoga and figning the convention.

I cannot but confider it as one encouragement under this appeal, and it is no fmall one, that though very few parts of my preceding conduct have efcaped the fcrutiny of crofs-examination, not a material tranfaction of this crifis has been controverted or glanced at, I beg leave to recapitulate the tranfactions upon which I rely.

It is proved by the evidence of the Earl of Harrington and Colonel Kingfton, that the enemy was pofted on the eaft fide the river to guard the ford.

Lord Harrington, 74 to 76.

It is further proved by the evidence of Lieut. Col. Kingfton, that in concert with the general officers, it was determined to try a night march on the eaft fide the river, abandoning the baggage ; and that the attempt was prevented by the impoffibility attending the delivery of neceffary provifion. The fame witnefs goes on to fhew, that the next day it was evident, that had the delivery been poffible, the attempt would ftill have failed, for we then received intelligence of the enemy being previoufly in poffeffion, in force, of the country on both fides the river between us and Fort Edward.*

Lieut. Col. Kingfton, 86. See the plan. Lieut. Col. Kingfton, 91, 92.

Lieut. Col. Kingfton, 93, 94, 95.

* It was alfo in contemplation to force a way back to Albany, had the enemy in the diftribution of their pofts weakened their right, fo as to have made the effort poffible. See Lord Harrington's evidence.

While

While the army was lying day and night upon their arms, " in anxious hope of fuccour from our friends, " or as the next defirable expectation, an attack from " the enemy,"* I cannot omit obferving from the *Lieut. Col. Kingftone, 88, 89, 90.* fame evidence (that of Colonel Kingfton) how near the laft expectation was being accomplifhed. It would be improper to pronounce pofitively what would have been the iffue : but I requeft the attention of my mili *See the plan. No. VII.* tary readers to the plan of the ground, as an argument of the probability of fuccefs. The difpofition of the enemy being to pafs the Fifh-Kill in different columns, and to make their great effort upon the plain, they muft have formed under the fire of all our park artillery, within reach of grape fhot, a crofs fire from the artillery and mufketry of the entrenched corps upon the hill, and the mufketry of the 20th regiment, which was at eafy diftance to be fupported by the Germans, in front; added to this would have been the advantage, which though always wifhed for we never had attained, of a charge upon an open plain. I am perfuaded the general judgement will go with me when I lament the accident that prevented the enemy's defign (when fo far advanced in it, as actually to have paffed the river with one column) as one of the moft adverfe ftrokes of fortune in the whole campaign.

Lord Harrington, 84, 85, 86. Lord Balcarras, from 60 to the end. Maj. Forbes, 22 to 29. Lord Balcarras, 64. The ftate of things after this difappointment is given by the Earl of Harrington : " It was as bad as poffi " ble ; the numbers of the army were few, their pro " vifions fhort, their pofition not a good one, owing " to the nature of the country." This ftate is corroborated by the evidence of the Earl of Balcarras and Major Forbes, with the additional circumftance, that there was not a fpot to be found in the whole pofition which was not expofed to cannon or rifle fhot.

The minutes of the firft council of war prove the unanimity of opinion for opening the treaty ; and it is proved by the evidence of Colonel Kingfton, that the force of the enemy was actually greater, and their

* Letter from Albany to the Secretary of State.

pofition

position stronger, than the intelligence I had received
and laid before the council of war represented them.

It is proved by the fulleft evidence, that the terms Maj. Forbes,
first proposed by the enemy were instantly and unani- 21 to 34.
mously rejected by the council of war as dishonourable. Lord Balcar-
as, 65 to 73.

The same unanimity in approving the terms I proposed and obtained, is equally inconteftibly eftabifhed.

And lastly, two papers are produced, and authenticated beyond a poffibility of cavil, the one General Appendix,
Gates's return figned by himfelf, fhewing the effective No. XVI.
strength prefent of the rebel army ; the other, the mi- No. XVII.
nutes of the last council of war, fhewing, that even fupported as I was by the unanimity of the former councils,
in opening and conducting the treaty, I was repugnant See alfo
Lord Bil-
to the figning of it, upon a flight hope entertained of a carras, 130,
remote relief——(a hope arifing from fome intelligence 131, 132,
received in the night of Sir Henry Clinton's moving up
the North River) and gave my voice againft a majority
accordingly ; that I at laft thought myfelf compelled to
yield to the majority upon " the uncertainty of the in-
" telligence, and the improbability of General Clinton's
" motions being effectual if true ; upon the doubts en-
" tertained of fome part of the troops, if the negotia-
" tion of the treaty ceafed, and of a greater part for
" want of bodily ftrength, if defperate enterprizes were
" to be afterwards undertaken ; and lastly, upon the
" reflection that a mifcarriage of fuch enterprizes muft
" be fatal to the whole army, and that even a victory
" could not fave it."

To this mafs of evidence, appofite and direct to every
fact effential to my juftification, I beg leave to add the
opinion of the army, that the terms obtained were bet- Lord Bal-
ter than the fituation of things gave us a right to expect. carras.
Lord Har-
For a proof that fuch was their opinion, I refer to the rington.
teftimony of Lord Balcarras.

A fair judgment upon recent events is hardly to be Reflections
expected, efpecially while many prejudices are alive. upon the
convention,
It will be allowed me to affume, what no one has ever
ventured to deny, that there may be a combination of
circumftances under which an army may be juftified in

N   treating

treating with an enemy. That the army under my command was under fuch circumftances at Saratoga is alfo
generally acknowledged : but what is not denied to me
from my own fituation, is attempted to be withheld, by
fome, on account of the quality of the enemy. They
fuggeft that there fhould be no treaty with rebels. It is
unneceffary in anfwer to have recourfe to hiftory. I
will not take defence from treaties between Spain, the
haughtieft power of the world, and the arch-rebel the
great Prince of Orange ; nor between Charles the Firft
and the arch-rebels the Englifh Parliament (for fuch in
both inftances they were called) I need only refer to the
examples exifting at that time in America, and fince
much improved on at home. My fuperior officer in
America, with the approbation of government, had
treated upon different occafions with General Wafhington. The Britifh government in its higheft collective
authority, the King in Parliament, has fince commif-
fioned five members of that Parliament, the one a peer,
the others of eminent ftation in military and civil capa-
cities, to *treat with* rebels, I had almoft faid to *fue* to
rebels for peace, by the furrender of almoft every principle for the maintenance of which they had profecuted
the war.

Thus highly juftified in treating with rebels, I am at
a lofs to difcover by what poffible mode of defence I
could have acquitted myfelf to God or my country, when
the brave and intelligent officers of my army unanimoufly
refolved, upon military principle, precedent and reafon,
that the treaty was expedient, and the terms honourable, if I had delivered them up to certain deftruction,
or even to be prifoners at difcretion.

If the informed and difpaffionate part of mankind
fhould agree in fentiment with the unanimous voice of
the army, upon the convention of Saratoga, furely to
impute to it the final lofs of the army is too palpable an
injuftice long to remain upon the minds of the moft prejudiced. The convention exprefsly preferved the army
for the fervice of the ftate. According to that convention

tion a truce was made during the war, between that army and the enemy, in America, and it now might have been acting against the House of Bourbon in any other part of the world. The army was loft by the non-compliance with the treaty on the part of the Congrefs; and that violation of faith no man will ever be found to juftify.

I will not decide how far it was encouraged in America, by the perfuafion that the miniftry of Britain had neither power nor fpirit to redrefs the wrong; and that they had funk the nation fo low, in point of refpect, that the world would overlook, where fhe was concerned, an action that would have excited, in any other cafe, univerfal cenfure and indignation. But whatever motives the Congrefs may have had, the tamenefs and filence with which the Britifh minifters have borne this outrage, is aftonifhing. That men fo conftant and fo prodigal in their anger againft the Congrefs, as never before to have failed in expreffing it, even in cafes where it bordered upon being ridiculous, fhould on a fudden become cold and mute, and dead to feeling, in a cafe were refentment was juftly founded, can hardly be accounted for, except upon the principle that it was better to fupprefs the jufteft cenfure upon a power they detefted, than that even a particle of unmerited odium fhould be wanting to load the man whom they were refolved to deprefs.

CON-

CONCLUSION.

I AM not aware that in the preceding Review of Evidence I have neglected any part effential to my defence. I do not reckon as fuch, that part which applies to the management of the public purfe. The calumny defigned to wound me upon that head was too grofs to fucceed : it perifhed in its birth, and fcorn is the only fentiment excited by the remembrance of its momentary exiftence. In regard to the more plaufible objections pointed againft my conduct, I have not only endeavoured to meet them in the crofs-examination, but have fearched for them in every place where I could fuppofe them to originate or be entertained. If fome have efcaped, I fhall ftand excufed, when it is recollected how they have grown and changed from one fhape to another, and that it has never been my fortune to be confronted with an avowed and regular accufer—I defpair of ever being fo : but I defire it to be underftood, that although I am earneft in this mode of defence, I am fo far from declining another, that I fhall think it one very happy circumftance of the paft enquiry, if any thing contained in it fhould have effect hereafter to produce an enquiry by court-martial.

It would not be an ungrateful tafk to follow the defence of the campaign with a detail of the occurrences which happened between the time of figning the convention and my leaving America. Many of them would be found curious ; and the cares and perplexities in which I bore a principal and moft painful part, would create a new intereft in the minds of my friends : but I do not think myfelf at liberty, upon the plan I laid down at

my

my outfet, to enter into matter where no blame is imputed or implied. If my proceedings during that interval deferve any credit, I am content with that teftimony of it, which I may affume from the filence of my enemies.

I have not the fame reafons for paffing over the tranfactions in which I have been engaged fince my return to England, becaufe blame, and of a very atrocious nature, *has* been imputed to me. But as the principal of thefe tranfactions are already before the public, I fhall mention them very briefly ; and merely to introduce connectedly fuch further thoughts upon them as could not with propriety be ftated upon any former occafion.

Immediately after my arrival, a board of general officers was appointed to enquire into the caufes of the failure of the expedition from Canada. This enquiry was made the foundation of an order againft my appearing at court.

The board reported, that they could not take cognizance of me being under parole—the prohibition from the King's prefence neverthelefs ftill remained in force.

I had recourfe to parliament for enquiry ; and openly, and repeatedly, and ftrenuoufly called upon the minifters to join iffue with me before that tribunal. Objection was taken againft immediate enquiry, becaufe Generals Sir Guy Carleton and Sir William Howe who might be parties were abfent ; but it was evidently the difpofition of the houfe, that an enquiry fhould be inftituted the enfuing feffion.

I pledged myfelf zealoufly to profecute that meafure ; I accufed minifters of injurious treatment towards myfelf ; and it became my duty, upon occafions with which my own affairs had no connection, to exprefs deeper refentments of their conduct towards the public.

In this ftate of things parliament was prorogued on the 3d of *June*. On the 5th of *June*, I received the firft order to repair to Bofton as foon as I had tried the Bath waters. The order and my anfwer, reprefenting the

N 3   hard-

hardſhip of being ſent back unheard, and the ſecond conditional order, with entire ſlight of my repreſentations, are too well known to require repetition : but there are two circumſtances attending the dates of theſe orders with which I was not acquainted till long after, and which have never yet been taken notice of.

The one is, that at the very time I was told that my preſence was *material*, and (as the ſecond letter from the ſecretary at war expreſſed) of *ſo much importance to the troops detained priſoners in New England*, that it muſt not be diſpenſed with—at that very time, it was determined to ratify the convention, according to the requiſition of the Congreſs ; and to tranſmit the ratification through other hands, and without any participation with me, or employment of me, in carrying it to a concluſion. It was very poſſible, the troops might have been ſailed for England before I had reached America, had I even complied as early as the condition of either order could poſſibly be conſtrued to preſcribe. But at all events, the circumſtance could not but ſerve to mark *to me* the true intent and meaning of the order beyond a poſſibility of miſtake—*that it was an order of vindictive puniſhment* ; and my preſence with the troops, if I reached America in time, was *material* and *important* to mark to *them* the degree of diſgrace to which I was reduced. The terms are a mockery, and an inſult upon common ſenſe, if applied, in the ſituation in which I was placed, to the ſervice of the King, or the conſolation of the troops. Such a diſplay of vengeance might indeed be intended to apply to their prudence, and to act as a caution and warning how at their return they ſhould ſupport a General under the extremity of the King's diſpleaſure *.

The

---

* In times when the maintenance of the conſtitution in its puritv is the ruling principle of an adminiſtration, the King's name is introduced by office only to denote an act of the executive part of the ſtate. In times when an adminiſtration meat to rule by the influence of monarchy, the language of office is to connect the royal perſon with

The other circumstance attending these dates is not less remarkable, viz.

The determination of changing the nature of the war, as afterwards declared by the commissioners in America, must have been taken at this time.

I am very much disinclined to believe, that the consideration of my person as a proper victim upon that occasion was ever regularly and formally debated in the cabinet; but I cannot think it uncharitable to the individual adviser of the Crown, whoever he was, who could project such an order, to suppose, that if upon the first exercise of *the extremes of war* on the one side, and in the ardour of retaliation on the other, it had so happened, that an object so well to be spared as an obnoxious and disgraced Lieutenant General, had opportunely presented itself to the enemy's rigour, and had been detained in their prisons, the order for the voyage would not have been thought, by that individual, quite thrown away. Detention, with or without the troops, of a troublesome and bold complainant, could not be immaterial or unimportant to such a person, and the order was of an import

" —To make assurance double sure—
" And take a bond of fate—
" That he might tell pale-hearted Fear it lied.

The living presence of an injured man is, perhaps, more offensive and insupportable to the sight of a mean injurer, than the spectre of him would be after death.

But to return to the facts I was recapitulating.

I remained under the conditional order in England.

The ensuing session, the parliamentary enquiry now laid before the public took place. It ended, as has been stated, in July, 1779.

with the act, and to give him attributes of passion and displeasure, from which in his political character he is held exempt. I disclaim language and ideas so unconstitutional and disrespectful, and never mean to allude to my Sovereign personally, but in acts of justice and mercy.

In September, I received a fevere reprimand, a denial of a court-martial, and a prohibition of serving my country in its exigence, though other officers precisely in my situation were employed—I resigned.

The blame laid upon me for the part I took in these transactions is, that intemperately and factiously I engaged in opposition ; that I was guilty of disobedience to the King's orders; and it has been added in a late publication, that even my defence of my conduct is a libel upon the King's government.

I think I have perceived, that the first part of these charges, a rash engagement in opposition, is not combated by some who wish me well so strenuously as other imputations have been. It may possibly have appeared to friendly and prudential observers, as a palliating plea for a restitution to favour upon some future occasion, to have to say, that I had acted upon the sudden impulse of passion ; and the sequel might be, that I had repented, and would offend no more.

Without doubting the kindness which suggests these excuses, I have been impelled by principles too forcible, and have taken my part too decidedly, to look for a resource in those or any other subterfuges. It would be inconsistent and dishonourable in me to withhold a public declaration upon this occasion, in addition to those I have made upon others, that I engaged in resistance to the measures of the court upon mature reflection; that after collecting in my mind all the lights upon men and things which my experience and observation could furnish, I believed that the constitution of England was betrayed : and neither blaming or suspecting any men who conceived different opinions, and acted upon them, I thought it a point of time in which a man believing as I did was called upon to sacrifice to his country. The test of this motive, it is true, must rest between God and my conscience : but let it not be supposed that I acted blindly—the path of interest, a broad and beaten track, lay clearly before me from the time I arrived in England. Supple joints, and an attentive eye, always

giving

giving way to power, on one fide, and fometimes puſh-ing my friends into the dirt on the other, would have carried me fafely through. I even believe, that the ad-vifer of the letters I lately alluded to would rather have feen me in that track, than in the other which he pre-fcribed for me acrofs the Atlantic.

As little would I be fuppofed to want difcernment of the path I took : for the barefaced preferences, rewards and puniſhments held forth for parliamentary conduct, were among the moſt glaring parts of the fyſtem I had contemplated. And it was impoffible to doubt, that as a delinquent *there*, I ſhould be preſſed both by art and vengeance to the end the enemies I had provoked fore-faw—the lofs of my profeffion and the impoveriſhment of my fortune. I truſt it will be an innocent revenge on my part, to ſhew them I can bear my condition firm-ly; and that I am incapable of redeeming what I have loſt, were it ever in my option, by the difavowal of a fingle principle I have profeffed.

I come now to the fecond charge, difobedience of orders; and in a point that fo nearly touches the very effence of military character, I truſt I ſhall not trefpafs upon the patience of the reader, if I treat it a little more at large than I have done in my correfpondence with the fecretary at war.

I admit that fubordination and implicit obedience, as applied to the operation of arms, are primary principles in the military fyſtem. An army is a mere name with-out them. The officer who hefitates to meet certain death upon command, deferves to receive it from the hand of the executioner.

But there are poſſible exceptions to thefe general prin-ciples, efpecially out of the field, in the moſt abfolute fervices ; and in the Britiſh fervice they are known and marked, and co-exiſtent with the military eſtabliſhment itfelf, in the mutiny act, which confines obedience to legal commands. An army muſt again be garbled like the army of Cromwell (which God avert!) before an

order

order could be executed, like that of Cromwell, for garbling the parliament.

A high spirit will contract the limits of obedience still more; with illegal, he will reject diſhonourable commands; and he will follow the reaſoning I have already premiſed, and ſtate it as a maxim thus; *he who obeys at the expence of fortune, comfort, health and life, is a ſoldier; he who obeys at the expence of honour is a ſlave.*

But I may be aſked by ſome diſciplinarians, who is to be the judge in theſe nice definitions of obedience? It is uncommon military doctrine, I may be told, to reaſon upon the King's orders—I confeſs it is ſo. Since the reign of James the Second, in the Britiſh ſervice it never has been neceſſary. We have been uſed in this age, to ſee the King's name give wings and inſpiration to duty. Diſcipline, in this country, has been raiſed upon perſonal honour—a firmer baſis than fear or ſervility ever furniſhed: and the miniſter who firſt ſhakes that happy confidence; who turns military command to political craft; who dares to uſe his gracious Sovereign's name as an engine of ſtate, to glut his own anger, or to remove his own fears, he is amongſt the worſt enemies to that Sovereign. But ſhould his purpoſes go further (a conſideration of far greater magnitude to the public) and ſhould it be ſeen that the royal name was brought forth for the *diſcipline* of parliament, the miniſter ſo uſing it would be not only an enemy to his Sovereign, but a traitor to the conſtitution of the ſtate.

I will cloſe the defence of my principles reſpecting military ſubordination by reference to an anecdote well authenticated and not very remote.

An officer in a neighbouring nation, for ſome error he had committed in a day of battle, received a blow from his prince who commanded in perſon. The officer drew a piſtol, and his firſt movement was to point it at his maſter; but the next (and it was inſtantaneous) was to turn the muzzle, and diſcharge the ball into his own heart. Though my caſe differs both in the provocation and the consequence, in many circumstances my conduct may justly be supported upon the same principle. I receive an affront that a liberal spirit cannot endure ; and in a name, against which no personal resentment can be pursued, nor indeed entertained : but a suicide of my professional existence (if I may be allowed the phrase) is preferable to the state in which the affront placed me. In one instance only I renounce the parallel.——God forbid I shoud be thought, even in a burst of passion, to have pointed at my Sovereign! It was not from his hand I received the blow.

I shall solicit the reader's attention very little further : but I feel the necessity of repeating my application to the candour of the public, both as a writer and an appellant. Defence, and imputation of blame to others, are naturally interwoven in my cause : it required a more distinct conception, and an abler hand than mine, to keep them always apart, and open to separate view. In some parts my defence may be weakened by this deficiency of skill ; but I have no right to offer the same excuse for suffering any blame to rest upon others beyond what I thought myself justified to support.

Upon this principle, I think it just, at taking leave of the secretary of state for the American department, briefly to enumerate the only facts and propositions respecting the plan of the expedition from Canada, that I think clearly maintainable against him.

First fact. It is clear that the plan of a junction of the greater part of the forces in Canada with the army of Sir William Howe, was formed in the year 1776, when Sir William Howe was in full success ; when his whole force was in the neighbourhood of New York, or in the Jersies, and Mr. Washington was beaten, and at the weakest.

Second fact. This plan of a junction was continued (and upon just reasoning) in the close of the year 1776, when Sir William Howe's first proposal of operations for the ensuing campaign arrived. Those proposals were made upon the datum of a number of troops, sufficient

ent

ent to furnish, besides the main army, an *offensive* army
of 10,000 men, rank and file, to act on the side of
Rhode Island, by taking possession of Providence, and
penetrating from thence into the country towards Boston ; and another *offensive* army, not less than 10,000,
to move up the North River to Albany, exclusive of
5000 for the defence of New York.

In either of the above cases, the plan of junction
could hardly have failed of success.

Third fact. On the 23d of February, Sir William
Howe's alteration of the first plan was received, and
he then proposed to act with the greater part of his
force on the side of Philadelphia, at the opening of the
campaign, and to enable him so to do, to defer the *offensive plan from Rhode Island till the reinforcements should
arrive*, and to destine only 3000 men to act *defensively*
upon the lower part of the Hudson's River.

Fourth fact. On the 3d of March, the secretary of
state signified his Majesty's entire approbation of this
deviation from the plan first suggested.

From these facts arises my first proposition, that at
the time the change of plan for Sir William Howe's
operations was adopted, by which no offensive force
was to remain upon the Hudson's River, nor a diversion
probably to take place from Rhode Island, the plan of
my operations, the success of which would probably
depend in a great degree upon co-operation and diversion, ought to have been changed likewise : instead
of that, it was enforced and made positive by the refusal of the latitude I had proposed of acting upon
the Connecticut, or, in case of exigency, embarking the
troops and effecting the junction by sea.

Fifth fact. On the 19th of March, a letter from Sir
William Howe, by the secretary of state, acquainting
him, that a brigade of British and some companies of
grenadiers and light infantry had been withdrawn from
Rhode Island, which made the force left there merely
defensive. The same letter mentions the prospects the
enemy had of bringing 50,000 men into the field.

Sixth

Sixth fact. I did not leave England till the beginning of April, by which time the fecretary of ftate muft have known, or ought to have known, that no dependance could be placed upon reinforcements from England arriving at New York in time for Sir William Howe to refume the intention he had deferred, viz. a diverfion from Rhode Ifland, or of making the force upon Hudfon's River adequate to offenfive operation.

Hence arifes my fecond propofition, that the latitude I had propofed, or other expedients of precaution, ought then at leaft to have been adopted : inftead of which, I was fuffered to fail, ignorant of Sir William Howe's plans, and ignorant of the defalcation or the delays in the reinforcements deftined for him. The confequence was, that neither his letter to Sir Guy Carleton, put into my hands after my arrival in Canada, nor his letter to me of the 17th of June, informing me of his deftination for Pennfylvania, removed my expectation of co-operation, becaufe I was to fuppofe, that fubfequent to the dates of either of thofe letters, he would receive orders from the fecretary of ftate refpecting the junction, and alfo a timely reinforcement.

Seventh fact. The fecretary of ftate makes no mention of the northern expedition in any of his difpatches to Sir William Howe at the end of March, when my orders were fixed, nor in the month of April. And it is a further fact, that I am perfuaded will not be contefted, that he did not mention any orders or recommendations relative to co-operation verbally to Sir William Howe's aid-de-camp, or any other confidential perfon who failed about that time.

The firft mention made of the neceffity of co-operation was in the fecretary of ftate's letter of the 18th of May, wherein his Lordfhip " Trufts that whatever he [Sir William Howe] may meditate, it will be executed in time to co-operate with the army ordered to proceed from Canada."

The propofition clearly juftified by thefe facts is, that if the fecretary of ftate had thought proper to fignify
the

the King's expectation of a co-operation to be made in my favour in the month of March or beginning of April, as in confiſtency he ought to have done, it would have arrived before Sir William Howe embarked his army, and in time for him to have made a new diſpoſition : but inſtead of that, this very material injunction was not diſpatched till it was almoſt phyſically impoſſible it ſhould have any effect. And ſo indeed it happened, for Sir William Howe received it on the 16th of Auguſt, at a diſtance from Hudſon's River too great for any detachment from his own army to be made in time, could it even have been ſpared ; and the reinforcement from England, upon which Sir William Howe depended to ſtrengthen Sir Henry Clinton, was much later ſtill—too late (as it has been ſhewn) to enable that general with all his activity and zeal to give any effectual ſupport.

Indeed the conduct of the ſecretary of ſtate, in inſerting this paragraph, in his letter of the 18th of May, when it could not avail, after omitting it when certainly it would have been timely, ſeems ſo prepoſterous, that it can only be explained by one fact. It tranſpired about that time, that Sir William Howe's army was deſtined for Pennſylvania, and people who had conſidered the force of the enemy to be collected from the northern provinces began to be alarmed for my army. It is well known (though I cannot aſcertain the date) that an officer of very great ability, and a perfect knowledge in the country through which I was to paſs, as ſoon as he heard that no diſpoſition was made for a ſupport from New York, foretold to the ſecretary of ſtate, or his near friends, the fall of my army. Under this apprehenſion it might appear to the ſecretary of ſtate a proper caution, that an expectation of co-operation ſhould exiſt under his hand.

If plans ſo inconſiſtently formed, and managed by the ſecretary of ſtate with ſo much ſeeming confidence, as to miſlead his generals, and ſo much real reſerve as to deſtroy them, ſhould be defended by that infatuated belief

lief then entertained of the inability of the enemy to refift, I fhould beg leave to ftate, as one propofition
more, that after the experience of their actions at
Trenton, and many other places, and the intelligence of
their new levies received from Sir William Howe, fuch
confidence was an additional fault, and perhaps a more
pernicious one than any I have ftated.

Thus much for the noble Lord in his public capacity.
What fhare of the perfecution I have fuftained (more
than I have directly expreffed in different parts of my
defence) are imputable to his private councils, is not
within my knowledge: but if in fpeaking of my perfe-
cutors in general, I may be thought fometimes to have
ufed ftrong terms, I have only to fay, that having advanced no fact which I am not able and refolved to
maintain, I have not felt myfelf called upon, in applying thofe facts for any further attention, than to preferve
the language of a gentleman, which is an attention due
to myfelf as well as to the public. It is open and manly
enmity alone that unites refpect with refentment.

I wifh I could as eafily apologife for all the other
faults with which this undertaking abounds as a com-
pofition. At a time when fo many pens are employed,
I muft not expect to be fpared. I fhall treat with filent
refpect any comments that are fairly founded and delivered with liberality; and with contempt, equally
filent, the common invectives of the political prefs.
This appeal is not to reft upon literary criticifm, or
party difputation, but upon the broad equity of my
country. I know that prejudice and malice will vanifh
before the man who dares to fubmit his actions to
that teft—If acquitted *there*, I feel I am not degrad-
ed; and I have not a fenfation within my breaft
which does not at the fame time affure me, I cannot
be unhappy.

J BURGOYNE.

APPENDIX.

Copy of a Letter from Lieutenant-General Burgoyne *to* No. I.
Lord George Germain, *dated* Hertford-Street, 1*st*
January, 1777.

MY LORD,

MY phyſician has preſſed me to go to Bath for a
ſhort time, and I find it requiſite to my health and
ſpirits to follow his advice ; but I think it a previous
duty to aſſure your Lordſhip, that, ſhould my attendance in town become neceſſary, relatively to information upon the affairs of Canada, I ſhall be ready to o-
bey your ſummons upon one day's notice.

Your Lordſhip being out of town, I ſubmitted the
above intentions, a few days ago, perſonally to his
Majeſty in his cloſet ; and I added, " That, as the
arrangements for the next campaign might poſſibly
come under his royal contemplation before my return,
I humbly laid myſelf at his Majeſty's feet for ſuch active employment as he might think me worthy of."

This was the ſubſtance of my audience on my part.
I undertook it, and I now report it to your Lordſhip,
in the hope of your patronage in this purſuit ; a hope,
my Lord, fonnded not only upon a juſt ſenſe of the
honour your Lordſhip's friendſhip muſt reflect upon me,
but alſo upon a feeling that I deſerve it, in as much as
a ſolid reſpect and ſincere perſonal attachment can con-
ſtitute ſuch a claim.

I leave in the hands of Mr. D'Oyley ſuch of the
memorandums confided to me by General Carleton as
require diſpatch, ſhould your Lordſhip think proper
to carry them into execution.

A   I alſo

I alfo leave in that gentleman's hands the copy of an application relative to boats for the artillery, and which I take the liberty to fubmit to your Lordfhip as well worthy of confideration, upon the fuppofition that the enemy fhould arm upon Lake George, and that any operation fhould be advifeable by that route.

I likewife leave the difpofition of winter quarters, which I received by the laft fhip from Canada. I find no difpatch is come to your Lordfhip by that occafion, and I conceived thofe papers might be of ufe.

I have the honour to be,

My Lord, &c.

J. BURGOYNE.

No. II. *Extract of a Letter from Lord* George Germain *to Sir* Guy Carleton, *dated* Whitehall, 22d Auguft, 1776.

THE rapid fuccefs of his Majefty's arms, in driving the rebels out of Canada, does great honour to your conduct; and I hope foon to hear that you have been able to purfue them acrofs the lakes, and to poffefs thofe pofts upon the frontiers which may effectually fecure your province from any future infult.

His Majefty, in appointing you commander in chief of his forces in Canada, was pleafed to extend your commiffion to the frontiers of his provinces bordering thereupon, wifely forefeeing that it might be neceffary for the completing your plan of operations that you fhould march your army beyond the limits of your own government. I truft, before this letter reaches you, that you will, by your fpirit and activity, have cleared the frontiers of Canada of all the rebel forces, and will have taken the proper meafures for keeping poffeffion of the lakes. That fervice being performed, his Majefty commands me to acquaint you, that there ftill remains another part of your duty to be under-

taken,

taken, which will require all your abilities and the strictest application, the restoring peace and the establishing good order and legal government in Canada. It is an object of the greatest importance to this country ; the difficulties attending it are immense ; but his Majesty depends upon your zeal, and upon your experience, for carrying it into execution. His Majesty, ever anxious for the happiness of his subjects, commands me to inform you, that no time should be lost in beginning so important a work, and that you do therefore return to Quebec, detaching Lieutenant-General Burgoyne, or such other officer as you shall think most proper, with that part of your forces which can be spared from the immediate defence of your province, to carry on such operations as shall be most conducive to the success of the army acting on the side of New-York ; and that you direct the officer so detached to communicate with, and put himself as soon as possible under the command of, General Howe: you will order such artillery as you shall judge necessary to proceed with this detachment; and, as a great quantity of heavy cannon and military stores were sent, upon the supposition that Quebec might have been in the hands of the rebels, you will, upon requisition from General Howe, supply him with such cannon and stores as may not be wanted for the protection of Canada.

Thoughts for conducting the War from the Side of Canada. No. III.

By Lieutenant-General Burgoyne.

WHEN the last ships came from Quebec, a report prevailed in Canada, said to have been founded upon positive evidence, that the rebels had laid the keels of several large vessels at Skenesborough and Ticonderoga, and had resolved to exert their utmost

A 2   powers

powers to conftruct a new and formidable fleet during the winter.

I will not, however, give credit to their exertions in fuch a degree as to imagine the King's troops will be prevented paffing Lake Champlain early in the fummer, but will fuppofe the operations of the army to begin from Crown-Point.

But as the prefent means to form effectual plans is to lay down every poffible difficulty, I will fuppofe the enemy in great force at Ticonderoga: the different works there are capable of admitting twelve thoufand men.

I will fuppofe him alfo to occupy Lake George with a confiderable naval ftrength, in order to fecure his retreat, and afterwards to retard the campaign; and it is natural to expect that he will take meafures to block up the roads from Ticonderoga to Albany by the way of Skenefborough, by fortifying the ftrong ground at different places, and thereby obliging the King's army to carry a weight of artillery with it; and, by felling trees, breaking bridges, and other obvious impediments, to delay, though he fhould not have power or fpirit finally to refift, its progrefs.

The enemy thus difpofed upon the fide of Canada, it is to be confidered what troops will be neceffary, and what difpofition of them will be moft proper to profecute the campaign with vigour and effect.

I humbly conceive the operating army (I mean exclufively of the troops left for the fecurity of Canada) ought not to confift of lefs than eight thoufand regulars, rank and file. The artillery required in the memorandums of General Carleton, a corps of watermen, two thoufand Canadians, including hatchet-men and other workmen, and one thoufand or more favages.

It is to be hoped that the reinforcement and the victualling-fhips may all be ready to fail from the Channel and from Corke on the laft day of March.

I am

I am perfuaded, that to fail with a fleet of tranfports earlier, is to fubject government to lofs and difappointment. It may reafonably be expected that they will reach Quebec before the 20th of May ; a period in full time for opening the campaign. The roads, and the rivers and lakes, by the melting and running off of the fnows, are in common years impracticable fooner.

But as the weather, long before that time, will probably have admitted of labour in the docks, I will take for granted that the fleet of laft year, as well bateaux as armed veffels, will be found repaired, augmen ed, and fit for immediate fervice. The magazines that remain of provifion (I believe them not to be abundant) will probably be formed at Montreal, Sorel, and Chamblée.

I conceive the firft bufinefs for thofe entrufted with the chief powers, fhould be to felect and poft the troops deftined to remain in Canada ; to throw up the military ftores and provifion with all poffible difpatch, in which fervice the above-mentioned troops, if properly pofted, will greatly affift ; and to draw the army, deftined for operation, to cantonments, within as few days march of St. John's as conveniently may be. I fhould prefer cantonments at that feafon of the year to encampment, as the ground is very damp, and confequently very pernicious to the men, and more efpecially as they will have been for many months before ufed to lodgings, heated with ftoves, or between decks in fhips : all thefe operations may be put in motion together, but they feverally require fome obfervation.

I fhould wifh that the troops left in Canada, fuppofing the number mentioned in my former memorandum to be approved, might be made as follows :

The

Rank and File.

The 31ft regiment, British, exclusive of their light company of grenadiers, — — —	448
Maclean's corps, — — — — — —	300
The 29th regiment, — — — — —	448
The ten additional companies from Great-Britain, — — — — — — —	560
Brunswic and Hesse Hanau to be taken by detachments or complete corps, as Major-General Reidesel shall recommend, leaving the grenadiers, light-infantry, and dragoons, complete, — — — — — —	650
Detachments from the other British brigades, leaving the grenadiers and light infantry complete, and squaring the battalions equally, — — — — — — —	600
	3006

My reason for selecting the 31ft regiment for this duty is, that when I saw it last it was not equally in order with the other regiments for services of activity.

I propose the 29th regiment, as it is not at present brigaded.

I propose Maclean's corps, because I very much apprehend desertion from such parts of it as are composed of Americans, should they come near the enemy.

In Canada, whatsoever may be their disposition, it is not so easy to effect it.

And I propose making up the residue by detachment, because, by selecting the men least calculated for fatigue or least accustomed to it, which may be equally good soldiers in more confined movements and better-provided situations, the effective strength for operation is much greater and the defensive strength not impaired.

I must beg leave to state the expeditious conveyance of provision and stores from Quebec and the several
other

other depositaries, in order to form ample magazines at Crown-Point, as one of the most important operations of the campaign, because it is upon that which most of the rest will depend. If sailing-vessels up the St. Lawrence are alone to be employed, the accident of contrary winds may delay them two months before they pass the Rapids of Richelieu, and afterwards St. Peter's-Lake; delays to that extent are not uncommon, and they are only to be obviated by having a quantity of small craft in readiness to work with oars. From the mouth of the Sorel to Chamblée, rowing and tacking is a sure conveyance if sufficient hands are found. From Chamblée to St. Therese (which is just above the Rapids) land-carriage must be used, and great authority will be requisite to supply the quantity necessary.

A business thus complicated in arrangement, in some parts unusual in practice, and in others perhaps difficult, can only be carried to the desired effect by the peremptory powers, warm zeal, and consonant opinion, of the governor ; and, though the former are not to be doubted, a failure, in the latter, vindicated, or seeming to be vindicated, by the plausible obstructions that will not fail to be suggested by others, will be sufficient to crush such exertions as an officer of a sanguine temper, entrusted with the future conduct of the campaign, and whose personal interest and fame therefore consequentially depend upon a timely out-set, would be led to make.

The assembly of the savages and the Canadians will also entirely depend upon the governor.

Under these considerations, it is presumed, that the general officer, employed to proceed with the army, will be holden to be out of the reach of any possible blame till he is clear of the province of Canada, and furnished with the proposed supplies.

The navigation of Lake Champlain, fecured by the fuperiority of our naval force, and the arrangements for forming proper magazines fo eftablifhed as to make the execution certain, I would not lofe a day to take poffeffion of Crown-Point with Brigadier Frafer's corps, a large body of favages, a body of Canadians, both for fcouts and works, and the beft of our engineers and artificers well fupplied with intrenching tools.

The brigade would be fufficient to prevent infult during the time neceffary for collecting the ftores, forming magazines, and fortifying the pofts; all which fhould be done, to a certain degree, previous to proceeding in force to Ticonderoga; to fuch a degree I mean as may be fuppofed to be effected in time of tranfporting artillery, preparing fafcines, and other neceffaries for artillery operations; and, by keeping the reft of the army back during that period, the tranfport of provifions will be leffened, and the foldiers made of ufe in forwarding the convoys.

But though there would be only one brigade at Crown-Point at that time, it does not follow that the enemy fhould remain in a ftate of tranquillity. Corps of favages, fupported by detatchments of light regulars, fhould be continually on foot to keep them in alarm; and within their works, to cover the reconnoitering of general officers and engineers; and to obtain the beft intelligence of their ftrength, pofition, and defign.

If due exertion is made in the preparations ftated above, it may be hoped that Ticonderoga will be reduced early in the fummer, and it will then become a more proper place for arms than Crown-Point.

The next meafure muft depend upon thofe taken by the enemy, and upon the general plan of the campaign as concerted at home. If it be determined that General Howe's whole forces fhould act upon Hudfon's-River, and to the fouthward of it, and that the only

object

object of the Canada army be to effect a junction with that force, the immediate poffeffion of Lake George would be of great confequence, as the moft expeditious and moft commodious route to Albany; and, fhould the enemy be in force upon that lake, which is very probable, every effort fhould be tried, by throwing favages and light troops round it, to oblige them to quit it without waiting for naval preparations. Should thofe efforts fail, the route by South-Bay and Skenef-borough might be attempted; but confiderable diffi-culties may be expected, as the narrow parts of the river may be eafily choked up and rendered impaffi-ble; and, at beft, there will be neceffity for a great deal of land-carriage for the artillery, provifion, &c. which can only be fupplied from Canada. In cafe of fuccefs alfo by that route, and the enemy not removed from Lake George, it will be neceffary to leave a chain of pofts, as the army proceeds, for the fecurities of your communication, which may too much weaken fo fmall an army.

Left all thefe attempts fhould unavoidably fail, and it become indifpenfably neceffary to attack the enemy by water upon Lake George, the army, at the out-fet, fhould be provided with carriages, implements, and artificers, for conveying armed veffels from Ticonde-roga to the lake.

Thefe ideas are formed upon the fuppofition that it be the fole purpofe of the Canada army to effect a junc-tion with General Howe; or, after co-operating fo far as to get poffeffion of Albany and open the communi-cation to New-York, to remain upon the Hudfon's-River, and thereby enable that general to act with his whole force to the fouthward.

But, fhould the ftrength of the main American ar-my be fuch as to admit of the corps of troops now at Rhode-Ifland remaining there during the winter, and acting feparately in the fpring, it may be highly wor-thy

thy confideration, whether the moſt important purpoſe to which the Canada army could be employed,
ſuppoſing it in poſſeſſion of Ticonderoga, would not
be to gain the Connecticut River.

The extent of country from Ticonderoga to the inhabited country upon that river, oppoſite to Charles-
Town, is about ſixty miles; and, though to convey
artillery and proviſion ſo far by land would be attended
with difficulties, perhaps more than thoſe above ſug-
geſted upon a progreſs to Skeneſborough, ſhould the
object appear worthy, it is to be hoped reſources might
be found; in that caſe, it would be adviſeable to fortify, with one or two ſtrong redoubts, the heights oppoſite to Charles-Town, and eſtabliſh poſts of ſavages
upon the paſſage from Ticonderoga to thoſe heights,
to preſerve the communication, and at the ſame time
prevent any attempt from the country above Charles-
Town, which is very populous, from moleſting the
rear or interrupting the convoys of ſupply, while the
army proceeded down the Connecticut. Should the
junction between the Canada and Rhode-Iſland armies
be effected upon the Connecticut, it is not too ſanguine
an expectation that all the New-England provinces will
be reduced by their operations.

To avoid breaking in upon other matter, I omitted
in the beginning of theſe papers to ſtate the idea of an
expedition at the out-ſet of the campaign, by the Lake
Ontario and Oſwego, to the Mohawk-River; which,
as a diverſion to facilitate every propoſed operation,
would be highly deſirable, provided the army ſhould
be reinforced ſufficiently to afford it.

It may at firſt appear, from a view of the preſent
ſtrength of the army, that it may bear the ſort of detachment propoſed by myſelf laſt year for this purpoſe;
but it is to be conſidered that at that time the utmoſt
object of the campaign, from the advanced ſeaſon and
unavoidable delay of preparation for the lakes, being
the

the reduction of Crown-Point and Ticonderoga, unless the success of my expedition had opened the road to Albany, no greater numbers were necessary than for those first operations. The case in the present year differs; because the season of the year affords a prospect of very extensive operation, and consequently the establishment of many posts, patroles, &c will become necessary. The army ought to be in a state of numbers to bear those drains, and still remain sufficient to attack any thing that probably can be opposed to it.

Nor, to argue from probability, is so much force necessary for this diversion this year as was required for the last; because we then knew that General Schuyler, with a thousand men, was fortified upon the Mohawk. When the different situations of things are considered, viz. the progress of General Howe, the early invasion from Canada, the threatening of the Connecticut from Rhode-Island, &c. it is not to be imagined that any detachment of such force as that of Schuyler can be supplied by the enemy for the Mohawk. I would not therefore propose it of more (and I have great diffidence whether so much can be prudently afforded) than Sir John Johnson's corps, a hundred British from the second brigade, and a hundred more from the 8th regiment, with four pieces of the lightest artillery, and a body of savages; Sir John Johnson to be with a detachment in person, and an able field-officer to command it. I should wish Lieutenant-Colonel St. Leger for that employment.

I particularise the second brigade, because the first is proposed to be diminished by the 31st regiment remaining in Canada, and the rest of the regiment, drafted for the expedition, being made also part of the Canada force, the two brigades will be exactly squared.

Should it appear, upon examination of the really effective numbers of the Canada army, that the force is not sufficient for proceeding upon the above ideas with

a

a fair profpect of fuccefs, the alternative remains of embarking the army at Quebec, in order to effect a junction with General Howe by fea, or to be employed feparately to co-operate with the main defigns, by fuch means as fhould be within their ftrength upon other parts of the continent. And though the army, upon examination of the numbers from the returns here, and the reinforcements defigned, fhould appear adequate, it is humbly fubmitted, as a fecurity againft the poffibility of its remaining inactive, whether it might not be expedient to entruft the latitude of embarking the army by fea to the commander in chief, provided any accidents during the winter, and unknown here, fhould have diminifhed the numbers confiderably; or that the enemy, from any winter fuccefs to the fouthward, fhould have been able to draw fuch forces towards the frontiers of Canada, and take up their ground with fuch precaution, as to render the intended meafure impracticable or too hazardous. But, in that cafe, it muft be confidered that more force would be required to be left behind, for the fecurity of Canada, than is fuppofed to be neceffary when an army is beyond the lakes; and I do not conceive any expedition from the fea can be fo formidable to the enemy, or fo effectual to clofe the war, as an invafion from Canada by Ticonderoga. This laft meafure ought not to be thought of, but upon pofitive conviction of its neceffity.

Hertford-Street,
Feb. 28th, 1777.

J. BURGOYNE.

No. IV. *Extract of a Letter from Lord* George Germain *to General* Carleton, *dated* Whitehall, 26*th* March, 1777.

MY letter of the 22d Auguft, 1776, was intrufted to the care of Captain Le Maitre, one of your aid-decamps; after having been three times in the Gulph of St. Lawrence he had the mortification to find it impoffible

poffible to make his paffage to Quebec, and therefore
returned to England with my difpatch; which, though
it was prevented by that accident from reaching your
hands in due time, I neverthelefs think proper to tranfmit to you by this earlieft opportunity.

You will be informed, by the contents thereof, that,
as foon as you fhould have driven the rebel forces from
the frontiers of Canada, it was his Majefty's pleafure
you fhould return to Quebec, and take with you fuch
part of your army as in your judgement and difcretion
appeared fufficient for the defence of the province;
that you fhould detach Lieutenant-General Burgoyne,
or fuch other officer as you fhould think moft proper,
with the remainder of the troops, and direct the officer
fo detached to proceed with all poffible expedition to
join General Howe, and to put himfelf under his command.

With a view of quelling the rebellion as foon as poffible, it is become highly neceffary that the moft fpeedy
junction of the two armies fhould be effected; and,
therefore, as the fecurity and good government of Canada abfolutely require your prefence there, it is the
King's determination to leave about 3000 men under
your command, for the defence and duties of that
province, and to employ the remainder of your army
upon two expeditions, the one under the command of
Lieutenant-General Burgoyne, who is to force his way
to Albany; and the other under the command of Lieutenant-Colonel St. Leger, who is to make a diverfion
on the Mohawk-River.

As this plan cannot be advantageoufly executed
without the affiftance of Canadians and Indians, his
Majefty ftrongly recommends it to your care, to furnifh both expeditions with good and fufficient bodies
of thofe men; and I am happy in knowing that your
influence among them is fo great, that there can be no

room

room to apprehend you will find it difficult to fulfil his Majesty's expectations.

In order that no time may be lost in entering upon these important undertakings, General Burgoyne has received orders to sail forthwith for Quebec ; and that the intended operations may be maturely considered, and afterwards carried on in such a manner as is most likely to be followed by success, he is directed to consult with you upon the subject, and to form and adjust the plan as you both shall think most conducive to his Majesty's service.

I am also to acquaint you, that, as soon as you shall have fully regulated every thing relative to these expeditions, (and the King relies upon your zeal, that you will be as expeditious as the nature of the business will admit,) it is his Majesty's pleasure that you detain, for the Canada service,

The 8th regiment, deducting 100 for the expedition to the Mohawk, — — — —	460
Battalion companies of the 29th and 31st regiments, — — — — — — —	896
Battalion companies of the 34th, deducting 100 for the expedition to the Mohawk, — —	348
Eleven additional companies from Great-Britain,	616
Detachments from the two brigades, — —	300
Detachments from the German troops, — —	650
Royal Highland emigrants, — — — —	500
	3770

You will naturally conclude that this allotment for Canada has not been made without properly weighing the several duties which are likely to be required. His Majesty has not only considered the several garrisons and posts which probably it may be necessary for you to take ; *viz* Quebec, Chaudiere, the disaffected parishes of Point Levi, Montreal, and posts between that town

town and Ofwegatche, Trois Rivieres, St. John's, Sele aux Noix, La Prairie, Vergere, and fome other towns upon the fouth fhore of St. Lawrence, oppofite the ifle of Montreal, with pofts of communication to St. John's, but he hath alfo reflected that the feveral operations, which will be carrying on in different parts of America, muft neceffarily confine the attention of the rebels to the refpective fcenes of action, and fecure Canada from external attacks; and that the internal quiet which at prefent prevails is not likely to be interrupted, or, if interrupted, will foon be reftored by your influence over the inhabitants; he therefore trufts that 3000 men will be quite fufficient to anfwer every poffible demand.

It is likewife his Majefty's pleafure that you put under the command of Lieutenant-General Burgoyne,

The grenadiers and light infantry of the army (except of the 8th regiment and the 24th regiment) as the advanced corps, under the command of Brigadier-General Frafer, — 1568
Firft brigade, battalion companies of the 9th, 21ft, and 47th, regiments, deducting a detachment of 50 from each corps, to remain in Canada, — — — — — — 1194
Second brigade, battalion companies of the 20th, 53d, and 62d, regiments, deducting 50 from each corps, to remain as above, — 1194
All the German troops, except the Hanau chaffeurs, and a detachment of 650, — — 3217
The artillery, except fuch parts as fhall be neceffary for the defence of Canada.

———
7173
———

Together with as many Canadians and Indians as may be thought neceffary for this fervice; and, after having furnifhed him in the fulleft and completeft manner with

with artillery, ftores, provifions, and every other article neceffary for his expedition, and fecured to him
every affiftance which it is in your power to afford and
procure, you are to give him orders to pafs Lake
Champlain ; and from thence, by the moft vigorous
exertion of the force under his command, to proceed
with all expedition to Albany, and put himfelf under
the command of Sir William Howe.

From the King's knowledge of the great preparations made by you laft year to fecure the command of
the lakes, and your attention to this part of the fervice during the winter, his Majefty is led to expect
that every thing will be ready for General Burgoyne's
paffing the lakes by the time you and he fhall have ad-
jufted the plan of the expedition.

It is the King's farther pleafure that you put under
the command of Lieutenant-Colonel St. Leger,

Detachment from the 8th regiment, — — —	100
Detachment from the 34th regiment, — —	100
Sir John Johnfon's regiment of New-York, —	133
Hanau chaffeurs, — — — — — —	342
	675

Together with a fufficient number of Canadians and
Indians ; and, after having furnifhed him with proper
artillery, ftores, provifions, and every other neceffary
article for his expedition, and fecured to him every affiftance in your power to afford and procure, you are
to give him orders to proceed forthwith to and down
the Mohawk-River to Albany, and put himfelf under
the command of Sir William Howe.

I fhall write to Sir William Howe, from hence, by
the firft packet ; but you will, neverthelefs, endeavour
to give him the earlieft intelligence of this meafure ;
and alfo direct Lieutenant-General Burgoyne and Lieutenant-Colonel St. Leger to neglect no opportunity of
doing

doing the fame, that they may receive inftructions from Sir William Howe. You will, at the fame time, inform them, that, until they fhall have received orders from Sir William Howe, it is his Majefty's pleafure that they act as exigences may require, and in fuch manner as they fhall judge moft proper for making an impreffion on the rebels, and bringing them to obedience; but that, in fo doing, they muft never lofe view of their intended junctions with Sir William Howe as their principal objects.

In cafe Lieutenant-General Burgoyne or Lieutenant-Colonel St. Leger fhould happen to die, or be rendered, through illnefs, incapable of executing thofe great trufts, you are to nominate, to their refpective commands, fuch officer or officers as you fhall think beft qualified to fupply the place of thofe whom his Majefty has, in his wifdom, at prefent appointed to conduct thefe expeditions.

Copy of a Letter from Lieutenant-General Burgoyne *to* No. V. *Lord* George Germain, *dated* Quebec, May 14, 1777.

My Lord,   [Private.]

I TAKE the opportunity of a veffel, difpatched by Sir Guy Carleton to England, to inform your Lordfhip of my arrival here the 6th inftant. And though my prefent fituation, as acting under a fuperior upon the fpot, may make an official correfpondence unneceffary, I cannot perfuade myfelf I fhall not appear guilty of impropriety in affuming the honour of a private and confidential one, relative to the objects of my deftination.

From my prefent information, I have reafon to expect the preparations for opening the campaign to be very forward on our part. Due exertions were ufed in the courfe of the winter, and the uncommon mild-

B   nefs

nefs of the weather greatly favoured them, to convey
provifions to Chamblée and St. John's. One large
victualler arrived after I left the St. Lawrence laft November; all refidues of other victuallers have been
collected; I am in hopes of finding a fufficiency of
provifion to enable me to crofs the Lake Champlain
at leaft, without the arrival of the Corke fleet. I hope
alfo to find artillery-ftores enough to feel the pulfe of
the enemy at Ticonderoga. Should their fituation
and refolution be fuch as to make great artillery preparations requifite, I fhall certainly be under the neceffity of waiting, at Crown-Point, the arrival of the
ordnance fhips from England. A good body of the
Indians, I am affured, are ready to move upon the
firft call, and meafures are taking for bringing them
forthwith to proper rendezvous.

I cannot fpeak with fo much confidence of the military affiftance I am to look for from the Canadians. The
only corps yet inftituted, or that I am informed can at
prefent be inftituted, are three independent companies
of 100 men each, officered by Seigneurs of the country, who are well chofen; but they have not been
able to engage many volunteers. The men are chiefly
drafted from the militia, according to a late regulation
of the legiflative council. Thofe I have yet feen afford no promife of ufe of arms; — aukward, ignorant,
difinclined to the fervice, and fpiritlefs. Various reafons are affigned for this change in the natives fince the
time of the French government. It may partly be
owing to a difufe of arms, but I believe principally to
the unpopularity of their Seigneurs, and to the poifon
which the emiffaries of the rebels have thrown into
their minds. Should I find the new companies up the
country better compofed, or that the well-affected parties can be prevailed upon to turn out volunteers,
though but for a fhort occafion, as they did laft year,
I fhall

I fhall move Sir Guy Carleton to exert farther meafures to augment my numbers.

The army will fall fhort of the ftrength computed
in England; the want of camp-equipage, clothing,
and many other neceffary articles, will caufe inconvenience; I have neverthelefs determined to put the troops,
deftined for my command, immediately in motion;
and, affifted by the fpirit and health in which they
abound, I am confident in the profpect of overcoming
difficulties and difappointments.

Having fettled all meafures with Sir Guy Carleton,
both for this purpofe and for the expeditious tranfport
of the ftores as they may arrive; and having already
difpatched inftructions to Captain Lutwidge, who commands the fleet upon Lake Champlain, to fecure the
navigation, in which I clearly fee he will find no
trouble, I fhall proceed in perfon this afternoon for
Montreal; and from thence make my final arrangements for purfuing the King's orders.

I fhould think myfelf deficient in juftice and in honour, were I to clofe my letter without mentioning the
fenfe I entertain of General Carleton's conduct; that
he was anxioufly defirous of leading the military operations out of the province, is eafily to be difcerned;
but his deference to his Majefty's decifion, and his
zeal to give effect to his meafures in my hands, are
equally manifeft, exemplary, and fatisfactory. I fhall
take every poffible means to tranfmit to your Lordfhip
an account of my proceedings from time to time. And
have the honour to be, with perfect refpect,

Your Lordfhip's moft obedient

And moft humble fervant,

J. BURGOYNE.

P. S. I have mentioned nothing of intelligence concerning the enemy, concluding that Sir Guy Carleton

B 2

will

will tranfmit the material part of it, and in a manner
more full than in my power to do.   I underftand they
have laboured hard to ftrengthen Ticonderoga, and
threaten a vigorous refiftance there ; and that they have
built fome veffels on Lake George, as your Lordfhip
may remember I had forefeen.

Second   *Copy of a Letter from Lieutenant-General* Burgoyne *to*
No. V.   *Lord* George Germain, *dated* Montreal, May 19,
            1777.

My Lord,

I HAD the honour to write to your Lordfhip the
day I left Quebec ; having reafon to imagine this letter
may reach that place in time to be difpatched with my
former one, I cannot omit the occafion to inform your
Lordfhip, that the hopes I expreffed of being able to
put the troops in motion, without waiting the arrival
of the fleets from England and Ireland, are confirmed.

The only delay is occafioned by the impracticability
of the roads, owing to late extraordinary heavy rains ;
and this difficulty will be fpeedily removed, by exerting the fervices of the parifhes as foon as the weather
clears.   In the mean time, I am employing every
means, that water-carriage will admit of, for drawing
the troops and ftores towards their point.   I truft I
fhall have veffels fufficient to move the army and ftores
together ; and, in that cafe, will take poft at once,
within fight of Ticonderoga, and only make ufe of
Crown-Point for my hofpital and magazine.

A continuation of intelligence, from different fpies
and deferters, confirms the defign of the enemy to difpute Ticonderoga vigoroufly.   They are alfo building
bow-gallies at Fort George, for the defence of that
Lake, &c. fortifying on the road to Skenefborough.

It is configned to the New-England colonies to
furnifh fupplies of men and provifion to oppofe the
progrefs

progress of my army; and they have undertaken the task, upon condition of being exempt from supplying Mr. Washington's main army.

It is my design, while advancing to Ticonderoga, and during the siege of that post, (for a siege I apprehend it must be,) to give all possible jealousy on the side of Connecticut. If I can, by manœuvre, lead the enemy to suspect, that, after the reduction of Ticonderoga, my views are pointed that way, the Connecticut forces will be very cautious of leaving their own frontier, and I may gain a start that may much expedite and facilitate my progress to Albany.

Your Lordship may rest assured, that, whatever demonstration I may endeavour to impose on the enemy, I shall *really* make no movement that can procrastinate the great object of my orders.

I have the honour to be, &c.

J. BURGOYNE.

Substance of the Speech of Lieutenant-General Burgoyne **No. VI.** *to the* Indians, *in Congress, at the Camp upon the River* Bouquet, June 21, 1777; *and their Answer, translated.*

[*In Lieutenant-General* Burgoyne's, June 22, 1777.]

CHIEFS and WARRIORS,

THE great King, our common father, and the patron of all who seek and deserve his protection, has considered, with satisfaction, the general conduct of the Indian tribes from the beginning of the troubles in America. Too sagacious and too faithful to be deluded or corrupted, they have observed the violated rights of the parental power they love, and burned to vindicate them. A few individuals alone, the refuse of a small tribe, at the first were led astray; and the mis-

B 3   representations,

reprefentations, the fpecious allurements, the infidious promifes, and diverfified plots, in which the rebels are exercifed, and all of which they employed for that effect, have ferved only in the end to enhance the honour of the tribes in general, by demonftrating to the world how few and how contemptible are the apoftates. It is a truth known to you all, that, thefe pitiful examples excepted, (and they probably have before this day hid their faces in fhame,) the collective voices and hands of the Indian tribes, over this vaft continent, are on the fide of juftice, of law, and of the King.

The reftraint you have put upon your refentment in waiting the King your father's call to arms, the hardeft proof, I am perfuaded, to which your affection could have been put, is another manifeft and affecting mark of your adherence to that principle of connection, to which you were always fond to allude, and which it is mutually the joy and the duty of the parent to cherifh.

The clemency of your father has been abufed, the offers of his mercy have been defpifed, and his farther patience would, in his eyes, become culpable, in-as-much as it would withhold redrefs from the moft grievous oppreffions in the provinces that ever difgraced the hiftory of mankind. It therefore remains for me, the General of one of his Majefty's armies, and in this council his reprefentative, to releafe you from thofe bonds which your obedience impofed. — Warriors, you are free ; — go forth in might of your valour and your caufe ; — ftrike at the common enemies of Great-Britain and America ; — difturbers of public order, peace, and happinefs ; deftroyers of commerce ; parricides of the ftate.

The circle round you, the chiefs of his Majefty's European forces, and of the Princes, his allies, efteem you as brothers in the war : emulous in glory and in friendfhip, we will endeavour reciprocally to give and

to

to receive examples; we know how to value, and we will ftrive to imitate, your perfeverance in enterprife, and your conftancy to refift hunger, wearinefs, and pain. Be it our tafk, from the dictates of our religion, the laws of our warfare, and the principles and intereft of our policy, to regulate your paffions when they overbear, to point out where it is nobler to fpare than to revenge, to difcriminate degrees of guilt, to fufpend the up-lifted ftroke, to chaftife and not to deftroy.

This war to you, my friends, is new; upon all former occafions, in taking the field, you held yourfelves authorifed to deftroy wherever you came, becaufe every where you found an enemy. The cafe is now very different.

The King has many faithful fubjects difperfed in the provinces, confequently you have many brothers there; and thefe people are the more to be pitied, that they are perfecuted or imprifoned wherever they are difcovered or fufpected; and to diffemble is, to a generous mind, a yet more grievous punifhment.

Perfuaded that your magnanimity of character, joined to your principles of affection to the King, will give me fuller controul over your minds than the military rank with which I am invefted, I enjoin your moft ferious attention to the rules which I hereby proclaim for your invariable obfervation during the campaign.

I pofitively forbid bloodfhed, when you are not oppofed in arms.

Aged men, women, children, and prifoners, muft be held facred from the knife or hatchet, even in the time of actual conflict.

You fhall receive compenfation for the prifoners you take, but you fhall be called to account for fcalps.

In conformity and indulgence of your cuftoms, which have affixed an idea of honour to fuch badges of victory, you fhall be allowed to take the fcalps of the dead, when

B 4   killed

killed by your fire and in fair oppofition ; but, on no account, or pretence, or fubtlety, or p evarication, are they to be taken from the wounded, or even dying ; and ftill lefs pardonable, if pofible, will it be held, to kill men in that condition on purpofe, and upon a fuppofition that this protection to the wounded would be thereby evaded.

Bafe lurking affaffins, incendiaries, ravagers and plunderers of the country, to whatever army they may belong, fhall be treated with lefs referve ; but the la-titude muft be given you by order, and I muft be the judge of the occafion.

Should the enemy, on their part, dare to counte-nance acts of barbarity towards thofe who may fall in-to their hands, it fhall be yours alfo to retaliate ; but, till feverity be thus compelled, bear immoveable in your hearts this folid maxim, (it cannot be too deeply impreffed,) that the great effential reward, worthy fer-vice of your alliance, the fincerity of your zeal to the King, your father and never-failing protector, will be examined and judged upon the teft only of your fteady and uniform adherence to the orders and coun-fels of thofe, to whom his Majefty has entrufted the direction and the honour of his arms.

Anſwer from an old Chief of the Iroquois.

I STAND up in the name of all the nations prefent, to affure our father that we have attentively liftened to his difcourfe. We receive you as our father ; be-caufe, when you fpeak, we hear the voice of our great father beyond the great lake.

We rejoice in the approbation you have expreffed of our behaviour.

We have been tried and tempted by the Boftonians ; but we have loved our father, and our hatchets have been fharpened upon our affections.

In

In proof of the fincerity of our proffeffions, our whole villages, able to go to war, are come forth. The old and infirm, our infants and wives, alone remain at home.

With one common affent we promife a conftant obedience to all you have ordered, and all you fhall order; and may the Father of Days give you many and fuccefs.

Copy of a Letter from Lieutenant-General Burgoyne *to* No. VII.
Lord George Germain, *dated* Skenefborough, July 11th, 1777.

I HAVE the honour to inform your Lordfhip, that the enemy were diflodged from Ticonderago and Mount Independence on the 6th inftant, and were driven, on the fame day, beyond Skenefborough on the right, and to Humerton on the left, with the lofs of 128 pieces of cannon, all their armed veffels and bateaux, the greateft part of their baggage and ammunition, provifion, and military ftores, to a very large amount.

This fuccefs has been followed by events equally fortunate and rapid. I fubjoin fuch a detail of circumftances as the time will permit; and, for his Majefty's farther information, I beg leave to refer your Lordfhip to Captain Gardner, my aid-de-camp, whom I thought it neceffary to difpatch with news fo important to the King's fervice, and fo honourable to the troops under my command.

Journal of the late principal Proceedings of the Army.

Having remained at Crown-Point three days, to bring up the rear of the army, and to eftablifh the magazines and the hofpital, and to obtain intelligence of the enemy, on the 30th June
I ordered the advanced corps, confifting of the Britifh light-infantry and grenadiers, the 24th regiment,

ment, fome Canadians and Savages, and ten pieces
of light artillery, under the command of Brigadier-
General Frafer, to move from Putnam-Creek, where
they had been encamped fome days, up the weft fhore
of the lake to Four-Mile-Point, fo called from being
within that diftance off the fort of Ticonderoga. The
German referve, confifting of the Brunfwic chaffeurs,
light-infantry, and grenadiers, under Lieutenant-Colonel Breyman, were moved at the fame time to Richard-
fon's farm, on the eaft fhore, oppofite to Putnam-
Creek.

1ft July.　　The whole army made a movement forward.　Brigadier Frafer's corps occupied the ftrong poft, called
Three-Mile-Point, on the weft fhore ; the German referve, the eaft fhore oppofite : the army encamped in
two lines ; the right wing at the Four-Mile Point, the
left wing nearly oppofite, on the eaft fhore.

The Royal-George and Inflexible frigates, with the
gun-boats, were anchored at this time juft without the
reach of the enemy's batteries, and covered the lake
from the weft to the eaft fhores.　The reft of the fleet
had been fome time without guns, in order to affift in
carrying provifions over Lake Champlain.

The enemy appeared to be pofted as follows.　A
brigade occupied the old French lines on the height,
to the north of the fort of Ticonderoga.　Thefe lines
were in good repair, and had feveral intrenchments
behind them, chiefly calculated to guard the north-
weft flank, and were farther fuftained by a block-houfe.
They had, farther to their left, a poft at the faw-mills,
which are at the foot of the carrying-place to Lake
George, and a block-houfe upon an eminence above
the mills, and a block-houfe and hofpital at the entrance of the lake.

Upon the right of the lines, and between them and
the old fort, there were two new block-houfes, and a
confiderable battery clofe to the water edge.

It

It feemed that the enemy had employed their chief induſtry, and were in the greateſt force, upon Mount Independence, which is high and circular; and upon the ſummit, which is Table Land, was a ſtar fort, made of pickets, and well ſupplied with artillery, and a large ſquare of barracks within it. The foot of the hill, on the ſide which projects into the lake, was in-trenched, and had a ſtrong abattis cloſe to the water. This intrenchment was lined with heavy artillery, poin-ted down the lake, flanking the water-battery, above deſcribed, and ſuſtained by another battery about half-way up the hill. On the weſt ſide of the hill runs the main river, and in its paſſage is joined by the water which comes down from Lake George. The enemy had here a bridge of communication, which could not at this time be reconnoitred. On the eaſt ſide of the hill the water forms a ſmall bay, into which falls a ri-vulet, after having encircled in its courſe part of the hill to the ſouth eaſt. The ſide to the ſouth could not be ſeen, but was deſcribed as inacceſſible.

About nine in the morning a ſmoke was obſerved July 2. towards Lake George, and the Savages brought in a report, that the enemy had ſet fire to the farther block-houſe, and had abandoned the ſaw-mills, and that a conſiderable body was advancing, from the lines, to-wards a bridge upon the road which led from the ſaw-mills, towards the right of the Britiſh camp. A de-tachment of the advanced corps was immediately put in march, under the command of Brigadier Fraſer, ſupported by the ſecond brigade and ſome light artil-lery, under the command of Major-General Phillips, with orders to proceed to Mount Hope, which is to the north of the lines, to reconnoitre the enemy's poſition, and to take advantage of any poſt they might abandon or be driven from. The Indians, under Captain Fra-ſer, ſupported by his company of markſmen, were di-rected to make a circuit to the left of Brigadier Fraſer's line

line of march, and endeavoured to cut off the retreat of the enemy to their lines; but this design miscarried through the impetuosity of the Indians, who attacked too soon, and in front; and the enemy was thereby able to retire with the loss of one officer and a few men killed, and one officer wounded. Major-General Phillips took possession of the very advantageous post of Mount Hope this night, and the enemy was thereby entirely cut off from all communication with Lake George.

July 3. Mount Hope was occupied in force by General Fraser's whole corps; the first British brigade and two entire brigades of artillery. The second brigade, British, encamped upon the left of the first, and the brigade of Gall, having been drawn from the east shore, to occupy the ground where Fraser's corps had originally been, the line became complete, extending from Three-Mile-Point to the westernmost part of Mount Hope: on the same day, Major-General Reidesel encamped on the east shore, in a parallel line with Three-Mile-Point, having pushed the reserve forward, near the rivulet which encircles Mount Independence. The enemy cannonaded the camps of Mount Hope and of the German reserve during most part of this day, but without effect.

July 4. The army worked hard at their communications, and got up the artillery, tents, baggage, and provisions: the enemy, at intervals, continued the cannonade upon the camps, which was not in any instance returned.

The Thunderer radeau, carrying the battering train and stores, having been warped up from Crown-Point, arrived this day, and immediately began to land the artillery.

July 5. Lieutenant Twiss, the commanding engineer, was ordered to reconnoitre Sugar-Hill, on the south side of the communication from Lake George into Lake Champlain, which had been possessed in the night by a party ty of light infantry. It appeared at firſt to be a very advantageous poſt, and it is now known that the enemy had a council, ſome time ago, upon the expediency of poſſeſſing it; but the idea was rejected, upon the ſuppoſition that it was impoſſible for a corps to be eſtabliſhed there in force. Lieutenant Twiſs reported this hill to have the entire command of the works and buildings both of Ticonderoga and Mount Independence, at the diſtance of about 1400 yards from the former, and 1500 from the latter; that the ground might be levelled, ſo as to receive cannon, and that the road to convey them, though difficult, might be made practicable, in twenty-four hours. This hill alſo commanded, in reverſe, the bridge of communication, ſaw the exact ſituation of their veſſels, nor could the enemy, during the day, make any material movement or preparation, without being diſcovered, and even having their numbers counted.

It was determined that a battery ſhould be raiſed on Sugar-Hill for light twenty-four pounders, medium twelves, and eight-inch howitzers. This very arduous work was carried on ſo rapidly, that the battery would have been ready the next day.

It is a duty in this place to do ſome juſtice to the zeal and activity of Major-General Phillips, who had the direction of the operation; and, having mentioned that moſt valuable officer, I truſt it cannot be thought a digreſſion to add, that it is to his judicious arrangements and indefatigable pains, during the general ſuperintendency of preparation, which Sir Guy Carleton entruſted to him in the winter and ſpring, that the ſervice is indebted for its preſent forwardneſs. The prevalence of contrary winds and other accidents having rendered it impoſſible for any neceſſaries, prepared in England for the opening of the campaign, yet to reach the camp.

Soon

Soon after day-light, an officer arrived exprefs on-board the Royal George, where in the night I took up my quarters as the moft centrical fituation, with information from Brigadier Frafer, that the enemy was retiring, and that he was advancing with his picquets, leaving orders for the brigade to follow, as foon as they could accoutre, with intention to purfue by land. This movement was very difcernible, as were the Britifh colours, which the Brigadier had fixed upon the fort of Ticonderoga. Knowing how fafely I could truft to that officer's conduct, I turned my chief attention to the purfuit by water, by which route I underftood one column was retiring, in two hundred and twenty bateaux, covered by five armed galleys.

The great bridge of communication, through which a way was to be opened, was fupported by twenty-two funken piers of large timber, at nearly equal diftances; the fpace between was made of feparate floats, each about fifty feet long, and twelve feet wide, ftrongly faftened together by chains and rivets, and alfo faftened to the funken piers. Before this bridge was a boom, made of very large pieces of timber, faftened together by riveted bolts and double chains, made of iron an inch and a half fquare.

The gun-boats were inftantly moved forward, and the boom and one of the intermediate floats were cut with great dexterity and difpatch, and Commodore Lutwidge, with the officers and feamen in his department, partaking the general animation, a paffage was formed in half an hour for the frigates alfo, through impediments which the enemy had been labouring to conftruct fince laft autumn.

During this operation, Major General Reidefel had paffed to Mount Independence, with the corps, Breyman, and part of the left wing. He was directed to proceed by land, to fuftain Brigadier Frafer, or to act more to the left if he faw it expedient fo to do.

The

The 62d regiment, Britifh, and the Brunfwic regiment of Prince Frederick, were ftationed at Ticonderoga and Mount Independence, in the place of the parties of Frafer's brigade which had been left in pofſeſſion of the artillery and ſtores; and the reſt of the army was ordered to follow up the river as they could be collected, without regard to the place in the line.

About three in the afternoon I arrived, with the Royal George and Inflexible, and the beſt ſailing gun-boats, at South Bay, within three miles of Skeneſborough, at which latter place the enemy were poſted in a ſtockaded fort, and their armed gallies in the falls below.

The foremoſt regiments, viz. the 9th, 20th, and 21ſt, were immediately diſembarked, and aſcended the mountains with the intention of getting behind the fort and cutting off the retreat of the enemy; but their precipitate flight rendered this manœuvre ineffectual. The gun-boats and frigates continued their courſe to Skeneſborough Falls, where the armed veſſels were poſted. Captain Carter, with part of his brigade of gun-boats, immediately attacked, and with ſo much ſpirit, that two of the veſſels very ſoon ſtruck; the other three were blown up; and the enemy, having previouſly prepared combuſtible materials, ſet fire to the fort, mills, ſtorehouſes, bateaux, &c. and retired with the detachment left for that purpoſe, the main body having gone off when the troops were aſcending the mountain. A great quantity of proviſions and ſome arms were here conſumed, and moſt of their officers' baggage was burnt, ſunk, or taken. Their loſs is not known; about 30 priſoners were made, among which were two wounded officers.

During theſe operations upon the right, Brigadier General Fraſer continued his purſuit to Caſtletown till one o'clock, having marched, in a very hot day,

from

from four o'clock in the morning till that time. Some stragglers of the enemy were picked up, from whom the Brigadier learned, that their rear guard was composed of chosen men, and commanded by Colonel Francis, one of their best officers. During the time that the men were refreshing, Major General Reidesel came up, and, arrangements for continuing the pursuit having been concerted, Brigadier Fraser moved forward again, and during the night lay upon his arms, in an advantageous situation, three miles nearer the enemy.

7th July. At three in the morning he renewed his march, and about five his advanced scouts discovered the enemy's centries, who fired their pieces and joined the main body. The Brigadier, observing a commanding ground to the left of his light infantry, immediately ordered it to be possessed by that corps; and, a considerable body of the enemy attempting the same, they met. The enemy were driven back to their original post; the advanced guard, under Major Grant, was by this time engaged, and the grenadiers were advanced to sustain them and to prevent the right flank from being turned. The Brigadier remained on the left, where the enemy long defended themselves by the aid of logs and trees; and, after being repulsed, and prevented getting to the Castletown road, by the grenadiers, they rallied and renewed the action; and, upon a second repulse, attempted their retreat by Pitsford Mountain. The grenadiers scrambled up a part of that ascent, appearing almost inaccessible, and gained the summit before them, which threw them into confusion. They were still greatly superior in numbers, and consequently in extent; and the Brigadier, in momentary expectation of the Brunswickers, had laterally drawn from his left to support his right. At this critical moment, General Reidesel, who had pressed on, upon hearing the firing, arrived with the foremost

foremost of his columns, viz. the chaffeurs company and eighty grenadiers and light infantry. His judgement immediately pointed to him the course to take; he extended upon Brigadier Frafer's left flank. The chaffeurs got into action with great gallantry under Major Barner. They fled on all fides, leaving dead upon the field Colonel Francis and many other officers, with upwards of 200 men; above 600 were wounded, moft of whom perifhed in the woods attempting to get off; and one colonel, feven captains, ten fubalterns, and 210 men, were made prifoners; above 200 ftands of arms were alfo taken.

The number of the enemy before the engagement amounted to 2000 men. The Britifh detachment under Brigadier General Frafer (the parties left the day before at Ticonderoga not having been able to join) confifted only of 850 fighting men.

The bare relation of fo fignal an action is fufficient for its praife. Should the attack againft fuch inequality of numbers, before the German brigade came up, feem to require explanation, it is to be confidered, that the enemy might have efcaped by delay; that the advanced guard on a fudden found themfelves too near the enemy to avoid action without retreating; and that Brigadier Frafer had fuppofed the German troops to be very near. The difference of time in their arrival was merely accidental. The Germans pufhed for a fhare in the glory, and they arrived in time to obtain it. I have only to add, that the exertions of Brigadier Frafer on this day were but a continuance of that uniform intelligence, activity, and bravery, which diftinguifh his character upon all occafions, and entitle him to be recommended in the moft particular manner to his Majefty's favour.

The officers and foldiers of this brigade have prevented any diftinctions of individuals by a general and equal difplay of fpirit.

C

The

The country people about Skenefborough having reported that part of the enemy were ftill retreating, the 9th regiment was detached, with orders to take poft near Fort Anne and obferve the enemy's motions. This was effected, but with great difficulty, as the roads were almoft impracticable and the bridges broken. The other troops were employed all that day and night in dragging fifty bateaux over the carrying-place at Wood Creek, to facilitate the movement of the reft of the firft brigade to Fort Anne to diflodge the enemy.

8th July.

A report was received from Lieutenant Colonel Hill (9th regiment) that the enemy had been reinforced in the night by a confiderable body of frefh men; that he could not retire with his regiment before them, but he would maintain his ground. The two remaining regiments of the firft brigade were ordered to quicken their march, and upon fecond intelligence of the enemy, and firing being heard, the 20th regiment was ordered forward with two pieces of artillery, and Major General Phillips was fent to take the command. A violent ftorm of rain, which lafted the whole day, prevented the troops from getting to Fort Anne fo foon as was intended; but the delay gave the 9th regiment an opportunity of diftinguifhing themfelves, by ftanding and repulfing an attack of fix times their number. The enemy, finding the pofition not to be forced in front, endeavoured to turn it; and, from the fuperiority of their numbers, that inconvenience was to be apprehended; and Lieutenant Colonel Hill found it neceffary to change his pofition in the height of action. So critical an order was executed by the regiment with the utmoft fteadinefs and bravery. The enemy, after an attack of three hours, were totally repulfed, and fled toward Fort Edward, fetting fire to Fort Anne, but leaving

a faw-a faw-mill and a block-houfe in good repair, which were afterwards poffeffed by the king's troops.

The 9th regiment acquired, during their expedition, about thirty prifoners, fome ftores and baggage, and the colours of the 2d Hampfhire regiment.

One unlucky accident happened, to counterbalance in fome degree this fuccefs. Captain Montgomery, an officer of great merit, was wounded early in the action, and was in the act of being dreffed by the furgeon when the regiment changed ground; being unable to help himfelf, he and the furgeon were taken prifoners. I fince hear he has been well treated, and is in a fair way of recovery at Albany.

The army, very much fatigued, (many parts of it having wanted their provifions for two days, almoft the whole their tents and baggage,) affembled in their prefent pofition. The right wing occupies the heights of Skenefborough in two lines; the right flank to the mountains, covered by the regiment of Reidefel's dragoons, *en potence*; the left to the Wood Creek. *9th and 10th July.*

The Brunfwick troops under Major General Reidefel upon Caftletown River, with Breyman's corps upon the communication of roads leading to Putney and Rutland, the regiment of Heffe Hanau, are pofted at the head of Eaft Creek, to preferve the communication with the camp at Caftletown river and fecure the bateaux.

Brigadier Frafer's corps is in the center, and ready to move on either wing of the army.

The fcattered remains of the enemy are at Fort Edward, on the Hudfon's River, where they have been joined, as I am informed, by General Putnam with a confiderable corps of frefh troops.

Roads are opening for the army to march to them by Fort Anne, and the Wood Creek is clearing of fallen trees, funken ftones, and other obftacles, to give paffage to bateaux for carrying artillery, ftores,

C 2 provifions,

provifions, and camp equipage. Thefe are laboricus works, but the fpirit and zeal of the troops are fufficient to furmount them. Some little time muft alfo be allowed for the fupplies of provifions to overtake us. In the mean time all poffible diligence is ufing at Ticonderoga to get the gun-boats, provifion-veffels, and a proper quantity of bateaux, into Lake George. A corps of the army will be ordered to penetrate by that route, which will afterwards be the route for the magazines ; and a junction of the whole is intended at Fort Edward.

I tranfmit to your Lordfhip herewith, returns of the killed and wounded, and lifts of fuch parts of provifions and ftores, taken from the enemy, as could be collected in fo fhort a time.

I have the honour to be, with the greateft refpect,

Your Lordfhip's, &c.

No. VIII. *Copy of a Letter from Lieutenant General* Burgoyne *to Lord* George Germaine, *dated* Skenefborough, July 11, 1777.

[Private.]

My Lord,

H A V I N G given your Lordfhip a detail, in my public letter of this date, of the late tranfactions, I now do myfelf the honour to ftate to your Lordfhip fuch circumftances as appear to me more proper for a private communication.

Mr. Peters and Mr. Jeffup, who came over to Canada laft autumn, and propofed to raife battalions, one from the neighbourhood of Albany, the other from Charlotte county, are confident of fuccefs as the army advances. Their battalions are now in embryo, but very promifing ; they have fought, and with fpirit. Sir Guy Carleton has given me blank commiffions

commiffions for the officers to fill up occafionally; and the agreement with them is, that the commiffions are not to be fo effective till two thirds of the battalions are raifed. Some hundreds of men, a third part of them with arms, have joined me fince I penetrated this place, profeffing themfelves loyalifts, and wifhing to ferve, fome to the end of the war, fome for the campaign. Though I am without inftructions upon this fubject, I have not hefitated to receive them, and, as faft as companies can be formed, I fhall poft the officers till a decifion can be made upon the meafure by my fuperiors. I mean to employ them particularly upon detachments for keeping the country in awe and procuring cattle. Their real ufe I expect will be great in the prefervation of the national troops; but the impreffion which will be caufed upon public opinion, fhould provincials be feen acting vigoroufly in the caufe of the King, will be yet more advantageous, and I truft fully juftify the expence.

The manifefto, of which I enclofed your Lordfhip a copy in my laft difpatches, and herewith fend a duplicate, has great effect where the country is not in the power of the rebels; where it is, the committees turn all their efforts to counteract it. They watch or imprifon all fufpected perfons, compel the people in general to take arms, and to drive the cattle, and to burn the corn, under penalty of immediate death. Great numbers have been hanged. Should thefe wretches fucceed to make a defert of the country by fire and maffacre, it will at leaft be a pleafing reflection, that, while advantages are reaped from the clement part of the manifefto, they, and not the King's troops, are the executioners of its threats.

Your Lordfhip will have obferved I have made no mention of the Indians in the purfuit from Ticonderoga. It is not poffible to draw them in many ref-

pects

pects from the plunder of that place, and I confidentially acknowledge this is not the only inftance in
which I have found little more than a name. If, under the management of their conductors, they are indulged, for interefted reafons, in all the caprices and
humours of fpoiled children, like them they grow
more unreafonable and importunate upon every new favour. Were they left to themfelves, enormities too
horrid to think of would enfue: guilty and innocent,
women and infants, would be a common prey.

This is the character of the lower Canadian Indians, who alone have been with the army hitherto.
I am informed the Outawas, and other remote nations, who are within two days march of joining me,
are more brave and more tractable; that they profefs
war, not pillage. They are under the directions of a
M. St. Luc, a Canadian gentleman of honour and
parts, and one of the beft partizans the French had
laft war, and of one Langlade, the very man who
projected and executed, with thefe very nations, the
defeat of General Braddock. My firft intention was
to turn this whole corps to the Connecticut immediately, to force a fupply of provifions, to intercept
reinforcements, and to confirm the jealoufy I have in
many ways endeavoured to excite in the New-England
provinces: but, finding that the enemy are labouring to remove their magazines from Forts George and
Edward, and every where deftroying the roads, and
preparing to drive and burn the country towards Albany, I have determined to employ them, to prevent, if poffible, by their terror, the continuance of
thofe operations. And, after arriving at Albany,
they may be employed to renew the alarm towards
Connecticut and Bofton.

Your Lordfhip will pardon me if I a little lament,
that my orders do not give me the latitude I ventured to propofe, in my original project for the campaign,

paign, to make a real effort inftead of a feint upon New England. As things have turned out, were I at liberty to march in force immediately by my left, inftead of my right, I fhould have little doubt of fubduing, before winter, the provinces where the rebellion originated.

If my late letters reach Mr. Howe, I ftill hope this plan may be adopted from Albany; in the mean while my utmoft exertions fhall continue, according to my inftruΩions, to force a junΩion.

I have fent fome Indians through the woods, in the hope of their reaching St. Leger with the account of my progrefs : now is the critical time for his pufh upon the Mohawk. I have certain intelligence that all the country round Fort Stanwix is in alarm ; but I imagine it proceeds from the appearance of fome favages detached by Colonel Butler, not apprehending St. Leger can be got quite fo forward.

Camp near Saratoga, Auguft 20, 1777. Second No.VIII.

To Lord George Germaine.

My Lord,

IN my laft difpatch (a duplicate of which will be inclofed herewith) I had the honour to inform your Lordfhip of the proceedings of the army under my command to the 30th of July.

From that period to the 15th of Auguft every poffible meafure was employed to bring forward bateaux, provifions, and ammunition, from Fort George to the firft navigable part of Hudfon's River, a diftance of eighteen miles, the roads in fome parts fteep, and in others wanting great repair. Of the horfes, furnifhed by contraΩ in Canada, not more than a third part was yet arrived. The delay was not imputable to negleΩ, but to the natural accidents attending fo
long

long and intricate a combination of land and water carriage. Fifty team of oxen, which had been collected in the country through which I had marched, were added to affift the tranfport ; but thefe refources together were found far inadequate to the purpofes of feeding the army and forming a magazine at the fame time. Exceeding heavy rains augmented the impediments : it was often neceffary to employ ten or twelve oxen upon a fingle bateau; and, after the utmoft exertions for the fifteen days above ftated, there were not above four days provifion before hand, nor above ten bateaux in the river.

Intelligence had reached me, that Lieutenant Colonel St. Leger was before Fort Stanwix, which was defended. The main army of the enemy oppofed to me was at Stillwater, a place between Saratoga and the mouth of the Mohawk.

A rapid movement forward appeared to be of the utmoft confequence at this period. The enemy could not have proceeded up the Mohawk without putting themfelves between two fires, in cafe Colonel St. Leger fhould have fucceeded, and at beft being cut off by my army from Albany. They muft either, therefore, have ftood an action, have fallen back towards Albany, or have paffed the Hudfon's River, in order to fecure a retreat to New England, higher up. Which ever of thefe meafures they had taken, fo that the King's army had been enabled to advance, Colonel St. Leger's operations would have been affifted, a junction with him probably fecured, and the whole country of the Mohawk opened. To maintain the communication with Fort George during fuch a movement, fo as to be fupplied by daily degrees at a diftance continually increafing, was an obvious impoffibility. The army was much too weak to have afforded a chain of pofts. Efcorts for every feparate tranfport would have been a ftill greater drain; nor could

any

any have been made so strong as to force their way through such positions as the enemy might take in one night's march from the White Creek, where they had a numerous militia. Had the enemy remained supine, through fear, or want of comprehending so palpable an advantage, the physical impossibility of being supplied by degrees from Fort George was still in force, because a new necessity of land carriage for nine miles arises at Stillwater ; and, in the proportion that carriages had been brought forward to that place, the transport must have ceased behind.

The alternative, therefore, was short : either to relinquish the favourable opportunity of advancing upon the enemy, or to attempt other resources of supply.

It is well known that the enemy's supplies in live cattle, from a large tract of country, passed by the route of Manchester, Arlington, and other parts of the Hampshire Grants, to Benington, in order to be occasionally conveyed thence to the main army. A large deposit of corn and of wheel carriages was also formed at the same place, and the usual guard was militia, though it varied in numbers from day to day. A scheme was formed to surprise Benington. The possession of the cattle and carriages would certainly have enabled the army to leave their distant magazines, and to have acted with energy and dispatch ; success would also have answered many secondary purposes.

Lieut. Col. Baume, an officer well qualified for the undertaking, was fixed upon to command. He had under him 200 dismounted dragoons of the regiment of Reidesel, Captain Fraser's markfmen, which were the only British, all the Canadian volunteers, a party of the Provincials who perfectly knew the country, 100 Indians, and two light pieces of cannon; the whole detachment amounted to about 500 men. The instructions were positive, to keep the regular corps posted,

ted, while the light troops felt their way, and not to
incur the danger of being furrounded, or having a retreat cut off.

In order to facilitate this operation, and to be ready
to take advantage of its fuccefs, the army moved up
the eaft fhore of Hudfon's River. On the 14th, a
bridge was formed of rafts, over which the advanced
corps paffed and encamped at Saratoga. Lieutenant-
Colonel Breyman's corps were pofted near Batten-
Kill; and, upon intelligence, from Colonel Baume,
that the enemy were ftronger at Bennington than expected, and were aware of his attack, that corps, confifting of the Brunfwic grenadiers, light-infantry, and
chaffeurs, were fent forward to fuftain him.

It fince appears, that Lieutenant-Colonel Baume,
not having been able to complete his march undifcovered, was joined at a place called Sancoix-Mills, about
four miles fhort of Bennington, by many people profeffing themfelves to be Loyalifts. A provincial gentleman of confidence, who had been fent with the detachment, as knowing the country and the character
of the inhabitants, was fo incautious as to leave at liberty fuch as took the oath of allegiance.

His credulity and their profligacy caufed the firft
misfortune. Colonel Baume was induced to proceed
without fufficient knowledge of the ground. His defign was betrayed; the men who had taken the oaths
were the firft to fire upon him: he was attacked on all
fides; he fhewed great perfonal courage, but was overpowered by numbers.

During this time Lieutenant-Colonel Breyman was
upon the march through a heavy rain; and fuch were
the other impediments ftated in that officer's report, of
bad roads, tired horfes, difficulties in paffing artillery,
carriages, &c. that he was from eight in the morning
of the 15th to four in the afternoon of the following
day making about twenty-four miles.

He

He engaged, fought gallantly, and drove the enemy from three feveral heights ; but was too late to fuccour Colonel Baume, who was made prifoner, and a confiderable part of his dragoons were killed or taken. The failure of ammunition, from the accidental breaking to pieces of a tumbril, unfortunately obliged Lieutenant-Colonel Breyman to retire conquering troops, and to leave behind two pieces of cannon, befides two which had been loft by Lieutenant-Colonel Baume. The Indians made good their retreat from the firft affair, as did Captain Frafer, with part of his company, and many of the Provincials and Canadians.

The lofs, as at prefent appears, amounts to about 400 men, killed and taken in both actions, and twenty-fix officers, moftly prifoners; but men who were difperfed in the woods drop in daily. A correct return fhall be tranfmitted to your Lordfhip the firft opportunity.

This, my Lord, is a true ftate of the event. I have not dwelt upon errors, becaufe, in many inftances, they were counterbalanced by fpirit The enemy will of courfe find matter of parade in the acquifition of four pieces of cannon ; but, that apart, they have fmall caufe of exultation, their lofs, in killed and wounded, being more than double to ours, by the confeffion of their prifoners and deferters, and of many inhabitants who were witneffes to the burial of their dead.

The chief fubject of regret on our fide, after that which any lofs of gallant men naturally occafions, is the difappointment of not obtaining live cattle, and the lofs of time in bringing forward the magazines.

This heavy work is now nearly completed, and a new bridge of boats is thrown over the Hudfon's River, oppofite to Saratoga, the former one of rafts having been carried away by the fwell of water after the late continual rains. When enabled to move, nothing within my fcale of talent fhall be left unattempted to

fulfil

fulfil his Majefty's orders; and I hope circumftances
will be fuch, that my endeavours may be, in fome degree, affifted by the co-operation of the army under
Sir William Howe.

I have the honour to be, with great refpect,

Your Lordfhip's moft obedient

And moft humble fervant,

(Signed.)   J. BURGOYNE.*

No. IX. *Copy of a Letter from Lieutenant-General* Burgoyne *to
Lord* George Germaine, *dated Camp, near* Saratoga,
Auguft 20, 1777.

My Lord,   [Private.]

I NEED not enlarge upon the concern I have in
communicating any finifter events.   I am perfuadéd
your Lordfhip will give me credit for partaking every
fentiment that your Lordfhip, or any other man war-
med with principle and zeal in this conteft, can feel.

In regard to the affair of Saintcoick, I have only to
add to the public account, that, if ever there was a fituation to juftify enterprize and exertion, out of the
beaten track of military fervice, it was that in which I
found myfelf.   Had I fucceeded, I fhould have effected
a junction with St. Leger, and been now before Albany.   And I flatter myfelf, I need only mention thofe
views, to fhew, that, in hazarding this expedition, I
had the foundeft principles of military reafoning on my
fide, viz. that the advantages to be expected from fuccefs were, in a great degree, fuperior to the evils that
could attend mifcarriage.   The fecondary purpofes,
to which I alluded in the public letter, were to try the
affections of the country, to complete the Provincial
corps,

* The letter that follows, No. IX. is alfo materially referable
to No. VIII.

corps, many recruits for which were unable to escape from their villages without a force to encourage and protect them, and to distract the councils of the enemy, by continuing their jealousy towards New-England.

Major-General Reidesel has pressed upon me repeatedly the mounting his dragoons; the men were animated with the same desire, and I conceived it a most favourable occasion to give into their ideas and solicitations, because, in exerting their zeal to fulfil their favourite purpose, they necessary would effect the greater purpose of my own. The rest of the troops were selected from such as would least weaken the solid strength of the army, in case of ill success; and I thought it expedient to make a little trial of the Provincials and Canadians, before I might have occasion for them in more important actions.

The original detachment could not have been made larger without opening roads, and other preparations of time, nor should I have thought it justifiable to expose the best troops to loss upon a collateral action. Had my instructions been followed, or could Mr. Breyman have marched at the rate of two miles an hour, any given twelve hours out of the two and thirty, success would probably have ensued; misfortune would certainly have been avoided. I did not think it prudent, in the present crisis, to mark these circumstances to the public so strongly as I do in confidence to your Lordship; but I rely, and I will venture to say I expect, because I think justice will warrant the expectation, that while, for the sake of public harmony, that necessary principle for conducting nice and laborious service, I colour the faults of the execution, your Lordship will, in your goodness, be my advocate to the King and to the world, in vindication of the plan.

The consequences of this affair, my Lord, have little effect upon the strength or spirits of the army; but the prospect of the campaign, in other respects, is far

less

lefs profperous than when I wrote laft. In fpite of St.
Leger's victory, Fort Stanwix holds out obftinately.
I am afraid the expectations of Sir J. Johnfon greatly
fail in the rifing of the country. On this fide I find
daily reafon to doubt the fincerity of the refolution of
the profeffing loyalifts. I have about 400, but not
half of them armed who may be depended upon; the
reft are trimmers merely actuated by intereft. The
great bulk of the country is undoubtedly with the Congrefs, in principle and zeal; and their meafures are executed with a fecrecy and difpatch that are not to be
equalled. Wherever the King's forces point, militia,
to the amount of three or four thoufand, affemble in
twenty-four hours; they bring with them their fubfiftence, &c. and, the alarm over, they return to their
farms. The Hampfhire Grants, in particular, a
country unpeopled, and almoft unknown the laft war,
now abounds in the moft active and moft rebellious
race of the continent, and hangs like a gathering ftorm
upon my left. In all parts, the induftry and management, in driving cattle and removing corn, are indefatigable and certain; and it becomes impracticable to
move without portable magazines. Another moft em-
barraffing circumftance is the want of communication
with Sir William Howe; of the meffengers I have
fent, I know of two being hanged, and am ignorant
whether any of the reft arrived. The fame fate has
probably attended thofe difpatched by Sir William
Howe; for only one letter is come to hand, informing
met hat his attention is for Pennfylvania; that Wafhington has detached Sullivan, with 2500 men, to Albany; that Putnam is in the Highlands with 4000 men.
That, after my arrival at Albany, the movements of
the enemy muft guide mine; but that he wifhed the
enemy might be driven out of the province, before any
operation took place againft the Connecticut; that Sir
Henry Clinton remained in the command in the neighbourhood

bourhood of New-York, and would act as occurrences might direct.

No operation, my Lord, has yet been undertaken in my favour; the Highlands have not even been threatened. The confequence is, that Putnam has detached two brigades to Mr. Gates, who is now ftrongly pofted near the mouth of the Mohawk-River, with an army fuperior to mine in troops of the Congrefs, and as many militia as he pleafes. He is likewife far from being deficient in artillery, having received all the pieces that were landed from the French fhips which got into Bofton.

Had I a latitude in my orders, I fhould think it my duty to wait in this pofition, or perhaps as far back as Fort Edward, where my communication with Lake George would be perfectly fecure, till fome event happened to affift my movement forward; but my orders being pofitive, to " force a junction with Sir William Howe," I apprehend I am not at liberty to remain inactive longer than fhall be neceffary to collect twenty-five days provifion, and to receive the reinforcement of the additional companies, the German drafts and recruits, now (and unfortunately only now) on Lake Champlain. The waiting the arrival of this reinforcement is of indifpenfible neceffity; becaufe, from the hour I pafs the Hudfon's river and proceed towards Albany, all fafety of communication ceafes. I muft expect a large body of the enemy, from my left, will take poft behind me. I have put out of the queftion the waiting longer than the time neceffary for the foregoing purpofes, becaufe the attempt, then critical, depending on adventure and the fortune that often accompanies it, and hardly juftifiable but by orders from the ftate, would afterwards be confummately defperate. I mean, my Lord, that, by moving foon, though I fhould meet with infurmountable difficulties to my progrefs, I fhall at leaft have the chance of fighting my
way

way back to Ticonderoga; but the season a little farther advanced, the distance encreased, and the march unavoidably tardy, because surrounded by enemies, a retreat might be shut by impenetrable bars, or the elements, and, at the same time, no possible means of existence remain in the country.

When I wrote more confidently, I little foresaw that I was to be left to pursue my way through such a tract of country, and hosts of foes, without any co-operation from New-York; nor did I then think the garrison of Ticonderoga would fall to my share alone; a dangerous experiment would it be to leave that post in weakness, and too heavy a drain it is upon the life-blood of my force to give it due strength.

I yet do not despond. — Should I succeed in forcing my way to Albany, and find that country in a state to subsist my army, I shall think no more of a retreat, but at the worst fortify there, and await Sir W. Howe's operations.

Whatever may be my fate, my Lord, I submit my actions to the breast of the King, and to the candid judgement of my profession, when all the motives become public; and I rest in the confidence, that, whatever decision may be passed upon my conduct, my good intent will not be questioned.

I cannot close so serious a letter, without expressing my fullest satisfaction in the behaviour and countenance of the troops, and my complete confidence, that, in all trials, they will do whatever can be expected from men devoted to their King and country.

I have the honour to be, &c.

J. Burgoyne.

P. S. Upon re-perusing this letter, I am apprehensive that the manner in which I have expressed myself, respecting the reinforcement being only upon Lake
Champlain,

Champlain, may seem ambiguous.—I do not mean to impute the delay to any thing but accidents, nor do I mean to contest Sir Guy Carleton's reasoning, upon not complying with my requisitions to garrison Ticonderoga; I only lament it.

Copy of a Letter from Sir William Howe *to Lieutenant-General* Burgoyne, *dated* New-York, July *the* 17th, 1777.

No. X.

DEAR SIR,

I HAVE received yours of the second instant on the 15th; have since heard from the rebel army of your being in possession of Ticonderoga, *which is a great event, carried without loss.* I have received your two letters, *viz.* from Plymouth and Quebec, your last of the 14th May, and shall observe the contents. There is a report of a messenger of yours to me having been taken, and the letter discovered in a double wooden canteen: you will know if it was of any consequence; nothing of it has transpired to us. I will observe the *same rules* in writing to you as you propose in your letters to me. Washington is waiting our motions here, and has detached Sullivan, with about 2500 men, as I learn, to Albany. My intention is for Pennsylvania, where I expect to meet Washington; but, if he goes to the northward, contrary to my expectations, and you can keep him at bay, be assured I shall soon be after him to relieve you.

After your arrival at Albany, the movements of the enemy will guide yours ; but my wishes are, that the enemy be driven out of this province before any operation takes place in Connecticut. Sir Henry Clinton remains in the command here, and will act as occurrences may direct. Putnam is in the highlands, with about 4000 men. Success be ever with you.

Yours, &c. WILLIAM HOWE.

D

Sir

A P P E N D I X.

Sir Guy Carleton's *Letter.**

S I R,   *Quebec, November* 12, 1777.

I received your letter of the 20th of October, with your public difpatches, by Captain Craig, the 5th inftant, and heartily condole with you upon the very difagreeable accounts they contain ; all which I fincerely lamented, both on the public account and your own.

This unfortunate event, it is to be hoped, will in future prevent minifters from pretending to direct operations of war, in a country at three thoufand miles diftance, of which they have fo little knowledge as not to be able to diftinguifh between good, bad, or interefted, advices, or to give pofitive orders in matters, which, from their nature, are ever upon the change ; fo that the expedience or propriety of a meafure, at one moment, may be totally inexpedient or improper in the next.

Having given over all hopes of being relieved this fall, I determined upon fending home Captain Foy, to furnifh his majefty's confidential fervants, and my fucceffor, with the beft information, in my power, of the ftate of affairs in this province, that they may form the better judgement of what they have to do.

I am, &c.

Army from Canada *under Lieutenant-General* Burgoyne.

Total Rank and File, 1ft of July, 1777. [*Sick included.*]

British.		British.	Brought over 2660
9th regiment — — — — 542		53d — — — — — — 537	
20th — — — — — 528		62d — — — — — — 541	
21ft — — — — — 538		Grenadiers and light-infantry com-	
24th — — — — — 528		panies from the 29th, 31ft, and	
47th — — — — — 524		34th, regiments — — — 329	
Carried over 2660		Carried over 4067	

* This letter, which was never printed before, only regards the view of the evidence, towards the beginning.

Brought over 4067
Left in Canada out of the above 343

British. Total 3724
Germans, 1ft July 3727
Left in Canada 711

For the campaign, Germans 3016

Regular troops. Total 6740
Garrifon left out of the above at Ticonderoga.
Britifh rank and file 462
German rank and file 448

910

To force a paffage to Albany 5830
1ft July, Britifh artillery — — 257
German artillery — 100
Bat men, fervants, &c. in the above.
Recruits under Lieutenant Nutt 154
Canadians — — — 148
Indians never more than 500

Before Septemb. fell off to 90
Provincials at moft — 682
1ft Oct. no more than 456

In September the additional companies joined near Fort Miller, in all — — — — — 300

Regulars killed, wounded, and prifoners, in the campaign, 1777.

	Kill	Wo.	Prif.	Tot.
Britifh.				
Officers	26	47	19	
Serjeants	15	33	14	
Drummers	3	5	6	
R. & File	207	549	449	1285
Germans.				
Officers	10	16	29	
Serjeants	12	28	59	
Drummers	1	8	18	
R. & File	141	225	575	941

Firft Application from Major-General Phillips, *relative* No. XII.
to Horfes. Dated Montreal, June 4, 1777.

SIR,

I TAKE the liberty of informing your Excellency, that there has yet been no arrangement made for marching the field-artillery by land, fhould the corps of troops upon an expedition under your command, in the courfe of the campaign, quit the lakes Champlain and George, and the rivers.

I have, upon the ftricteft information which could be procured, reafon to believe, that neither carriages nor horfes will be to be had nearer than Albany, fhould the route of your army be that way ; and, even in that country, it will neceffarily require a confiderable time before any can be got ; all which muft neceffarily delay the operations of the campaign, after the reduction of Ticonderoga. I therefore fubmit to your Excellency's confideration, whether horfes, and fuch ammunition-carriages as may be wanted, fhould not be procured for the fervice of the campaign, for

the

the field-artillery attached to the corps of troops your Excellency is to command this campaign ?

I have the honour to be, Sir,

With the greatest respect,

Your Excellency's most obedient

And most humble servant,

M. PHILLIPS, Major-General, commanding the royal artillery in Canada.

His Excellency
Lieutenant-General Burgoyne.

Copy of a Letter to Major-General Phillips, *respecting Horses.* Dated Montreal, June 4, 1777.

SIR,

I HAVE the honour of your letter of this day's date, informing me that no arrangement has yet been made for moving the field-artillery by land ; and that, upon the best information you can obtain, neither carriages nor horses can be procured on the other side Lake Champlain nearer than Albany.

In consequence of this representation, I have to request you, to give in your opinion upon the mode of procuring horses and carriages from this country, combining the considerations of dispatch, sufficiency, œconomy towards government ; and I wish to know the opinion as soon as possible.

I am, with truest regard, Sir,

Your obedient humble servant,

J. BURGOYNE, Lieutenant-General.

Major-General Phillips.

Extracts

Extracts of Letters from Major-General Phillips, *&c.*

Extract of a Letter from Major-General Phillips *to Lieutenant-General* Burgoyne.

Montreal, June 5, 1777.

I HAVE the honour of your Excellency's letter to me of yesterday, in answer to one I wrote on the subject of the field-artillery being supplied with horses, &c. &c.

You are pleased, Sir, to order me to give an opinion upon the mode of procuring horses and carriages from this country ; combining the consideration of dispatch, sufficiency, and œconomy towards government.

There are but two modes of procuring horses for the service, supposing the country is not to furnish them upon corvées ; the one is by purchasing of horses upon the account of government, the other by contract.

The first of these modes has always appeared, to me, difficult, uncertain, and full of openings for every species of imposition, and the expence uncertain. — Government must trust various people to buy horses ; and, in this country, it will not be possible to procure any persons who will not immediately pursue the views of gaining money to themselves, with a consideration for the King's service. Add to this, that it will become such a charge, that many commissaries must be appointed, and various other officers of that sort, &c. which being a mixture of inspectors into the purchases of horses, and necessarily also at times the being purchasers, it will be difficult ever to ascertain the price, and seldom that the goodness of horses can be depended on.

I have seen, in my service, this mode attempted ; but it has, to my knowledge, failed. I must allow,

that,

that, could it be carried into execution complete, it would be the cheapeſt for government: but, taking into conſideration the various impoſitions which will ariſe, and that the ſetting out on a plan of this nature will require a very large ſum of money, perhaps from 20,000l. to 30,000l. to be intruſted into various hands, I freely give it as my opinion that it is not a perfect plan. The contracting for a certain number of horſes, at a fixed price for the hire by day, reduces the whole to a very ſimple, and therefore generally a certain, plan. It depends on the ſetting out, by making as cheap, as fair, and juſt, a bargain, on the part of government, as can be: And, being ſo made, that the military and civil officers do their duty, by attending to the receiving of horſes only as they are fitting for ſervice. The contractor has his intereſt ſo directly connected with fulfilling his contract, (as upon failure it ceaſes,) that he will exert all means to do it, and the care of government will be, that it be done honeſtly and completely.

I have thus obeyed your Excellency's orders, and given an opinion which I ſubmit entirely to your conſideration.

Extract of a Letter to Nathaniel Day, *Eſq. Commiſſary-General, &c. Dated* Montreal, *June 4th*, 1777.

I BEG the favour of you to calculate what number of horſes and carriages (ſuppoſing them ſuch as are in common uſe in Canada) will be ſufficient for conveying, by land, thirty days proviſion for 10,000 men, together with about 1000 gallons of rum; and you will pleaſe to make me your report as ſoon as poſſible.

Extract

Extract of a Letter to Sir Guy Carleton.

Montreal, June 7, 1777.

HAVING had the honour to reprefent to your Excellency the neceffity of being provided with a certain number of horfes and carriages for the artillery, victuals, and other indifpenfable purpofes of the army, when it fhall be obliged to quit the borders of the lakes and rivers ; and having underftood from your Excellency that fuch provifion could not be made by the ordinary methods of corvée ; and that, if propofed without compulfion upon the country, the effect would be precarious, dilatory, and expenfive ; I have the honour now to lay before your Excellency propofals for contracts for an expeditious fupply of horfes for the artillery, and 500 carts, with two horfes each, for the other purpofes.

I am too ignorant of the prices of the country to offer any judgement upon the reafonablenefs of thefe propofals ; nor have I any long acquaintance with Mr. Jordan, or other motive for wifhing him the preference, if other perfons can be found equally capable, refponfible, and expeditious. I have only thus far interfered, upon a conviction, (after confidering the route the King's orders direct, and taking all poffible methods of information upon the fupply to be expected as we proceed,) that to depend upon the country altogether would be to hazard the expedition.

Your Excellency will obferve, that, in order to fave the public expence as much as poffible, I have reduced this requifition much below what would be adequate for the fervice, and I mean to truft to the refources of the expedition for the reft : 500 carts will barely carry fourteen days provifions at a time, and Major-General Phillips means to demand as few horfes as poffible, fubject to whatever future augmentations future fervices may require : the prefent number

D 4

wanted

wanted will be about 400 ; there will then remain un-
provided for (for expeditious movement) the tranfport of bateaux from Lake George to Hudfon's River,
and the carriage of the tents of the army, and many
other contingencies that I need not trouble your Excellency to point out to you.

Extract of a Letter to General Harvey.

Montreal, May 19, 1777.

YOU have permitted me, as formerly, to write to
you confidentially. I take the firft conveyance to renew a correfpondence fo pleafing and honourable to
myfelf, and that may, in fome cafes, become benefi-
cial to the public fervice. It fhall never be employed
but to convey tru hs, to do juftice to facts and perfons,
and to fecure myfelf in the continuance of an efteem fo
valuable to me as yours, againft appearances and mif-
reprefentations.

I have reafon to be exceedingly fatisfied with all that
has been done, and with moft things that are doing :
exertions have been made during the winter, which
was remarkably favourable, in all the departments, and
preparations are very forward ; thofe that have been
committed to the directions of General Phillips have
b en executed with a diligence, precifion, and fore-
fight, that entitle him to the fulleft praife. The troops
are in a ftate of health almoft unprecedented, and their
fpirits and general improvement are equally objects of
great pleafure and promife. To this agreeable reprefentation I have the happinefs to add, that Sir Guy
Carleton has received me, and the orders I brought, in
a manner that, in my opinion, does infinite honour to
his public and private character.

That he fhould have wifhed for the lead in active
and important military operations is very natural.
That he thinks he has fome caufe of refentment for the
general

general tenor of treatment he has received from some of the ministers is discernible ; but neither his disappointment nor his personal feelings operate against his duty ; and I am convinced he means to forward the King's measures, entrusted to my hands, with all the zeal he could have employed had they rested in his own.

My intention is, during my advance to Ticonderoga, and siege of that post, (for a siege I apprehend it must be,) to give all possible jealousy on the side of Connecticut. If I can, by manoeuvre, make them suspect that, after the reduction of Ticonderoga, my views are pointed that way, it may make the Connecticut forces very cautious of leaving their own frontiers, and much facilitate my progress to Albany. I mention this intention only to Lord George and yourself, and I do it left, from any intelligence of my motions that may reach England indirectly, it should be supposed I have suffered myself to be diverted from the main object of my orders. The King and his Majesty's ministers may rest assured, that, whatever demonstrations I may endeavour to impose upon the enemy, I shall really make no movement that can procrastinate my progress to Albany.

One thing more occurs. I had the surprise and mortification to find a paper handed about at Montreal, publishing the whole design of the campaign, almost as accurately as if it had been copied from the Secretary of State's letter. My own caution has been such, that not a man in my own family has been let into the secret. Sir Guy Carleton's, I am confident, has been equal ; I am therefore led to doubt whether imprudence has not been committed from private letters from England, and wish you would ask my friend D'Oyley, to whom my very affectionate compliments, whether there is any person within the line of ministerial communication that he can suspect to be so unguarded ?

It

It is not of great confequence here, except as far as regards St. Leger's expedition ; but fuch a trick may be
of moft prejudicial confequence in other cafes, and
fhould be guarded againft.

Extract of a Letter to General Harvey.

*Camp on the River Bouquet, near
Lake Champlain, June 22, 1777.*

I HAVE had to contend againft wet weather that
rendered the roads almoft impracticable at the carrying places, and confequently the paffage of the bateaux, &c. exceedingly dilatory ; befides a great deal
of contrary wind. Indeed, the combination of land
and water movement, bad roads, inactivity, and fometimes difobedience in the country, and a thoufand other
difficulties and accidents, unknown in other fervices,
difconcert all arrangements. I do not mention this
upon my own account, as I do not hold myfelf refponfible for delays within the province of Canada ; but I
mention it to do juftice to others, who, I really think,
have infinite merit in overcoming the obftructions we
have met with, and who ought to be juftified againft
fome acquaintances of yours and mine, who travel a-
crofs a map very faft, and are very free in their comments, when others, who have ten times their knowledge
and refources, do not anfwer their predictions and expectations.

I have been exceedingly diftreffed in regard to the
brigadiers of this army. Sir Guy Carleton, the day I
took leave of him, put into my hands an extract of a
letter from the Secretary of War, approving the ap-
pointment of thofe gentlemen, but obferving, that
whenever any of them fhould *lead their brigades out of
the province of Canada, in order to join the troops under
General Howe*, there would be a neceffity for their command ceafing as brigadiers, &c.

Were

Were this to be put in execution, according to the letter of the order and the geographical limits of Canada, and suppofing Major-General Phillips at the fame time to be employed folely in the artillery, I fhould find myfelf at the head of an army to undertake a fiege, and afterwards purfue objects of importance, and poffibly of time, without a fingle intermediate Britifh officer between the lieutenant-general, commanding *pro tempore* in chief, and a lieutenant-colonel. It would be prepofterous and impertinent in me to fay one word more to you, as an officer, upon the impof-fibility of methodifing or conducting fuch an army with fuch a total deficiency of ftaff. Had Lord Barrington condefcended to have communicated his intentions to me in London, I think I could have convinced him of the impropriety. As it is, I muft conclude that the fpirit of the order goes only to prevent thofe gentle-men bearing a higher rank and pay than fenior lieute-nant-colonels ferving in the fame army; and that there-fore there can be no fault in keeping it dormant till the junction takes place. In other words, I look upon mine to be the Canada army till fuch time as I am in communication with General Howe, fo as to make part of his force, and confequently, without meafuring degrees north and fouth, that the arrangements made in Canada, and approved of by the King, remain in force till that time.

I am perfuaded, my dear General, you will fupport me in this liberty, if fuch it is to be called, not only as the abfolute order and method of the fervice depends upon it, but alfo to avoid to thefe gentlemen, who have really great merit, the vexation and the ridicule of being deprived of their rank and pay in the hour of that very fervice, with a view to which their ap-pointment was originally made. I think I can anfwer, that, the junction made, and the reafons for reverting

to

to their forrmer ranks become obvious, they will fubmit to his Majefty's pleafure without a murmur.

Extract of a Letter from Lieutenant-General Burgoyne
to General Harvey.

Head-Quarters, Skenefborough, July 11, 1777.

THE mere compliment of fervice I have given to
the troops in orders, and in the relation defigned for
the Gazette, is not doing them fufficient juftice. It
is a duty in me farther, through you, and I know I
fhall impofe a pleafing tafk on you, to affure the King
that their behaviour is as uniformly good in the camp
as in action.

After what I have publicly mentioned of Frafer, I
am fure I need not prefs you in his favour. I cannot
but feel confident in the hope that his Majefty's grace
will find its way through all obftacles to prevent fo
difcouraging a circumftance as the return of this gallant
officer to the mere duty of lieutenant-colonel, at the
head of one battalion, after having given afcendancy to
the King's troops, and done honour to his profeffion,
by the moft fpirited actions in critical periods of two
fucceffive campaigns.

You will obferve, Sir, both in the public letter and
in the order of battle, which captain Gardner will put
into your hands, that Major-General Phillips is occafionally employed feparately from the ftrict line of his
department. This does not proceed from inattention
to the explanation of his Majefty's pleafure two years
ago, but from abfolute neceffity. The ftaff being compofed without any Britifh major-general, Brigadier Frafer being pofted where he is of infinite ufe, at the head
of the advanced corps, the fervice would fuffer in the
moft material degree if the talents of General Phillips
were not fuffered to extend beyond the limits of the artillery,

tillery, and I hold myself fully juftified in continuing the great ufe of his affiftance under this extenfion, by what I underftand to be the fignification of the King's pleafure to Sir Guy Carleton, viz. *That this meafure muft not be made a precedent*, but not forbidding it during the prefent exigency.

I flatter myfelf the King will be fatisfied with the diligence ufed in taking the field, as well as with the fubfequent operations; if not, my difappointment can only proceed from my own deficiency in ftating the embarraffments I found, notwithftanding previous preparations and cordial affiftances. Remote fituations of the troops, currents, winds, roads, want of materials for caulking the veffels, inactivity and defertion of the Canadian corvees, were all againft me. A great difficulty lay in providing horfes and carriages for the bare tranfport of provifions and tents, when we fhould arrive at Fort George, or any other place where the army fhould have no refource of water-carriage. I found an active, and I think a reafonable, contractor, who fupplied this neceffity at a much cheaper rate than could have been done any other way. I inclofe a copy of the contract to the treafury, to which I refer you. You will obferve that I have limited the number to the mere indifpenfible purpofes of provifions and tents; trufting to the country for the farther affiftance of officers baggage and the other attirail of an army. Experience already fhews me that I judged right in not trufting to the country for more; for, had this precaution been omitted, I fhould be bound faft to the fpot where I am, or obliged to return by water to Ticonderoga.

I avow alfo to you my advice to General Carleton to grant commiffions to two provincial battalions, to be raifed from Albany and Charlotte County, by a Mr. Jeffup and a Mr. Peters, upon condition that the commiffions fhould not take place till two-thirds of the

corps

corps fhould be effective; provincial corps, acting zea-loufly in the King's caufe, muft have great impreffion upon public opinion, and will, befides, in fact, be of fingular ufe to the eafe and prefervation of the regular troops.

Upon this principle, therefore, I have not hefitated farther to receive and to pay fuch loyalifts as have come in with their arms fince the fuccefs of Ticonderoga, and wifh to be employed. Though I have not power to grant commiffions, I poft the officers, and form them into companies till the meafure can be decided by thofe who have more authority.

I hope all thefe articles of expence will meet with the fupport of your opinion; and have only to add, that as no job fhall be done by myfelf, fo will I ufe all efforts to prevent fuch being done by others.

I am indifpenfably obliged to wait fome time on this pofition, to clear roads and make bridges, which is great labour in this country, and to bring up a ftock of provifion, and alfo to give time to the gun-boats, bateaux, and provifion-veffels, to be put into Lake George, to fcour that lake and fecure the future route of the magazines. I propofe to poffefs Fort Edward at the fame time that the force is ready to move down the lake; by which means, if the enemy do not eva-cuate Fort George, the garrifon muft inevitably be caught. In the mean while I have ordered Reidefel to make roads, reconnoitre the country, and make all other poffible feints of a march to the Connecticut, and, by fome other meafures, I hope to give alarms that way.

INSTRUC-

Amendments made by General Burgoyne.

INSTRUCTIONS for Lieutenant-Colonel Baume, *on a secret expedition to the Connecticut River.*

[*The erasures were made by General Burgoyne.**]

THE object of your expedition is to try the affections of the country, to disconcert the councils of the enemy, to mount the Reidesel's dragoons, to complete Peters's corps, and to obtain large supplies of cattle, horses, and carriages.

The several corps, of which the inclosed is a list, are to be under your command.

The troops must take no tents, and what little baggage is carried by officers must be on their own bat horses.

You are to proceed *by the route* from Batten Kill to Arlington, and take post there, *so as to secure the pass from Manchester. You are to remain at Arlington* till the detachment of the Provincials, under the command of Captain Sherwood, shall join you from the southward.

You are then to proceed to Manchester, where you will take post so as to secure the pass of the mountains on the road from Manchester to

Rockingham;

* The erasures are printed in Italics, and the amendments in the opposite column.

Amendments made by General Burgoyne.

Rockingham ; hence you will detach the Indians and light troops to the northward, toward Otter Creek. On their return, and also receiving intelligence that no enemy is in force *in the neighbourhood of Rockingham,* (1) you will proceed by the road over the mountains to Rockingham, where you will take poft. This will be the moft diftant part on the expedition. (2)

You are to remain there *as long as neceffary to fulfil the intention of the expedition from thence,* (3) and you are afterwards to defcend *by* the Connecticut River to Brattlebury, and from that place, by the quickeft march, you are to return by the great road to Albany.

During your whole progrefs, your detachments are to have orders to bring in to you all horfes fit to mount the dragoons under your command, or to ferve as bat horfes to the troops, *they are likewife to bring in* (4) faddles and bridles as can be found. (5)

Your parties are likewife to bring in waggons and other convenient carriages, with as many draft oxen as will be neceffary to draw them, and all cattle fit for flaughter, (milch cows excepted,) which are to be left for the ufe of the inhabitants. Regular re-

(1) *upon the Connecticut River,*

(2) *And muft be proceeded upon with caution, as you will have the defile of the mountains behind you, which might make a retreat difficult ; you muft therefore endeavour to be well informed of the force of the enemy's militia in the neighbouring country.*
Should you find it may with prudence be effected.
(3) *while the Indians and light troops are detached up the river.*

(4) *together with as many*
(5) *The number of horfes requifite, befides thofe neceffary for mounting the regiment of dragoons, ought to be 1300. If you can bring more for the ufe of the army, it will be fo much the better.*

ceipts,

Amendments made by General Burgoyne.

ceipts, in the form hereto fub-joined, are to be given, in all places where any of the above-mentioned articles are taken, to fuch perfons as have remained in their habitations, and otherwife complied with the terms of General Burgoyne's manifefto; but no receipts to be given to fuch as are known to be acting in the fervice of the rebels. (6)

(6) *As you will have with you perfons perfectly acquainted with the abilities of the country, it may perhaps be advifeable to tax the feveral diftricts with the portions of the feveral articles, and limit the hours for their delivery; and, fhould you find it neceffary to move before fuch delivery can be made, hoftages of the moft refpectable people fhould be taken, to fecure their following you the enfuing day. All poffible means are to be ufed to prevent plundering.*

As it is probable that Captain Sherwood, who is already detached to the fouthward and will join you at Arlington, will drive in a confiderable quantity of cattle and horfes to you, you will therefore fend in this cattle to the army, with a proper detachment from Peters's corps to cover them, in order to difencumber yourfelf; but you muft always keep the regiments of dragoons compact.

The dragoons themfelves muft ride, and take care of the horfes of the regiment. Thofe horfes
which

Amendments made by General Burgoyne.

which are destined for the use of the army must be tied together by strings of ten each, in order that one man may lead ten horses. You will give the unarmed men of Peters's corps to conduct them, and inhabitants whom you can trust. You must always take your camps in good position; but at the same time where there is pasture; and you must have a chain of centinels round your cattle and horses when grazing.

Colonel Skeene will be with you as much as possible, in order to assist you with his advice, to help you to distinguish the good subjects from the bad, to procure you the best intelligence of the enemy, and to choose those people who are to bring me the accounts of your progress and success.

When you find it necessary to halt for a day or two, you must always entrench the camp of the regiment of dragoons, in order never to risk an attack or affront from the enemy.

As you will return with the regiment of dragoons mounted, you must always have a detachment of Captain Fraser's or Peters's corps in front of the column, and the same in the rear, in order to prevent your falling into an ambuscade when you march through the woods.

You will use all possible means to make the country believe that the troops under

your

your command are the advanced corps of the army, and that it is intended to pass the Connecticut on the road to Boston. You will likewise *have it insinuated,* (7) that the main army from Albany is to be joined at Springfield by a corps of troops from Rhode. Island.

You will send off occasionally cattle or carriages, to prevent being too much incumbered; and will give me as frequent intelligence of your situation as possible.

It is highly probable that the corps under Mr. Warner, now supposed to be at Manchester, will retreat before you; but, should they, contrary to expectation, be able to collect in great force, and post themselves advantageously, it is left to your discretion to attack them or not; always bearing in mind, that your corps is too valuable to let any considerable loss be hazarded on this occasion.

Should any corps be moved from Mr. Arnold's main army, in order to intercept your retreat, you are to take as strong a post as the country will afford, and send the quickest intelligence to me; and you may depend on my making such a movement as shall put the enemy between two fires, or otherwise effectually sustain you.

It is imagined the progress of the whole of this expedi-

Amendments made by General Burgoyne.

(7) *insinuate,*

tion.

tion may be effected in about a fortnight; but every movement of it muft depend upon your fuccefs in obtaining fuch fupply of provifions as will enable you to fubfift till your return to the army, in cafe you can get no more. (8)

All perfons acting in committees, or any officers acting under the directions of Congrefs, either civil or military, are to be made prifoners.

Amendments made by General Burgoyne.

(8) *And, fhould not the army be able to reach Albany before your expedition fhould be completed, I will find means to fend you notice of it, and give your route another direction.*

SIR,   *Batten-Kill,* 12*th Auguft,* 1777.
I HAD the honour of acquainting your Excellency, by a man fent yefterday evening by Colonel Skeene to head-quarters, of the feveral corps under my command being encamped at Saratoga, as well as of my intention to proceed the next morning at five o'clock; the corps moved at that time, and marched a mile, when I received a letter from Brigadier General Frafer, fignifying your Excellency's order to poft the corps advantageoufly on Batten-Kill, till I fhould receive frefh inftructions from your Excellency: the corps is now encamped at that place, and wait your Excellency's orders. I will not trouble you, Sir, with the various reports which fpread, as they feem rather to be founded on the different interefts and feelings of the people who occafion them.

I have the honour to be, moft refpectfully,
Your Excellency's moft obedient
And humble fervant,
F. BAUME,

The reinforcement of fifty chaffeurs, which your Excellency was pleafed to order, joined me laft night at eleven o'clock.
General Burgoyne.

SIᴰ

Cambridge, 13*th August*, 1777.

SIR,

IN consequence of your Excellency's orders I moved this morning, at four o'clock, with the corps under my command; and, after a march of sixteen miles, arrived at Cambridge at four in the evening. On the road I received intelligence of forty or fifty of the rebels being left to guard some cattle. I immediately ordered thirty of the provincials and fifty savages to quicken their march, in hopes to surprise them. They took five prisoners in arms, who declared themselves to be in the service of the Congress; yet the enemy received advice of our approach, and abandoned the house they were posted in. The provincials and savages continued their march about a mile, when they fell in with a party of fifteen men, who fired upon our people, and immediately took to the woods with the greatest precipitation. The fire was quick on our side, but I cannot learn if the enemy sustained any loss. A private of Captain Sherwood's company was the only one who was slightly wounded in the thigh. From the many people who came from Bennington, they agree that the number of the enemy amounted to 1800. I will be particularly careful, on my approach at that place, to be fully informed of their strength and situation, and take the precautions necessary to fulfil both the orders and instructions of your Excellency.

I cannot ascertain the number of cattle, carts, and waggons, taken here, as they have not been as yet collected. A few horses have been also brought in, but am sorry to acquaint your Excellency that the savages either destroy or drive away what is not paid for with ready money. If your Excellency would allow me to purchase the horses from the savages, stipulating the price, I think they might be procured cheap, otherwise they ruin all they meet with, their officers and interpreters not having it in their power to controul

E 3   them.

them. Your Excellency may depend on hearing how I proceed at Bennington, and of my fuccefs there : praying my refpectful compliments to General Rei-defel,

I am, moft refpectfully, Sir,

Your moft obedient and humble fervant,

F. BAUME.

P. S. The names of the men taken in arms are as follow :

George Duncan,	John Bell,
David Slarrow,	Matt. Bell.
Samuel Bell,	

Hugh More, a noted rebel, furrendered himfelf yefterday evening.

The exprefs left Cambridge at four o'clock, on the morning of the 14th of Auguft.

Sanccick, 14th Auguft, 1777, 9 o'Clock.

SIR,

I HAVE the honour to inform your Excellency, that I arrived here at eight in the morning, having had intelligence of a party of the enemy being in poffeffion of a mill, which they abandoned at our approach ; but, in their ufual way, fired from the bufhes, and took their road to Bennington ; a favage was flightly wounded ; they broke down the bridge, which has retarded our march above an hour ; they left in the mill about 78 barrels of very fine flour, 1000 bufhels of wheat, 20 barrels of falt, and about 1000l. worth of pearl and pot afh. I have ordered thirty provincials and an officer to guard the provifion and the pafs of the bridge. By five prifoners taken here, they agree that 1500 to 1800 men are at Bennington ; but are fuppofed to leave it on our approach. I will proceed fo far to-day as to fall on the enemy to-morrow early, and make fuch difpofition position as I think neceffary from the intelligence I may receive. People are flocking in hourly, but want to be armed : the favages cannot be controuled, they ruin and take every thing they pleafe.

I am your Excellency's

Moft obedient humble fervant,

F. BAUME.

Beg your Excellency to pardon the
hurry of this letter, it is written on
the head of a barrel.

General Burgoyne.

Inftructions to Colonel Skeene, *upon the expedition to Bennington.*

SIR,

I REQUEST the favour of you to proceed with Lieutenant-Colonel Baume, upon an expedition of which he has the command, and which will march this evening or to-morrow morning.

The objects of his orders are to try the affections of the country ; to difconcert the councils of the enemy ; to mount the regiment of Reidefel's dragoons ; to complete Lieutenant-Colonel Peters's corps ; and to procure a large fupply of horfes for the ufe of the troops, together with cattle and carriages.

The route marked for this expedition is to Arlington and Manchefter ; and, in cafe it fhould be found that the enemy is not in too great force upon the Connecticut-river, it is intended to pafs the mountains to Rockingham, and defcend the river from thence to Brattlebury. Some hours before the corps marches for Arlington, Colonel Peters, with all his men, are to fet forward for Bennington, and afterwards are to join at Arlington.

APPENDIX.

Receipts are ordered to be given for all horses and cattle taken from the country.

Lieutenant-Colonel Baume is directed to communicate to you the rest of his instructions, and to consult with you upon all matters of intelligence, negotiation with the inhabitants, roads, and other means depending upon a knowledge of the country, for carrying his instructions into execution.

I rely upon your zeal and activity for the fullest assistance, particularly in having it understood in all the country through which you pass, that the corps of Lieutenant-Colonel Baume is the first detachment of the advanced guard, and that the whole army is proceeding to Boston, expecting to be joined upon the route by the army from Rhode-Island.

I need not reccommend to you to continue the requisites of the service with every principle of humanity in the mode of obtaining them; and it may be proper to inform the country, that the means to prevent their horses being taken for the future, will be to resist the enemy when they shall presume to force them, and drive them voluntarily to my camp.

I have the honour to be, &c. &c. &c.

J. BURGOYNE.

CAL

CALCULATIONS of the Number of Carts that will carry Provisions for the following Number of Men.

Number of Men for	1 Day	2 Days	3 Days	4 Days	5 Days	6 Days	7 Days	8 Days	9 Day	10 Days	11 Days	12 Days	13 Days	14 Days	15 Days	16 Days	17 Day	18 Days	19 Days	20 Days	30 Days	60 Days	90 Days
10000 Men, Carts	38	75	113	150	188	226	263	300	338	375	413	452	490	526	564	600	638	678	716	750	1125	2250	3375
5000 Men, Carts	19	38	57	75	94	113	132	150	169	188	207	226	245	263	282	300	319	339	358	375	563	1125	1688
4000 Men, Carts	15	30	45	60	75	90	105	120	135	150	165	180	195	210	225	240	255	270	285	300	450	900	1350
3000 Men, Carts	12	23	34	45	57	68	79	90	102	113	124	135	147	158	169	180	192	203	214	225	338	676	1014
2000 Men, Carts	8	15	23	30	38	45	53	61	68	75	83	90	98	105	113	120	128	135	143	150	225	450	675
1000 Men, Carts	4	8	12	15	19	23	27	31	35	39	42	45	49	53	57	60	64	68	72	75	113	226	339
500 Men, Carts	2	4	6	8	10	12	14	16	18	20	21	23	25	27	29	30	32	34	36	38	57	113	171

The above Table is made, allowing 3 pounds weight to the Ration and 800 pounds to the Cart-load.

NATHANIEL DAY, Commissary-General.

Extract of a Letter from Lieutenant General Burgoyne
to Sir Guy Carleton, *dated Head-Quarters, at
Skenesborough House,* 11th *July,* 1777.

I REQUEST your Excellency to take into confideration the expediency of fupplying, from Canada,
a garrifon for Ticonderoga.

My communication will widen fo much as I proceed, the drain upon the army for pofts will be fo
confiderable, not to fpeak of detachments and fafeguards to protect and to awe the country, that, if that
firft diminution be not replaced, my effective ftrength
may become inadequate to the fervices intended.
My prefent intelligence is, that Putnam is collecting
an army to oppofe me at Saratoga. Fort Edward is
alfo talked of to fuftain a fiege.

Your Excellency will, I am fure, agree with me,
that Ticonderoga, or fome other fortified poft on the
fouth part of Lake Champlain, ought to be confidered on the frontiers of the province of Canada. I am
aware of the difficulties that arife from the manner in
which the Secretary of State's orders are penned : but
I fubmit to your Excellency, whether, under the
principle laid down in the beginning of the order,
and afterwards repeated, *that* 3000 *men were held fufficient for the defence of that province,* you would not
be juftified in fparing, for the purpofe of this garrifon, the overplus of the 3000 that may remain after
completing my army.

And, notwithftanding the corps for the Canada fervice are precifely named by the Secretary of State, I
would farther fubmit whether, upon my preffing requifition, the garrifon might not juftifiably be furnifhed by detachment, even though there were no
overplus, under the following words of the order :
after having fecured to him (Lieutenant General Burgoyne)

goyne) *every affiftance which it is in your power to afford and procure.* Your Excellency's zeal for the fervice and favour towards me will be better interpreters for the latitude I propofe than any thing I can farther fuggeft. My prefent purpofe, Sir, is to get a fufficient number of gun-boats upon the Lake George to fcour that lake as expeditioufly as poffible, to fupport them with a proper force to attack Fort George on that fide, while, with the main of the army, as foon as refrefhed and fupplied, I attack Fort Edward from hence, and thereby cut off the communication from Albany to Fort George, and confequently prevent the fuccour or retreat of that garrifon.

Extract of a Letter from Lieutenant General Burgoyne *to Sir* Guy Carleton. *Head-Quarters, near Fort Anne, July* 29*th,* 1777.

THE conftruction your Excellency puts upon the orders of the Secretary of State is too full and decifive for me to prefume to trouble you farther upon the fubject of a garrifon for Ticonderoga from Canada. I muft do as well as i can ; but I am fure your Excellency, as a foldier, will think my fituation a little difficult. A breach into my communication muft either ruin my army entirely, or oblige me to return in force to reftore, which might be the lofs of the campaign. To prevent a breach, Ticonderoga and Fort George muft be in very refpectable ftrength, and I muft befides have pofts at Fort Edward and other carrying-places. Thefe drains, added to common accidents and loffes of fervice, will neceffarily render me very inferior in point of numbers to the enemy, whom I muft expect always to find ftrongly pofted. I afk pardon for dwelling fo much upon this fubject, and have only to add my requeft to your Excellency, to forward

forward the additional companies as expeditiously as may be.

Copy of Lieutenant General Burgoyne's *Letter to Colonel* Baume.

Near Saratoga, August 14, 1777. *Seven at night.*

SIR,

THE accounts you have sent me are very satisfactory, and I have no doubt of every part of your proceeding continuing to be the same.

I beg the favour of you to report, whether the road you have passed is practicable; and, if so, if it is convenient for a considerable corps with cannon.

Should you find the enemy too strongly posted at Bennington, and maintaining such a countenance as may make an attack imprudent, I wish you to take a post where you can maintain yourself till you receive an answer from me; and I will either support you in force or withdraw you.

You will please to send off to my camp, as soon as you can, waggons and draft cattle, and likewise such other cattle as are not necessary for your subsistence.

Let the waggons and carts bring off all the flour and wheat they can, that you do not retain for the same purpose. This transport must be under the charge of a commission officer.

I will write you at full tomorrow in regard to getting the horses out of the hands of the savages.

In the mean time, any you can collect from them, fit to mount the regiments, at a low price, shall be allowed.

I am, with great esteem, Sir,

Your most obedient humble servant,

J. BURGOYNE.

Colonel

Colonel St. Leger's *Account of Occurrences at* Fort Stan- No. XIII.
wix.

A MINUTE detail of every operation fince my leaving La Chine, with the detachment entrufted to my care, your Excellency will permit me to referve to a time of lefs hurry and mortification than the prefent, while I enter into the interefting fcene before Fort Stanwix, which I invefted the 3d of Auguft, having previoufly pufhed forward Lieutenant Bird, of the King's regiment, with thirty of the King's troops, and two hundred Indians, under the direction of Captains Hare and Wilfon and the chiefs Jofeph and Bull, to feize faft hold of the lower landing-place, and thereby cut off the enemy's communication with the lower country. — This was done with great addrefs by the lieutenant, though not attended with the effect I had promifed myfelf, occafioned by the flacknefs of the the Meffafagoes : the brigade of provifion and ammunition boats I had intelligence of being arrived and difembarked before this party had taken poft.

The fourth and fifth were employed in making arrangements for opening Wood Creek, (which the enemy, with the indefatigable labour of one hundred and fifty men for fourteen days, had moft effectually choked up,) and the making a temporary road from Pine Ridges upon Fifh Creek, fixteen miles from the fort, for a prefent fupply of provifions and the tranfport of our artillery. The firft was effected by the diligence and zeal of Captain Bouville, affifted by Captain Herkimer of the Indian department, with one hundred and ten men, in nine days ; while Lieutenant Lundy, acting as affiftant quarter-mafter general, had rendered the road, in the worft of weather, fufficiently practicable to pafs the whole artillery and ftores, with feven days provifion, in two days.

On

On the 5th, in the evening, intelligence arrived, by my difcovering-parties on the Mohawk River, that a reinforcement of eight hundred militia, conducted by General Herkimer, were on their march to relieve the garrifon, and were actually at that inftant at Orifka, an Indian fettlement twelve miles from the fort. The garrifon being apprifed of their march by four men, who were feen to enter the fort in the morning through what was thought an impenetrable fwamp, I did not think it prudent to wait for them, and thereby fubject myfelf to be attacked by a fally from the garrifon in the rear, while the reinforcement employed me in front. I therefore determined to attack them on the march, either openly or covertly, as circumftances fhould offer. At this time I had not two hundred and fifty of the King's troops in camp, the various and extenfive operations I was under an abfolute neceffity of entering into having employed the reft, and therefore could not fend above eighty white men, rangers and troops included, with the whole corps of Indians. Sir John Johnfon put himfelf at the head of this party, and began his march that evening at five o'clock, and met the rebel corps at the fame hour the next morning. The impetuofity of the Indians is not to be defcribed on the fight of the enemy (forgetting the judicious difpofition formed by Sir John, and agreed to by themfelves, which was, to fuffer the attack to begin with the troops in front, while they fhould be on both flanks and rear): they rufhed in, hatchet in hand, and thereby gave the enemy's rear an opportunity to efcape. In relation to the victory, it was equally complete as if the whole had fallen; nay more fo, as the two hundred who efcaped only ferved to fpread the panic wider. But it was not fo with the Indians: their lofs was great (I muft be underftood Indian computation; being only about thirty killed, and the like number wounded, and in that number fome some of their favourite chiefs and confidential warriors were slain). On the enemy'y side, almost all their principal leaders were slain. General Herkimer has since died of his wounds. It is proper to mention, that the four men, detached with intelligence of the march of the reinforcement, set out the evening before the action, and consequently the enemy could have no account of the defeat, and were in possession only of the time appointed for their arrival ; at which, as I suspected, they made a sally, with two hundred and fifty men, towards Lieutenant Bird's post, to facilitate the entrance of the relieving corps, or bring on a general engagement with every advantage they could wish.

Captain Hoyes was immediately detached to cut in upon their rear, while they engaged the lieutenant. Immediately upon the departure of Captain Hoyes, having learned that Lieutenant Bird, misled by the information of a cowardly Indian that Sir John was pressed, had quitted his post to march to his assistance, I marched the detachment of the King's regiment in support of Captain Hoyes, by a road in sight of the garrison, which, with executive fire from his party, immediately drove the enemy into the fort, without any farther advantage than frightening some squaws, and pilfering the packs of the warriors which they left behind them. After this affair was over, orders were immediately given to complete a two-gun battery, and mortar-beds, with three strong redoubts in the rear, to enable me, in case of another attempt to relieve the garrison by their regimented troops, to march out a larger body of the King's troops.

Captain Lernoult was sent with 110 men to the lower landing place, where he established himself with great judgement and strength, having an enclosed battery of a three-pounder opposed to any sally from the fort, and another to the side of the country where a

relief

relief muſt approach ; and the body of his camp deeply intrenched and abbatiſed.

When, by the unabating labour of officers and men, (the ſmallneſs of our numbers never admitting of a relief, or above three hours ceſſation for ſleep or cooking,) the batteries and redoubts were finiſhed, and new cheeks and axle-trees made for the ſix-pounders, thoſe that were ſent being reported rotten and unſerviceable.

It was found that our cannon had not the leaſt effect upon the ſod-work of the fort, and that our royals had only the power of teazing, as a ſix-inch plank was a ſufficient ſecurity for their powder-magazine, as we learnt from the deſerters. At this time, Lieutenant Glenie of the artillery, whom I had appointed to act as aſſiſtant-engineer, propoſed a converſion of the royals (if I may uſe the expreſſion) into howitzers. The ingenuity and feaſibility of this meaſure ſtriking me very ſtrongly, the buſineſs was ſet about immediately, and ſoon executed ; when it was found that nothing prevented their operating with the deſired effect but the diſtance, their chambers being too ſmall to hold a ſufficiency of powder. There was nothing now to be done but to approach the town by ſap, to ſuch a diſtance that the rampart might be brought within their portice, at the ſame time all materials were preparing to run a mine under their moſt formidable baſtion.

In the midſt of theſe operations, intelligence was brought in, by our ſcouts, of a ſecond corps of 1000 men being on their march. The ſame zeal no longer animated the Indians ; they complained of our thinneſs of troops, and their former loſſes. I immediately called a council of the chiefs ; encouraged them as much as I could ; promiſed to lead them on myſelf, and bring into the field 300 of the beſt troops. They liſtened to this, and promiſed to follow me, and a-
greed

greed that I fhould reconnoitre the ground propereft
for the field of battle, the next morning, accompanied by fome of their chief warriors, to fettle the plan
of operations. When upon the ground appointed for
the field of battle, fcouts came in with the account of
the firft number, fwelled to 2000 ; immediately after,
a third, that General Burgoyne's army was cut to
pieces, and that Arnold was advancing, by rapid and
forced marches, with 3000 men. It was at this moment I began to fufpect cowardice in fome, and trea-
fon in others : however, I returned to camp, not
without hopes, with the affiftance of my gallant co-
adjutor, Sir John Johnfon, and the influence of the
fuperintending colonels, Claus and Butler, of indu-
cing them to meet the enemy. A council, according
to their cuftom, was called, to know their refolu-
tions ; before the breaking up of which I learned that
200 were already decamped. In about an hour they
infifted that I fhould retreat, or they would be obliged
to abandon me. I had no other party to take ; (and a
hard party it was, to troops who could do nothing
without them, to yield to their refolves ;) and therefore propofed to retire at night, fending on before
my fick, wounded, artillery, &c. down the Wood-
Creek, covering them by our line of march.

This did not fall in with their views ; which were
no lefs than treacheroufly committing ravage upon
their friends, as they had loft the opportunity of doing
it upon their enemies. To effect this, they artfully
caufed meffengers to come in, one after the other,
with accounts of the nearer approaches of the rebels ;
one and the laft affirmed, that they were within two
miles of Captain Lernoult's poft. Not giving entire
credit to this, and keeping to my refolution of retiring by night, they grew furious and abandoned ;
feized upon the officers liquor and clothes, in fpite of
the efforts of their fervants ; and became more formi-

dable

dable than the enemy we had to expect. I now
thought it time to call in Captain Lernoult's poft,
retiring with the troops in camp to the ruined fort,
called William, in the front of the garrifon, not only
to wait the enemy if they thought proper to fally, but
to protect the boats from the fury of the favages, having fent forward Captain Hoyes, with his detachment, with one piece of cannon, to the place where
Bull-Fort ftood, to receive the troops who waited the
arrival of Captain Lernoult. Moft of the boats were
efcorted that night beyond Canada-Creek, where no
danger was to be apprehended from the enemy. The
creek at this place, bending from the road, has a
deep cedar fwamp between. Every attention was now
turned to the mouth of the creek ; which the enemy
might have poffeffed themfelves of by a rapid march
by the Oneyda-Caftle. At this place the whole of the
little army arrived by twelve o'clock at night, and
took poft in fuch a manner as to have no fears of any
thing the enemy could do. Here we remained till
three o'clock next morning ; when the boats which
could come up the creek arrived, or rather that the
rafcally part of all nations of the Indians would fuffer
to come up ; and proceeded acrofs Lake Oneyda to
the ruined fort of Brereton, where I learned that fome
boats were ftill labouring down the creek, after being
lightened of the beft part of their freight by the Meffafagoes. Captain Lernoult propofed, with a boat
full of armed men, to repafs the lake that night, to
relieve them from their labour, and fupply them with
provifion. This tranfaction does as much honour to
the humanity, as to the gallantry, of this valuable
officer.

On my arrival at the Onondago-Falls, I received an
anfwer to my letter from your Excellency ; which
fhewed, in the cleareft light, the fcenes of treachery
that had been practifed upon me. The meffenger had
heard,

heard, indeed, on his way, that they were collecting the fame kind of rabble as before; but that there was not an enemy within forty miles of Fort-Stanwix.

Soon after my arrival here, I was joined by Captain Lernoult, with the men and boats he had been in search of. I mean immediately to send off, for the use of the upper garrison, all the overplus provision I shall have, after keeping a sufficiency to carry my detachment down; which I mean to do, with every expedition in my power, the moment this business is effected; for which purpose I have ordered here the snow. The sloop is already gone from this, with her full lading.

Officers from each corps are sent to Montreal to procure necessaries for the men, who are in a most deplorable situation from the plunder of the savages, that no time may be lost to join your army.

I have the honour to be, with the greatest respect,

Sir, your Excellency's most obedient

And most faithful servant,

Ofwego, Aug. 27,   BARRY ST. LEGER.
1777.
His Excellency General Burgoyne.

Extract of a Letter from Lieutenant-General Burgoyne *to* No. XIV.
Lord George Germaine, *dated at* Albany, 20*th*
October, 1777.

My Lord,

NO possibility of communication with your Lordship having existed since the beginning of September, (at which time my last dispatch was sent away,) I have to report to your Lordship the proceedings of the army under my command from that period; a series of hard toil, incessant effort, stubborn action; till dis-

abled

abled in the collateral branches of the army by the total defection of the Indians; the defertion or timidity of the Canadians and Provincials, fome individuals excepted; difappointed in the laft hope of any timely co-operation from other armies; the regular troops reduced by loffes from the beft part to 3500 fighting-men, not 2000 of which were Britifh; only three days provifions upon fhort allowance in ftore; invefted by an army of 16,000 men, and no apparent means of retreat remaining; I called into council all the generals, field-officers, and captains commanding corps, and by their unanimous concurrence and advice I was induced to open a treaty with Major-General Gates.

Your Lordfhip will fee, by the papers tranfmitted herewith, the difagreeable profpect which attended the firft overtures; and, when the terms concluded are compared, I truft that the fpirit of the councils I have mentioned, which under fuch circumftances dictated inftead of fubmitting, will not be refufed a fhare of credit.

Before I enter upon the detail of thefe events, I think it a duty of juftice, my Lord, to take upon myfelf the meafure of having paffed the Hudfon's River, in order to force a paffage to Albany. I did not think myfelf authorifed to call any men into council, when the peremptory tenor of my orders and the feafon of the year admitted no alternative.

Provifions for about thirty days having been brought forward, the other neceffary ftores prepared, and the bridge of boats comp eted, the army paffed the Hudfon's River on the 13th and 14th of September, and encamped on the heights and in the plain of Saratoga, the enemy being then in the neighbourhood of Stillwater.

15th. The whole army made a movement forward, and encamped in a good pofition in a place called Dovacote.

It

It being found that there were several bridges to 16th. repair, that work was begun under cover of strong detachments, and the same opportunity was taken to reconnoitre the country.

The army renewed their march, repaired other 17th. bridges, and encamped upon advantageous ground about four miles from the enemy.

The enemy appeared in considerable force, to ob- 18th. struct the farther repair of bridges, and with a view, as it was conceived, to draw on an action where artillery could not be employed. A small loss was sustained in skirmishing; but the work of the bridges was effected.

The passages of a great ravine, and other roads to- Sept. 19. wards the enemy, having been reconnoitred, the army advanced in the following order.

Brigadier-General Fraser's corps, sustained by Lieutenant-Colonel Breyman's corps, made a circuit, in order to pass the ravine commodiously, without quitting the heights, and afterwards to cover the march of the line to the right. These corps moved in three columns, and had the Indians, Canadians, and Provincials, upon their fronts and flanks. The British line, led by me in person, passed the ravine in a direct line south, and formed in order of battle as fast as they gained the summit, where they waited to give time to Fraser's corps to make the circuit, and to enable the left wing and artillery (which, under the commands of Major-General Phillips and Major-General Reidesel, kept the great road and meadows near the river in two columns, and had bridges to repair) to be equally ready to proceed. The 47th regiment guarded the bateaux.

The signal-guns, which had been previously settled to give notice of all the columns being ready to advance, having been fired between one and two o'clock, the march continued. The scouts and flankers of the

column

column of the Britiſh line were ſoon fired upon from ſmall parties, but with no effect.   After about an hour's march, the picquets, which made the advanced guard of that column, were attacked in force, and obliged to give ground ; but they ſoon rallied and were ſuſtained.

On the firſt opening of the wood I formed the troops.   A few cannon-ſhot diſlodged the enemy, at a houſe from whence the picquets had been attacked ; and Brigadier-General Fraſer's corps had arrived with ſuch preciſion, in point of time, as to be found upon a very advantageous height on the right of the Britiſh.

In the mean time, the enemy, not acquainted with the combination of the march, had moved in great force out of their intrenchments, with a view of turning the line upon the right ; and, being checked by the diſpoſition of Brigadier-General Fraſer, countermarched, in order to direct their great effort to the left of the Britiſh.

From the nature of the country, movements of this ſort, however near, may be effected without a poſſibility of their being diſcovered.

About three o'clock the action began by a very vigorous attack on the Britiſh line, and continued with great obſtinacy till after ſunſet.   The enemy being continually ſupplied with freſh troops, the ſtreſs lay upon the 20th, 21ſt, and 62d, regiments, moſt parts of which were engaged near four hours without intermiſſion ; the 9th had been ordered early in the day to form in reſerve.

The grenadiers and 24th regiment were ſome part of the time brought into action, as were part of the light infantry ; and all theſe corps charged with their uſual ſpirit.

The riflemen, and other parts of Breyman's corps, were alſo of ſervice ; but it was not thought adviſeable to evacuate the heights, where Brigadier-General

Fraſer

Frafer was pofted, otherwife than partially and occafionally.

Major-General Phillips, upon firft hearing the firing, found his way through a difficult part of the
wood to the fcene of action, and brought up with him
Major Williams and four pieces of artillery; and
from that moment I ftood indebted to that gallant and
judicious fecond for inceffant and moft material fervices; particularly for reftoring the action in a point
which was critically preffed by a great fuperiority of
fire, and to which he led up the 20th regiment at the
utmoft perfonal hazard.

Major-General Riedefel exerted himfelf to bring up
a part of the left wing, and arrived in time to charge
the enemy with regularity and bravery.

Juft as the light clofed, the enemy gave ground on
all fides, and left us completely mafters of the field of
battle, with the lofs of about five hunded men on
their fide, and, as fuppofed, thrice that number wounded.

The darknefs preventing a purfuit, the prifoners
were few.

The behaviour of the officers and men in general was
exemplary. Brigadier-General Frafer took his pofition
in the beginning of the day, with great judgement, and
fuftained the action with conftant prefence of mind and
vigour. Brigadier-General Hamilton was the whole
time engaged, and acquitted himfelf with great honour, activity, and good conduct.

The artillery in general was diftinguifhed, and the
brigade under Captain Jones, who was killed in the
action, was confpicuoufly fo.

The army lay upon their arms the night of the 19th,
and the next day took a pofition nearly within cannon-
fhot of the enemy, fortifying their right, and extending their left to the brow of the heights, fo as to cover the meadows through which the great river runs,

F 4   and

and where their bateaux and hospitals were placed. The 47th regiment, the regiment of Hesse Hanau, and a corps of provincials, encamped in the meadows as a farther security.

It was soon found that no fruits, honour excepted, were attained by the preceding victory, the enemy working with redoubled ardour to strengthen their left: their right was already unattackable.

On our side it became expedient to erect strong redoubts for the protection of the magazines and hospital, not only against a sudden attack, but also for their security in case of a march, to turn the enemy's flank.

Sept. 21.   A messenger arrived from Sir Harry Clinton with a letter in cipher, informing me of his intention to attack Fort Montgomery in about ten days from the date of his letter, which was the 12th instant. This was the only messenger of many that I apprehend were dispatched by Sir William Howe, and he that had reached my camp since the beginning of August. He was sent back the same night to inform Sir Harry of my situation, and of the necessity of a diversion to oblige General Gates to detach from his army, and my intention to wait favourable events in that position, if possible, to the 12th of October.

In the course of the two following days, two officers in disguise, and other confidential persons, were dispatched, by different routes, with verbal messages to the same effect; and I continued fortifying my camp and watching the enemy, whose numbers increased every day.

I thought it adviseable on the 3d of October to diminish the soldiers' ration, in order to lengthen out the provisions; to which measure the army submitted with the utmost cheerfulness. The difficulties of a retreat to Canada were clearly foreseen; as was the dilemma, should the retreat be effected, of leaving at liberty

liberty fuch an army as General Gates's to operate againft Sir William Howe.

This confideration operated forcibly to determine me to abide events as long as poffible, and I reafoned thus. The expedition I commanded was evidently meant at firft to be *hazarded*. Circumftances might require it fhould be *devoted*. A critical junction of Mr. Gates's force with Mr. Wafhington might poffibly decide the fate of the war; the failure of my junction with Sir Harry Clinton, or the lofs of my retreat to Canada, could only be a partial misfortune.

In this fituation things continued till the 7th, when no intelligence having been received of the expected co-operation, and four or five days for our limited ftay in the camp only remained, it was judged advifeable to make a movement to the enemy's left, not only to difcover whether there were any poffible means of forcing a paffage, fhould it be neceffary to advance, or of diflodging him for the convenience of a retreat, but alfo to cover a forage of the army, which was in the greateft diftrefs on account of the fcarcity.

A detachment of fifteen hundred regular troops, with two twelve pounders, two howitzers, and fix fixpounders, were ordered to move, and were commanded by myfelf, having with me Major-General Phillips, Major-General Reidefel, and Brigadier-General Frafer.

The guard of the camp upon the heights was left to Brigadier-General Hamilton and Specht; the redoubts and the plain to Brigadier-General Gall; and, as the force of the enemy immediately in their front confifted of more than double their numbers, it was not poffible to augment the corps that marched beyond the numbers above ftated.

I formed the troops within three-quarters of a mile of the enemy's left; and Captain Frafer's rangers, with Indians and Provincials, had orders to go by fecret

paths

paths in the woods to gain the enemy's rear, and by
shewing themselves there to keep them in a check.

The farther operations intended were prevented by
a very sudden and rapid attack of the enemy on our
left, where the British grenadiers were posted to support the left wing of the line.   Major Acland, at the
head of them, sustained the attack with great resolu-
tion; but the enemy's great numbers enabling them
in a few minutes to extend the attack along the front
of the Germans, which were immediately on the right
of the grenadiers, no part of that body could be removed to make a second line to the flank, where the
stress of the fire lay.   The right was at this time engaged, but it was soon observed that the enemy were
marching a large corps round their flank, to endeavour cutting off their retreat.   The light infantry and
part of the 24th regiment, which were at that post,
were therefore ordered to form a second line, and to
secure the return of the troops into camp.   While this
movement was proceeding, the enemy pushed a fresh
and strong reinforcement to renew the action upon the
left; which, overpowered by a great superiority, gave
way, and the light infantry and 24th regiment were
obliged to make a quick movement to save that point
from being entirely carried; in doing which, Brigadier-
General Fraser was mortally wounded.

The danger to which the lines were exposed, becoming at this moment of the most serious nature,
orders were given to Major-General Phillips and Reidefel to cover the retreat, while such troops as were
most ready for the purpose returned for the defence of
them.   The troops retreated, hard pressed, but in good
order; they were obliged to leave six pieces of cannon, all the horses having been killed; and most of
the artillery-men, who had behaved as usual with the
utmost bravery under the command of Major Williams, being either killed or wounded.

The

The troops had fcarcely entered the camp when it was ftormed with great fury, the enemy rufhing to the lines under a fevere fire of grape-fhot and fmall arms. The poft of the light infantry, under Lord Balcarras, affifted by fome of the line, which threw themfelves, by order, into the intrenchments, was defended with great fpirit; and the enemy, led on by General Arnold, was finally repulfed, and the General wounded; but unhappily the intrenchments of the German referve, commanded by Lieutenant-Colonel Breyman, who was killed, were carried; and, although ordered to be recovered, they never were fo; and the enemy, by that misfortune, gained an opening on our right and rear. The night put an end to the action.

Under the difadvantages, thus apparent in our fituation, the army was ordered to quit the prefent pofition during the night, and take poft upon the heights above the hofpital.

Thus, by an entire change of front, to reduce the enemy to form a new difpofition, this movement was effected in great order and without lofs, though all the artillery and camp were removed at the fame time. The army continued offering battle to the enemy, in their new pofition, the whole day of the 8th.

Intelligence was now received that the enemy were marching to turn the right; and no means could prevent that meafure but retiring towards Saratoga. The army began to move at nine o'clock at night, Major-General Reidefel commanding the van-guard, and Major-General Phillips the rear.

This retreat, though within mufquet-fhot of the enemy, and encumbered with all the baggage of the army, was made without lofs; but a very heavy rain, and the difficulties of guarding the bateaux, which contained all the provifions, occafioned delays which prevented the army reaching Saratoga till the night of the 9th, and the artillery could not pafs the fords of the Fifh-Kill till the morning of the 10th. At

At our arrival near Saratoga, a corps of the enemy, between five and six hundred, were difcovered throwing up intrenchments on the heights, but retired over a ford of the Hudfon's River at our approach, and joined a body pofted to oppofe our paffage there.

It was judged proper to fend a detachment of artificers, under a ftrong efcort, to repair the bridges and open a road to Fort-Edward on the weft fide of the river. The 47th regiment, Captain Frafer's markfmen, and Mackoy's Provincials, were ordered for that fervice; but, the enemy appearing on the heights of the Fifh-Kill in great force, and making a difpofition to pafs and give us battle, the 47th regiment and Frafer's markfmen were recalled : the Provincials, left to cover the workmen at the firft bridge, ran away upon a very flight attack of a fmall party of the enemy, and left the artificers to efcape as they could, without a poffibility of their performing any work.

During thefe different movements the bateaux with provifions were frequently fired upon from the oppofite fide of the river, and fome of them were loft, and feveral men were killed and wounded in thofe which remained.

Oct. 11. The attacks upon the bateaux were continued ; feveral were taken and re-taken, but their fituation being much nearer to the main force of the enemy than to ours, it was found impoffible to fecure the provifions any otherwife than by landing them and carrying them upon the hill. This was effected under fire, and with great difficulty.

The poffible means of farther retreat were now confidered in councils of war, compofed of the general officers ; minutes of which will be tranfmitted to your Lordfhip.

The only one that feemed at all practicable was, by a night-march to gain Fort-Edward, with the troops

carrying

carrying their provifion upon their backs : the impoffibility of repairing bridges putting a conveyance of
artillery and carriages out of the queftion, it was propofed to force the ford at Fort Edward, or the ford
above it. Before this attempt could be made, fcouts
returned, with intelligence that the enemy were intrenched oppofite thefe fords, and poffeffed a camp
in force on the high ground, between Fort-Edward
and Fort-George, with cannon. They had alfo parties, down the whole fhore, to watch our motions,
and pofts fo near to us, upon our own fide of the water, as muft prevent the army moving a fingle mile
undifcovered.

The bulk of the enemy's army was hourly joined
by new corps of militia and volunteers, and their
numbers together amounted to upwards of 16,000
men. Their pofition, which extended three parts in
four of a circle round us, was, from the nature of
the ground, unattackable in all parts.

In this fituation, the army took the beft pofition
poffible, and fortified, waiting till the 13th at night,
in the anxious hope of fuccours from our friends, or
the next defirable expectation, an attack from our
enemy.

During this time, the men lay continually upon
their arms, and were cannonaded in every part : even
rifle-fhot and grape-fhot came into all parts of the
line, though without any confiderable effect.

At this period, an exact account of the provifions
was taken, and the circumftances ftated in the opening of this letter became complete.

The council of war was extended to all the field-
officers and captains commanding corps of the army,
and the event enfued which I am fure was inevitable,
and which, I truft, in that fituation was honourable,
but which it would be fuperfluous and melancholy to
repeat.

After

After the execution of the treaty, General Gates drew together the force that had furrounded my pofition, and I had the confolation to have as many witneffes, as I have men under my command, of its amounting to the numbers mentioned above.

During the events ftated above, an attempt was made againft Ticonderoga by an army affembled under Major-General Lincoln, who found means to march with a confiderable corps from Huberton undifcovered, while another column of his force paffed the mountains between Skenefborough and Lake-George; and, on the morning of the 18th of September, a fudden and general attack was made upon the carrying-place at Lake-George, Sugar-Hill, Ticonderoga, and Mount-Independence. The fea-officers commanding the armed floop ftationed to defend the carrying-place, as alfo fome of the officers commanding at the pofts of Sugar-Hill and at the Portage, were furprifed, and a confiderable part of four companies of the 53d regiment were made prifoners: a block-houfe, commanded by Lieutenant Lord of the 53d, was the only poft on that fide that had time to make ufe of their arms; and they made a brave defence, till cannon, taken from the furprifed veffel, was brought againft them.

After ftating and lamenting fo fatal a want of vigilance, I have to inform your Lordfhip of the fatiffactory events which followed.

The enemy, having twice fummoned Brigadier-General Powell, and received fuch anfwer as became a gallant officer entrufted with fo important a poft, and having tried, during the courfe of four days, feveral attacks, and being repulfed in all, retreated, without having done any confiderable damage.

Brigadier-General Powell, from whofe report to me I extract this relation, gives great commendations to the regiment of Prince Frederick, and the other troops

troops ſtationed at Mount-Independence. The Brigadier alſo mentions, with great applauſe, the behaviour of Captain Taylor of the 21ſt regiment, who was accidentally there on his route to the army from the hoſpital; and Lieutenant Beecroft of the 24th regiment, who, with the artificers in arms, defended an important battery.

On the 24th inſtant, the enemy, enabled, by the capture of the gun-boats and bateaux, which they had made after the ſurpriſe of the ſloop, to embark upon Lake George, attacked Diamond Iſland in two diviſions.

Captain Aubrey, and two companies of the 47th regiment, had been poſted at that iſland from the time the army paſſed the Hudſon's River, as a better ſituation, for the ſecurity of the ſtores at the ſouth end of Lake George, than Fort George, which is on the continent, and not tenable againſt artillery and numbers. The enemy were repulſed by Captain Aubrey with great loſs, end purſued by the gun-boats under his command, to the eaſt ſhore, where two of their principal veſſels were retaken, together with all the cannon. They had juſt time to ſet fire to the other bateaux, and retreated over the mountains.

I beg leave to refer your Lordſhip for farther particulars to my aid-de-camp, Lord Peterſham, and I humbly take occaſion to recommend to his Majeſty's notice that nobleman, as one endued with qualities to do important ſervices to his country in every ſtation to which his birth may lead. In this campaign, in particular, his behaviour has been ſuch as to entitle him to the fulleſt applauſe; and I am confident his merit will be thought a ſufficient ground for preferment, though deprived of the _eclat_ and ſort of claim which generally attends the delivery of fortunate diſpatches.

I have only to add, my Lord, a general report of the killed and wounded. I do not give it correct;
the

the hurry of the time and the feparation of the corps
having rendered it impoffible to make it fo. The
Britifh officers have bled profufely and moft honoura-
bly ; thofe who remain unwounded have been equally
forward ; and the general officers, from the mode of
fighting, have been more expofed than in other fervices. Among the reft of this ftation, I have had my
efcapes. It depends upon the fentence his Majefty
fhall pafs upon my conduct, upon the judgement of
my profeffion, and of the impartial and refpectable
parts of my country, whether I am to efteem them
bleffings or misfortunes.

I have the honour to be, &c.

(Signed.)

J. Burgoyne.

Second
No. XIV. *Copy of a Letter from Lieutenant-General* Burgoyne *to*
Lord George Germaine, *dated* Albany, 20*th* Octo-
ber, 1777.

[*Private, by Lord* Peterfham.]

My Lord,

I HAVE little to add to my public letter refpecting
the courfe of unfuccefsful events therein detailed. I
reft my confidence in the juftice of the King and his
councils, to fupport the General they thought proper
to appoint to as arduous an undertaking, and under as
pofitive a direction, as perhaps a cabinet ever framed.
It will, I am fure, be remembered, my Lord, that
a preference of exertions was the only latitude given
me ; and that to force a junction with Sir William
Howe, or at leaft a paffage to Albany, was the principle, the letter, and the fpirit, of my orders.

Indeed the appearances at the time I paffed the Hudfon's River, though fubject to doubt in fome inftances, as I then wrote to your Lordfhip, were, upon a
general view, fuch as I am perfuaded would have rendered

dered inaction cenfurable, had my orders, inftead of being peremptory, been difcretionary. Promifes of the profeffing loyalifts were not then brought to the teft; the fpirit of the enemy, in combat againft regular Britifh troops, had only been tried at Ticonderoga, at Huberton, at Skenefborough, and Fort Anne, in all which places it had failed; the total difappointment of effectual co-operation could not be forefeen or fuppofed; and, fure I am, had I then made fuppofition that any thing like what has happened might have happened, and remained cautioufly pofted, no exertion attempted, my conduct would have been held indefenfible by every clafs and diftinction of men, in government, in the army, and in the public.

The expediency of advancing being admitted, the confequences have been honourable misfortunes. The Britifh have perfevered in a ftrenuous and bloody progrefs. Had the force been all Britifh, perhaps the perfeverance had been longer; but, as it was, will it be faid, my Lord, that, in the exhaufted fituation defcribed, and in the jaws of famine, and invefted by quadruple numbers, a treaty, which faves the army to the ftate for the next campaign, was not more than could have been expected? I call it faving the army; becaufe, if fent home, the ftate is thereby enabled to fend forth the troops now deftined for her internal defence; if exchanged, they become a force to Sir William Howe as effectually as if any other junction had been made.

I fhould now hold myfelf unjuftifiable if I did not confide to your Lordfhip my opinion, upon a near infpection, of the rebel troops. The ftanding corps which I have feen are difciplined: I do not hazard the term, but apply it to the great fundamental points of military inftitution, fobriety, fubordination, regularity, and courage. The militia are inferior in method and movement, but not a jot lefs ferviceable in woods.

G   My

My conjectures were very different after the affair of Ticonderoga; but I am convinced they were delusive, and it is a duty to the state to confess it.

The panic of the rebel troops is confined, and of short duration ; the enthusiasm is extensive and permanent.

It is a justice to Major-General Phillips to inform your Lordship, that, when the crisis of our situation at Saratoga arrived, he very handsomely offered to hazard his person by making a circuit through the woods, and attempt to throw himself into Ticonderoga, to defend that place, should it be the object of the enemy to endeavour the retaking it.

In regard to myself, I am sunk in mind and body ; but, while I have a faculty of either, it shall be exerted for the King's service. I shall wait, in the neighbourhood of Boston, the orders of Sir William Howe.

I have the honour to be, &c.

J. BURGOYNE.

No. XV. *Minutes of a Council of War, holden on the Heights of Saratoga, Oct.* 12.

PRESENT.

Lieut. Gen. BURGOYNE,   Major Gen. PHILLIPS,
Major Gen. REIDESEL,   Brig. Gen. HAMILTON.

The Lieutenant-General states to the council the present situation of affairs.

The enemy, in force, according to the best intelligence he can obtain, to the amount of upwards of 14000 men, and a considerable quantity of artillery, are on this side the Fish-Kill, and threaten an attack. On the other side the Hudson's River, between this army and Fort Edward, is another army of the enemy, the numbers unknown ; but one corps, which there has

has been an opportunity of obferving, is reported to be about 1500 men. They have likewife cannon on the other fide the Hudfon's River, and they have a bridge below Saratoga church, by which the two armies can communicate.

The bateaux of the army have been deftroyed, and no means appear of making a bridge over the Hudfon's River, were it even practicable, from the pofition of the enemy.

The only means of retreat, therefore, are by the ford at Fort Edward, or taking the mountains, in order to pafs the river higher up by rafts, or by any other ford which is reported to be practicable with difficulty, or by keeping the mountains, to pafs the head of Hudfon's River, and continue to the weftward of Lake George all the way to Ticonderoga: it is true, this laft paffage was never made but by Indians or very fmall bodies of men.

In order to pafs cannon or any wheel carriages from hence to Fort Edward, fome bridges muft be repaired under fire of the enemy, from the oppofite fide of the river, and the principal bridge will be a work of fourteen or fifteen hours: there is no good pofition for the army to take to fuftain that work, and, if there were, the time ftated as neceffary would give the enemy, on the other fide the Hudfon's River, an opportunity to take poft on the ftrong ground above Fort Edward, or to difpute the ford, while General Gates's army followed in the rear.

The intelligence, from the lower part of Hudfon's River, is founded upon the concurrent reports of prifoners and deferters, who fay it was the news in the enemy's camp, that Fort Montgomery was taken; and one man, a friend to government, who arrived yefterday, mentions fome particulars of the manner in which it was taken.

The

The provisions of the army may hold out to the 20th; there is neither rum nor spruce beer.

Having committed this state of facts to the consideration of the council, the General requests their sentiments on the following propositions:

1st. To wait, in the present position, an attack from the enemy, or the chance of favourable events.

2d. To attack the enemy.

3d. To retreat, repairing the bridges as the army moves for the artillery, in order to force the passage of the ford.

4th. To retreat by night, leaving the artillery and the baggage; and, should it be found impracticable to force the passage with musquetry, to attempt the upper ford, or the passage round Lake George.

5th. In case the enemy, by extending to their left, leave their rear open, to march rapidly for Albany.

Upon the first proposition, resolved, that the situation would grow worse by delay, that the provision now in store is not more than sufficient for the retreat, should impediments intervene, or a circuit of country become necessary; and, as the enemy did not attack when the ground was unfortified, it is not probable they will do it now, as they have a better game to play.

The second unadviseable and desperate, there being no possibility of reconnoitring the enemy's position, and his great superiority of numbers known.

The third impracticable.

The fifth thought worthy of consideration by the Lieutenant-General, Major-General Phillips, and Brigadier-General Hamilton; but the position of the enemy yet gives no opening for it.

Resolved, that the fourth proposition is the only resource; and that, to effect it, the utmost secrecy and silence is to be observed; and the troops are to be put in motion from the right, in the still part of the night, without any change in the disposition.

N.B.

N.B. It depended upon the delivery of six days provision in due time, and upon the return of scouts, who had been sent forward, to examine by what route the army could probably move the first four miles undiscovered, whether the plan should take place on that day or on the morrow.

The scouts, on their return, reported, that the enemy's position on the right was such, and they had so many small parties out, that it would be impossible to move without our march being immediately discovered.

Minutes and Proceedings of a Council of War consisting of all the general Officers and Field Officers, and Captains commanding Corps, on the Heights of Saratoga, *October 13.*

THE Lieutenant-General having explained the situation of affairs, as in the preceding council, with the additional intelligence, that the enemy was intrenched at the fords of Fort Edward, and likewise occupied the strong position on the Pine-plains between Fort George and Fort Edward, expressed his readiness to undertake, at their head, any enterprise of difficulty or hazard that should appear to them within the compass of their strength or spirit. He added, that he had reason to believe a capitulation had been in the contemplation of some, perhaps of all, who knew the real situation of things; that, upon a circumstance of such consequence to national and personal honour, he thought it a duty to his country and to himself, to extend his council beyond the usual limits; that the assembly present might justly be esteemed a full representation of the army, and that he should think himself unjustifiable in taking any step in so serious a matter, without such a concurrence of sentiments, as should make a treaty the act of the army, as well as that of the general.

The

The firſt queſtion, therefore, he deſired them to decide was, Whether an army of 3500 fighting men, and well provided with artillery, were juſtifiable, upon the principles of national dignity and military honour, in capitulating in any poſſible ſituation?

Reſolved, nem. con. in the affirmative.

Queſtion 2. Is the preſent ſituation of that nature?

Reſolved, nem. con. That the preſent ſituation juſtifies a capitulation upon honourable terms.

The Lieutenant-General then drew up the meſſage, marked No. 2, and laid it before the council. It was unanimouſly approved; and, upon that foundation, the treaty opened.

October 14. Major Kingſton, having delivered the meſſage, marked No. 2, returned with the propoſals, marked No. 3; and the council of war being aſſembled again, the Lieutenant-General laid the propoſals before them, when it was reſolved unanimouſly to reject the 6th article, and not to admit of it in any extremity whatever.

The Lieutenant-General then laid before the council the anſwers to Major-General Gates's propoſals, as marked in the ſame paper, together with his own preliminary propoſals, which were unanimouſly approved of.

October 15. The council being aſſembled again, Major-General Gates's anſwers to Lieutenant-General Burgoyne's propoſals were laid before them, whereupon it was reſolved, that they were ſatisfactory, and a ſufficient ground for proceeding to a definitive treaty.

No. 2. *Major* Kingſton *delivered the following Meſſage to Major-General* Gates, October 14.

AFTER having fought you twice, Lieutenant-General Burgoyne has waited ſome days, in his preſent poſition, pofition, determined to try a third conflict againft any force you could bring to attack him.

He is apprifed of the fuperiority of your numbers, and the difpofition of your troops to impede his fupplies, and render his retreat a fcene of carnage on both fides. In this fituation he is impelled by humanity, and thinks himfelf juftifiable by eftablifhed princples and precedents of ftate and of war, to fpare the lives of brave men upon honourable terms. Should Major-General Gates be inclined to treat upon that idea, General Burgoyne would propofe a ceffation of arms during the time neceffary to communicate the preliminary terms by which, in any extremity, he and his army mean to abide.

No. 3. *Major-General* Gates's *Propofals*; *together with Lieutenant-General* Burgoyne's *Anfwers.*

I. General Burgoyne's army being exceedingly reduced by repeated defeats, by defertion, ficknefs, &c. their provifions exhaufted ; their military horfes, tents, and baggage, taken or deftroyed ; their retreat cut off, and their camp invefted, they can only be allowed to furrender prifoners of war.

Anfwer. Lieutenant-General Burgoyne's army, however reduced, will never admit that their retreat is cut off, while they have arms in their hands.

II. The officers and foldiers may keep the baggage belonging to them. The generals of the United States never permit individuals to be pillaged.

III. The troops under his Excellency General Burgoyne will be conducted by the moft convenient route to New-England, marching by eafy marches, and fufficiently provided for by the way.

Anfwer. This article is anfwered by General Burgoyne's firft propofal, which is here annexed.

IV. The officers will be admitted on parole ; may wear their fide-arms, and will be treated with the liberality

rality cuſtomary in Europe, ſo long as they, by proper behaviour, continue to deſerve it; but thoſe who
are apprehended, having broken their parole, as ſome
Britiſh officers have done, muſt expect to be cloſe confined.

Anſwer.   There being no officer in this army under, or capable of being under, the deſcription of
breaking parole, this article needs no anſwer.

V. All public ſtores, artillery, arms, ammunition,
carriages, horſes, &c. &c. muſt be delivered to commiſſaries appointed to receive them.

Anſwer.   All public ſtores may be delivered, arms
excepted.

VI. Theſe terms being agreed to and ſigned, the
troops under his Excellency General Burgoyne's command may be drawn up in their encampments, where
they will be ordered to ground their arms, and may
thereupon be marched to the river ſide, to be paſſed
over in their way towards Bennington.

Anſwer.   This article inadmiſſible in any extremity.
Sooner than this army will conſent to ground their
arms in their encampment, they will ruſh on the enemy, determined to take no quarter.

VII. A ceſſation of arms to continue till ſun-ſet, to
receive General Burgoyne's anſwer.

(Signed)

HORATIO GATES.

Camp, at Saratoga, Oct. 14.

Major Kingſton met the Adjutant-General of Major-General Gates's army, October 14th, at ſun-ſet,
and delivered the following meſſage.

If General Gates does not mean to recede from the
6th article, the treaty ends at once.

The army will, to a man, proceed to any act of
deſperation, rather than ſubmit to that article.

The ceſſation of arms ends this evening.

No. XVI.   A RE-

APPENDIX.

Extracts from the Minutes of the last Council of War, No.XVII *excepting the Names of the Officers, and the Notes they gave.*

Question.

General Gates having, in answer to General Burgoyne's message, given a solemn affirmation, on his honour, that no detachment has been made from his army during the negotiation of the treaty, is the treaty, in its present situation, binding on this army, or is the general's honour engaged for the signing it?

[Here follow the names of the officers as they voted.]

The lieutenant-general's opinion being clear, that he is not bound by what has passed, he would not execute the treaty upon the sole consideration of the point of honour, notwithstanding the respectable majority against him.

He is likewise far from being convinced that this army, by great exertions and by great enduring in point of provisions, might not yet be relieved; but he is compelled to yield on the following considerations:

The treaty was generally thought a most advantageous one before the intelligence arrived. That intelligence is refuted, and ocular demonstration of its falsity pledged as far as relates to General Gates's force; the other parts are only founded on hearsay, and not to be depended upon.

Should General Clinton be where reported, yet the distance is such as to render any relief from him improbable during the time our provisions could be made to last.

- - - - - - - declares his post untenable; and says, if this convention is not signed, he apprehends there will be considerable desertion.

- - says,

- - - - - - - - ſays, he thinks the 47th regiment is not to be depended on.

- - - - - - - - is of the ſame opinion.

- - - - - - - - thinks the 62d regiment is diſhearten-ed by the ſituation of their poſt, and not equal to their former exertions.

Several officers think the men in general ſeem to have got the convention in their heads as deſirable.

Many of the beſt officers are abſent, by ſickneſs and wounds, from all the corps.

Though the other officers, at the head of the Britiſh corps, think that they can anſwer for the ſpirit of their men, if attacked on their preſent ground, it is evident the moſt ſanguine do not think any part of the army in that elevation and alacrity of ſpirit neceſſary for un-dertaking deſperate enterpriſes.

To break off the treaty now renders a future renewal of it hopeleſs, as our condition muſt every hour grow worſe.

A defeat is fatal to the army. A victory does not ſave it, as they have neither proviſions to advance nor retreat againſt an enemy, who, by experience, we know are capable of rallying at every advantageous poſt.

And that the life and property of every provincial and dependent of this army depends upon the execu-tion of this treaty.

POST

POSTSCRIPT to the APPENDIX.

[Though the following Letters are not referred to in any Part of the Defence, it is hoped they will not be deemed fuperfluous.]

Extract of a Letter from Major-General Phillips to Lieutenant-General Burgoyne, dated Cambridge, September 29, 1778.

My dear Sir,

THE Bofton news-papers have given extracts from Englifh and New-York papers, wherein you are mentioned; your arrival, your fpeeches in parliament, and a variety of other matters concerning you. I do not always give credit to news-papers, and therefore the publifhers at Bofton will excufe me, if, in the inftance of news, I do not give them, in my opinion, more veracity than I allow the news compilers at London.

I will not plague you about our fituation, as you will know it by my affuring you it is almoft exactly as you left us; fo no more about it. The troops here depend upon you, their chief, in whatever may relate to them, their intereft, their honour. It is not doubted but you will exert yourfelf, that the officers may gain preferment in common with other parts of the army; that you will have the goodnefs to exert yourfelf in behalf of their fituation, refpecting the very great expence of living, and endeavour to procure the allowance of forage money; and, in fhort, that you will ufe all your powers of perfuafion and intereft for thefe troops, which have ferved under you with zeal and with honour; and endeavour, by ferving their fituation and promoting their honour, to alleviate misfortunes which nor fortitude nor valour could prevent,

and

and which they fuffer, however, with refignation and patience. I am moft perfectly convinced of your affectionate, I will fay your grateful, regard for us all; and I leave myfelf and the troops to your friendly care, to your humanity, to your honour.

You cannot expect a letter of entertainment; I have not even a power of making it one of intelligence; it fhall be, however, a letter of perfect fincerity; and, in the fulleft fenfe of it, I profefs to be,

My dear Sir,

Your very fincere friend and faithful fervant,

(Signed.)   W. PHILLIPS.

P. S. I enclofe you the Copy of a Memorial to the Secretary at War; I am fure you will affift it.

Copy of a Letter from Lieutenant-General Burgoyne *to Lord* Amherft, *inclofing the Memorial referred to in the above, dated* November 6, 1778.

MY LORD,

THE heavy misfortune I fuftain, in being precluded the King's prefence, touches me in no point more nearly than in the prevention of doing juftice to the various and extenfive merits of the army I had the honour to command. That the confequences of my fuppofed or real errors fhould involve pretenfions and interefts of fo many gallant officers, is a painful reflection; and it can only be alleviated by the trueft fenfe of the truft to be repofed in your Lordfhip, for the general protection of the fervice. The inclofed memorial was accompanied with expreffions of reliance, in the name of the whole army, upon my efforts to fupport it. The officers in New-England little conceive my prefent fituation. I take the firft opportunity

portunity to tranfmit their caufe to your Lordfhip's happier aufpices, with this folemn declaration, (which I have mentioned upon different public occafions, and which I can omit no occafion to repeat,) that there is not a Britifh officer, who ferved under me during the campaign of 1777, to whom I can impute blame; that the inftances are very numerous wherein particular diftinction is due; and, as a body, they have a claim to my fincereft refpect, for their zeal in the King's fervice; and to my utmoft gratitude, for their attention to me perfonally.

I have the honour to be, &c. &c. &c.

J. BURGOYNE.

F I N I S.